Imitating God

Imitating God

The Allegory of Faith in *Piers Plowman* B

Pamela Raabe

The University of Georgia Press

Athens and London

© 1990 by the University of Georgia Press
Athens, Georgia 30602
All rights reserved
Designed by Mary Mendell
Set in Trump Medieval
The paper in this book meets the guidelines for
permanence and durability of the Committee on
Production Guidelines for Book Longevity of the
Council on Library Resources.
Printed in the United States of America
94 93 92 91 90   5   4   3   2   1

Library of Congress Cataloging in Publication Data
Raabe, Pamela.
Imitating God : the allegory of faith in Piers Plowman B /
Pamela Raabe. p. cm.
Includes bibliographical references (p.).
ISBN 0-8203-1205-3 (alk. paper)
1. Langland, William, 1330?–1400? Piers the Plowman.   2. Faith
in literature.   3. Allegory.   I. Title.
PR2017.F33R3   1990
821'.1—dc20   89-28364 CIP
British Library Cataloging in Publication Data available

Contents

Imitating God

Introduction
Beginning with Faith

◆

"**C**rede ut intelligas"—this is the advice St. Augustine gives to anyone who wishes to learn the Truth. As Etienne Gilson puts it in his study of Augustine's philosophy, "The first step along the path leading the mind to God is to accept Revelation by faith." Gilson readily admits this to be a breach of logic, "inasmuch as it means accepting at the outset without proof precisely the things Augustine wishes to prove"; but he explains that Augustine is speaking from personal experience, which had taught him that "faith held possession in perpetuity of the very truth his reason had been unable to grasp."[1] Our attempt as modern readers to comprehend this very paradox will demonstrate Augustine's point: we perceive the paradox of faith's primacy as a logical dilemma, and resolve to withhold faith until such time as demonstration may make the paradox appear logical. But the paradox can never be demonstrated logically; we must accept it before we can understand the unified cosmic vision it unfolds. In the order of logic, paradox is a problem; but in the order of faith, it is the solution to a problem.

In recent years it has become increasingly popular for critics of *Piers Plowman* B, finding structural and thematic paradoxes in Langland's text, to cite them as proof of the poet's growing doubt and anxiety, not only concerning church doctrine as an adequate account of reality, but also concerning language, poetry, and allegory itself— that paradoxical literary union of spirit and flesh—as adequate signifiers of this reality. The justification for such a modern, skeptical approach to theological and literary paradox would seem to reside in prior critical assertions, such as those by Rosemary Woolf and Charles Muscatine, that *Piers* reflects the breakdown of the medieval system of life and thought: Woolf emphasizes the poem's "nonmedieval qualities," and Muscatine describes its strained allegory as a sign of "Gothic tension."[2] Once it has been suggested that Langland and his poem are not entirely medieval—an assertion that has been fairly made of any number of medieval poets and poems—critics tend with increasing ease to offer approaches to the poem that are almost entirely modern. It is no longer necessary, or even desirable, to assume any faith on Langland's part in which we cannot share, and his poem, so often disparaged for its frustrating opacity, now makes itself valuable as a gratifying reflection of our own disbelief.

The two critics in whom this trend is perhaps most completely embodied are Priscilla Martin and Mary Carruthers; both see in the poem an obsession with language's inability to express reality, and both see this obsession as a reflection of the poet's own moral and spiritual doubts. Martin, equating allegory with "simplification" and with "clear-cut moral distinctions," defines the structural basis of *Piers* as the interplay between the literal (i.e., realistic) mode and the no longer viable mode of allegory, concluding that "allegorization itself comes under increasing suspicion" in the process of the poem. This is essentially her argument in her later, full-length analysis of the poem as well, where she describes the poet as deliberately sabotaging his own allegory to prove its inadequacy as a way of perceiving reality. Carruthers, in *The Search for St. Truth*, contends that *Piers* is actually "an epistemological poem," focusing on Will's efforts to discover the meaning of Dowel despite its definitive basis in "a knowledge which is no longer secure." "In a very real sense," she argues, "Dowel is a word in search of a referent in this poem—hence the multitude of its definitions, the felt inadequacy of all of them, the confusion which results in a term which should be, by its very nature, perfectly clear."[3]

But even critics who are not centrally concerned with the question of anxiety and disbelief in the poem more and more readily assume it in the course of their arguments: thus in two separate articles explaining the tension between tenor and vehicle in Langland's allegory as a sign of the poet's opposition to the hypocrisy and formalism of social institutions, John Burrow argues that the poet fears the inadequacy of words and of poetic images to express the good life, and he describes the poem's quick movement from one allegory to the next as a series of increasingly frustrated "substitutions."[4] David Mills, in discussing the poet's legitimate "problem of talking about an ideal infinite with the outlook, and language, of a corrupt finite," ends by equating the human poet with his omniscient narrator, thus calling into question the reliability of the dream vision itself, and depicting Langland's various allegorical images as suffering a "breakdown" owing to the failure of finite vision to express infinity adequately. Anne Middleton focuses on Langland's grammatical metaphor to show his attempts to deal with his "moral doubts about whether a narrative fiction can adequately embody the truth." Barbara Nolan concludes her study of apocalyptic visionary poetry with a chapter on *Piers* in which, after asserting Langland's "theological skepticism," she argues that "[t]he artistic order Langland manages in his poem reflects a near breakdown of a familiar form in the face of impossible worldly pressures." John Bowers's theory that Will's (and Langland's) principal sin is *acedia* is founded on the assumption that *Piers* is "charged with anxiety" not only concerning religion but also "concerning the actual writing of poetry." And even Daniel Murtaugh's analysis of *Piers*, based on the highly orthodox medieval notion that humanity and the cosmos are created in God's image, nevertheless concludes that Langland's "structures and his metaphors constantly break down before his growing, evolving vision of a truth they can no longer embody." The specific focus of analysis changes from critic to critic, but the overall movement is unified in the desire to see modern difficulties with *Piers* as the poet's own difficulties, or as Muscatine applaudingly describes it, "to suggest the validity of the results of modern criticism—namely, its extraordinary inconclusiveness—and the validity of the meaning of those results: that *Piers Plowman* must in important ways *be* inconclusive; that its form and style are symptomatic of some sort of breakdown."[5] Our disbelief is simply Langland's disbelief, and a new critical tradition for the poem is born through the repetition of the same set of emotionally charged words: "tension," "doubt," "inadequacy," "fear," "crisis," "breakdown."

This new critical tradition arose in response to a real need that the larger and older tradition failed to fill; in their efforts to establish the unity and significance of *Piers Plowman* as a medieval work reflecting the usual medieval conventions and dogmas, most critics from Henry W. Wells and T. P. Dunning to R. W. Frank and D. W. Robertson, Jr., either ignored the poem's allegorical tensions and paradoxes altogether or explained them as lapses in poetic skill. The newer tradition strives to account for these moments of tension as integral parts of the poem's whole meaning, and succeeds in unearthing a rich and important stratum of the poem's significance; much of what these critics say about the poem is valid, even vital to our understanding of it. But the repeated emphasis on tension for its own sake has produced its own kinds of distortions, and some of the most recent criticism seems simply to reflect the modern taste for conflict and opposition, asserting the primary importance of these elements even in scenes in the poem where opposition is plainly invoked only to exhibit its resolution. Thus George Kane, who once described Langland's strained allegories in the old tradition's rhetoric of tropes and conceits, now not only employs the new terminology of doubt but even sides with the blaspheming doubters whom Dame Study derides in Passus X when he suggests that Dame Study's angry insistence on faith is an insufficient response to their doubts.[6] And thus Middleton, in positing the episode of combat and conflict as the basic structural unit of the poem, emphasizes the dispute between Wit and Study over Wit's immediate capitulation, stresses the parting of Clergy and Conscience over their friendly agreement to meet again, and points up the conflict Will perceives between Abraham/ Faith, Moses/Hope, and the Samaritan/Charity over the Samaritan's assurances that they are all one.[7] Read in this way, the paradox of the Trinity itself becomes a problem rather than a solution, a trio in conflict rather than a unity dissolving conflict. And this is just the point: increasingly the tendency is to assume that Langland's tensions reflect modern rather than medieval attitudes toward paradox, and that they arise from the poet's distaste for allegory, distrust of poetry, and disbelief in the Christian allegorical world view. Certainly Robertson's vision of the Middle Ages as a time of social and intellectual unity is overstated at best; certainly the late fourteenth century in England was a period of particular conflict and crisis, and Langland's satire addresses many of the social problems of his day. But it does not necessarily follow that his perspective on these problems, or on reality itself, is a modern one. It is one thing to suggest that Langland subscribed to the commonly held classical and medieval belief that the world is in a state of degeneration, and quite another to imply that he foresaw the end of the Middle Ages.[8]

As modern readers we should ask ourselves some crucial questions: is it the poet's anxiety we are reading in *Piers*, or our own? In imitating Will's willful withholding of faith until Dowel may be logically explained, are we doing what Langland believes is right— are we doing well? Where and to what extent does the poet evince doubt about allegory as a signifying mode, or about his poetic undertaking in general? We must begin our approach to the poem in good faith, in the assumption that the poet means what he says, likes what he does, and does more or less what he likes in the poem. Most critics in the new tradition, like most earlier critics of *Piers*, are in fact quick to agree that Langland's theology, as expressed by Dame Holy Church and other characters, is thoroughly orthodox and conservative. The tendency is to begin with a statement of Langland's orthodoxy and then to list a series of "buts": "but" he advocates reform and questions church authority, "but" he seems awkwardly to shift allegories in midstream, "but" he cannot seem to organize his material. This last "but" is by far the most damaging; it was the failure of earlier attempts to find some unifying order in the poem that led critics to seek significance in its disorder, where Will's frustrated quest for meaning seemed invitingly to mirror their own. Certainly no one could convincingly argue that Langland's orthodox faith reveals itself in the tidy hierarchies of the *Divina commedia*; but there must be some question about the propriety of siding with a character named Will against a figure named Holy Church in a Christian allegorical poem. The real basis of the argument for doubt and anxiety lies not in the poem's theology but in its poetics—especially in its allegory, and in the question of that allegory's interpretation.

The belief that Langland had serious reservations about writing poetry, even though he appears to have devoted much of his life to the undertaking, is founded largely on a single passage in the poem. At the beginning of Passus XII a character named Imaginative appears and, among other things, criticizes Will for writing:

"And þow medlest þee wiþ makynges and myȝtest go
    seye þi sauter,
And bidde for hem þat ȝyueþ þee bread, for þer are bokes
    y[n]owe
To telle men what dowel is, dobet and dobest boþe,
And prechours to preuen what it is of many a peire freres."

(XII.16–19)[9]

Out of context this might look like a serious confession of self-doubt; but when we see that it follows a scene in which Justice (Lewte) himself justifies with quotations from Scripture Will's desire to write about his dreams, and that it is followed not only by Will's own efforts to justify himself but also by Imaginative's lengthy exoneration of writing and study based on classical and Christian tradition, we begin to understand that Langland is allegorically expressing the inner debate that led to his decision to write. The allegory tells us that while imagination initially balks at the task, justice has exhorted the poet to go on—and he does so for several thousand lines. Still, this expression of self-doubt in the middle of the poem may perhaps appear excessively modest, until it is placed in the perspective of the long classical and medieval tradition of rhetoric expressing inadequacy. E. R. Curtius outlines this tradition in his discussions of "affected modesty" and the humility and inexpressibility topoi. The assertion of self-doubt is common not only in secular literature but also in religious texts, where the rhetoric of inadequacy naturally intensifies, since the subject undertaken is sacred. In *The Mirror of Language*, a study of medieval epistemology from St. Augustine to Dante, Marcia Colish describes the Christian writers' sense of the impossibility of their duty:

> They had been called, they believed, not only to attain a knowledge of God themselves, but also to convey the knowledge of God to the world. To this task they bent at once the resources of their Divine commission and the various techniques of thought and communication that human nature and their historical situation had imposed upon them and placed at their disposal. The acutely paradoxical implications of their mission did not fail to inspire in them mingled feelings of enthusiasm and unworthi-

ness. God had commanded them to express the Inexpressible, in terms accessible to the speaker and the audience alike. These very terms, however, would remain permanently inadequate to the assignment.

The solution to this paradox of necessity and inadequacy, of course, was faith in Christ, who "renewed and restored" the human faculties of language and cognition, "re-enabling them to become God-like": "Medieval thinkers drew an important epistemological corollary from this doctrine. In the Christian dispensation, human modes of thought and expression, although still limited by the human condition, could now worthily take on the tasks assigned to them by God. Human language, reborn through the Incarnation, could now assist God in spreading the effects of the Incarnation to the world."[10] The inadequacy of human language, then, and its ability nevertheless to convey the Truth through faith in the Word of God, had long been assumed when Langland wrote, and among medieval Christian writers the classical rhetoric of inadequacy had become a conventional but not necessarily insincere plea for the grace of both God and the reader. Finally, Imaginative's complaint is less that Will is doing a poor job of expressing the Truth than that he is saying nothing new and therefore wasting his time. Langland does not claim to make any bold new statements in his poem; he conceives of his work as another in a long line of traditional works about how to do well, all written in the understanding that human language is in itself inadequate to the task. The real difference between earlier literary statements of self-doubt and Langland's is that Langland converts even the rhetoric of inadequacy into allegory.

Carruthers's argument that "[i]f the poem lacks coherence, it is only because the Truth it so urgently seeks is not coherent in terms of those signs which Langland employs to conduct his search," suggests either that earlier, "coherent" poets never encountered the problem of the obvious gap between human signs and divine significance, or that unlike his predecessors Langland could not accept faith in the Word as the only power to bridge that gap. Eugene Vance, pointing out that "a radical anxiety about the sign and its functions has always marked the consciousness of the West," shows that in Western thought it has always been understood that linguistic signs are merely conventional, possessing in themselves no real bond with their signifieds.[11] Augustine is clear on the subject of conventional signs, stating that "even signs given by God and contained in the Holy Scripture are of this type also, since they were presented to us by the men who wrote them."[12] But as Vance shows, Augustine also understands that people produce conventional signs out of their "will to signify (volens significandi)" and that thus "medieval thinkers grasped not only the relationship between free will and signification, but also the contractual basis of signification." The value of words is not determined by the inherent inadequacy of language; rather, as faith in God and charity toward others are matters of individual free will, so the power of language to convey Truth depends on the speaker's willing faithfulness to the Word as a contract with God and the other members of the Christian community. Everyone is free to use language in the good faith that renders it adequate to spread the Word, or to abuse language by faithlessly distorting the conventional bond between signifier and signified. Langland makes clear that such faithlessness sins against others as well as against God, and Vance's argument that in the Middle Ages "the order of discourse could be considered as the living expression of a social or political order"[13] is nowhere more evident than in Piers, where Dame Study's blasphemous lords not only fail to feed the poor at their stately feast but also uncharitably distort the Word of God in their dinner conversation:

> "I haue yherd heiȝe men etynge at þe table
> Carpen as þei clerkes were of crist and of hise myȝtes,
> And leyden fautes vpon þe fader þat formede vs alle,
> And carpen ayein cler[gie] crabbede wordes:
> 'Why wolde oure Saueour suffre swich a worm in his blisse
> That be[w]iled þe womman and þe [wye] after,
> Thorouȝ whic[h werk and wil] þei wente to helle,
> And al hir seed for his synne þe same deeþ suffrede?
> Here lyeþ youre lore,' þise lordes gynneþ dispute,
> 'Of þat [ye] clerkes vs kenneþ of crist by þe gospel:
> *Filius non portabit iniquitatem patris &c.*
> Why sholde we þat now ben for þe werkes of Adam
> Roten and torende? Reson wolde it neuere!
> *Vnusquisque portabit onus suum &c.'*

Swiche motyues þei meue, þise maistres in hir glorie,
And maken men in mys bileue þat muse on hire wordes."

(X.104–18)

The important point here is not that the Word of God, like all words,
may be distorted and abused; that is obvious. The point is that such
distortions invariably signify the faithless and perverse human will
that fails to uphold the divine contract. Dame Study's stern advice to
these men, whose study has clearly brought them learning without
understanding, addresses the problem of faith and the human will
rather than the problem of language:

"Austyn to swiche Argueres [he] telleþ þis teme:
Non plus sapere quam oportet.
Wilneþ neuere to wite why þat god wolde
Suffre Sathan his seed to bigile,
Ac bileueþ lelly in þe loore of holy chirche,
And preie hym of pardon and penaunce in þi lyue,
And for his muche mercy to amende [vs] here.
For alle þat wilneþ to wite þe [whyes] of god almyȝty,
I wolde his eiȝe were in his ers and his [hele] after,
That euere [eft] wilneþ to wite why þat god wolde
Suffre Sathan his seed to bigile,
Or Iudas [þe Iew] Iesu bitraye."

(X.120–31)

If the blasphemous lords believed the Word of God, they would
understand their duty of charity and pure speech to others and would
understand that they are in this way responsible for the sins of others,
as well as for their own; instead they twist the Word to absolve themselves of guilt, at the same time irresponsibly spreading their sin to
all who hear them. The allegory of Dame Study suggests that for
Langland the attainment of Truth is a matter of faith rather than of
semiotics; the poet's interest in language lies in his perception of the
ways in which its use may reveal truths about the human will. Of
course, Dame Study's entire speech is addressed to none other than
Will, and the central allegory of the poem, as we shall see, is devoted
to the problem of the will and its perverse quest for understanding
without faith.

And yet Langland is said to distrust allegory, to distrust it so in-
tensely that he cannot stop himself from continually calling attention to it, breaking down its similitudes, and abandoning one after
another in despair of finding any that is adequate to express the
Truth. A distinction must be made—and has not always been made
—between the argument that Langland distrusted allegory's effec-
tiveness as a mode for expressing reality, and the argument that he
feared its misinterpretation by literal-minded readers. The latter concern is endemic to the genre: throughout the early Christian and
medieval periods writers of various kinds frequently accompanied
their allegories with serious words of caution lest the reader should
misunderstand. For St. Augustine, the very salvation of the soul depends upon the correct reading of figurative speech:

> [Y]ou must be very careful lest you take figurative expressions
> literally. What the Apostle says pertains to this problem: "For
> the letter killeth, but the spirit quickeneth." That is, when that
> which is said figuratively is taken as though it were literal, it
> is understood carnally. Nor can anything more appropriately
> be called the death of the soul than that condition in which
> the thing which distinguishes us from the beasts, which is the
> understanding, is subjected to the flesh in the pursuit of the let-
> ter. He who follows the letter takes figurative expressions as
> though they were literal and does not refer things signified to
> anything else. . . . There is a miserable servitude of the spirit
> in this habit of taking signs for things, so that one is not able
> to raise the eye of the mind above things that are corporal and
> created to drink in eternal light.

Augustine's concern, however, does not prevent him from using
metaphor to make his point in the same work, once again cautioning
his reader not to misunderstand:

> Therefore, since that truth is to be enjoyed which lives immu-
> tably, and since God the Trinity, the Author and Founder of the
> universe, cares for His creatures through that Truth, the mind
> should be cleansed so that it is able to see that light and to cling
> to it once it is seen. Let us consider this cleansing to be as a
> journey or voyage home. But we do not come to Him who is

everywhere present by moving from place to place, but by good endeavor and good habits.

The exhortation to the reader to see beyond the literal sense to the life-giving spiritual meaning of the allegory had become so common by Langland's time that Chaucer's Nun's Priest can use it playfully to excuse his tale: "Taketh the fruyt, and lat the chaf be stille." But the dangers of purely literal interpretation were just as serious to the late fourteenth-century English writer as they had been to Augustine; in *The Cloud of Unknowing*, an anonymous mystical treatise of the same period, the writer begins by urging the reader not to lend the book to nonbelievers or hasty readers, who are liable to misinterpret his words, and he specifically tells the reader not to misunderstand the metaphorical nature of his title:

> Do not suppose that because I have spoken of darkness and of a cloud I have in mind the clouds you see in an overcast sky or the darkness of your house when your candle fails. If I had, you could with a little imagination picture the summer skies breaking through the clouds or a clear light brightening the dark winter. But this isn't what I mean at all so forget this sort of nonsense. When I speak of darkness, I mean the absence of knowledge. If you are unable to understand something or if you have forgotten it, are you not in the dark as regards this thing? You cannot see it with your mind's eye. Well, in the same way, I have not said "cloud," but *cloud of unknowing.* For it is a darkness of unknowing that lies between you and your God. [14]

There is nothing new, then, in Langland's fear that allegory may be misinterpreted, or in his decision to use allegory despite these fears. But he does differ in one respect from other medieval writers who are willing to risk the dangers of figurative language in order to reap its benefits: rather than directly warning his readers about how to read his allegory, he incorporates the warning into the allegory itself.

The point may be illustrated by Piers's allegorical description of the pilgrimage to St. Truth, dismissed in the old critical tradition as an example of the poet's ineptness, and used in the new to demonstrate his anxieties concerning allegory. The field full of folk, having been shriven by Repentance, are told by Reason to "[s]eke Seynt

Truþe" rather than "Seynt Iames and Seyntes [at] Rome" (V.56–57), and Sloth, the last to be shriven, concludes with the resolve that "I shal seken truþe er I se Rome" (V.460). The folk cry out for a guide to St. Truth and are presented first with a pilgrim who has been everywhere but never found St. Truth, and then with Piers the Plowman, who has never gone anywhere but knows exactly how to reach Truth's castle:

> "Ye moten go þoruȝ mekenesse, boþe men and wyues,
> Til ye come into Conscience þat crist wite þe soþe,
> That ye louen oure lord god leuest of alle þynges.
> And þanne youre neȝebores next in none wise apeire
> Oþerwise þan þow woldest [men] wrouȝte to þiselue.
> And so boweþ forþ by a brook, beþ-buxom-of-speche,
> [Forto] ye fynden a ford, youre-fadres-honoureþ:
> *Honora patrem & matrem &c*
> And ye shul lepe þe liȝtloker al youre lif tyme.
> So shaltow se swere-noȝt-but-it-be-for-nede-
> And-nameliche-on-ydel-þe-name-of-god-almyȝty.
> Thanne shaltow come by a croft, [ac] come þow noȝt þerInne;
> Th[e] crofte hatte Coueite-noȝt-mennes-catel-ne-hire-wyues-
> Ne-noon-of-hire-seruauntȝ-þat-noyen-hem-myȝte;
> Lokeþ [þow] breke no bowes þere but if it be [þyn] owene."
>
> (v.561–75)

And so on for another thirty lines, until his description brings us at last to the Castle of Truth:

> "And if grace graunte þee to go in [in] þis wise
> Thow shalt see in þiselue truþe [sitte] in þyn herte
> In a cheyne of charite as þow a child were,
> To suffren hym and segge noȝt ayein þi sires wille."
>
> (v.605–8)

The chief complaint critics have lodged against this passage is that it lacks a sustained literal level; that it does not really depict a physical pilgrimage and is therefore not really an allegory but a feeble sort of allegorical shorthand or weak personification.[15] The assumption is that Langland senses the need for a traditionally allegorical gesture but has no faith in the allegory; that in his day pilgrimage did not really reflect a spiritual journey; and that he undermines the allegory to make this point. This assumption is correct in a way; Langland quite clearly means, by pointing out the nonsimilitude between physical and spiritual pilgrimages, to condemn the contemporary abuse of pilgrimage, its use as a sign without a spiritual referent. This is why he pits St. Truth against St. James and opposes Piers the Plowman to the literal pilgrim, who bears many "signes" of his pilgrimages that have no reference to Truth (V.521, 524, 529). Langland is as concerned as Augustine to remind the reader that the journey he is describing is not spatial or temporal, and that there is in fact no access to God through the mere passage of time or movement through space; thus St. Truth is found in the pilgrim's own heart and is described by someone who has never gone on a pilgrimage. But Langland is also no less confident than Augustine that allegory may help to express a spiritual reality, as long as his readers read it allegorically. Just as a physical pilgrimage confers salvation only when it truly signifies penance and faith in the heart of the pilgrim, so our own good faith as readers must bind the vehicle of pilgrimage with the tenor of penance if we are to perceive the true similitude expressed in the allegory. Langland's problem with the allegory of pilgrimage is that it needs a new vehicle, a literal level that really suggests the spiritual tenor to his readers; and he finds such a vehicle in the Ten Commandments, which provide his allegory with a true literal level in the daily acting out of God's laws of love. Langland's point is strictly allegorical here: true penance is neither a vacation in Rome nor a vague abstraction, but a spiritual state that must be acted out in the works of love and obedience that express the "cheyne of charite," the bond of love that ties the soul to God and all people to one another. If we fail to read the passage allegorically, we fail to perceive the spirit-made-flesh that is Langland's message of salvation. The poet forestalls such misinterpretation by closing the scene with a presentation of a cutpurse, a pardoner, and a "comune womman," who mistake the Castle of Truth for a physical place where they must have literal "kin," rather than a "kind" spirit, in order to enter.

Langland incorporates virtually everything—including himself as the tedious and inadequate allegorist of the life of Dowel, and his audience as possible misinterpreters of the allegorical road to Truth —into the allegory of his poem. Yet it is increasingly assumed that he does not regard allegory as an adequate mode for expressing reality. In her article on "the frustration of allegory" in *Piers*, Priscilla Martin argues that critics concerned with allegory have "tended to overlook the literal elements in the poem," and suggests both that the "interplay" between literal and allegorical modes "forms the structural basis of the poem and that the contrast between the ranges of experience they can express is central to its meaning."[16] Because the allegorical mode suggests to Martin "idealization and therefore simplification," she assumes that the poet, equating the real with the literal, must constantly abandon allegory in favor of the literal mode, which she argues "presents a world of compromise, confusion and frequent indifference to moral issues." Thus in Martin's view the Prologue begins by promising a dream vision allegory like the *Roman de la rose*, but instead presents "the real everyday world in all its variety, and the Prologue ends, as if to assert its verisimilitude, with the ordinary street cries of London. Most of the inhabitants are heedless of their uncertain position between the tower and the dungeon and act with regard only to the laws of this world." The perspective here seems twisted: if the folk are not aware of the moral significance of their behavior, the reader, who sees them in the absolute contexts of heaven and hell, cannot fail to be. The *Roman de la rose* by no means constitutes the only standard of allegory against which *Piers* may be judged; there is also the example of the *Divina commedia*, in which real human beings and their literal actions are judged by their significance within an absolute ideological framework of good and evil represented by a hierarchically and analogically ordered cosmos. Indeed, the whole notion that the literal and allegorical modes are opposed and incompatible would have seemed strange to medieval orthodox Christians like Dante and Langland, who assumed that everyday reality reflected the truths of Christian ideology as vehicle reflects tenor. In Dante's view, the "polysemous" nature of allegory properly mimics the polysemousness of the Christian cosmos, and his allegory should be read both literally and allegorically, as humanity is both physically real and spiritually the image of God. Dante's famous explanation of his allegory in his letter to Can Grande makes this intention clear:

> [T]he subject, with regard to which the alternative meanings are brought into play, must be twofold. And therefore the subject of

this work must be considered in the first place from the point of view of the literal meaning, and next from that of the allegorical interpretation. The subject, then, of the whole work, taken in the literal sense only, is the state of souls after death, pure and simple. For on and about that the argument of the whole work turns. If, however, the work be regarded from the allegorical point of view, the subject is man according as by his merits or demerits in the exercise of his free will he is deserving of reward or punishment by justice.[17]

To Dante, both the literal and the spiritual senses of the allegory are necessary for its complete understanding, just as it is essential for Christians to believe that Christ is both man and god. To argue, then, that the literal and allegorical modes are at odds, is to approach a paradox from the perspective of disbelief rather than faith. Being a twentieth-century reader, Martin does not conceive the cosmos allegorically; thus she begins her argument by assuming that allegory is by nature incapable of expressing reality, and that everything Langland intends literally must be antiallegorical.[18]

Let us begin instead with the supposition that an allegorist—as Langland is almost universally acknowledged to be—thinks allegorically. Let us assume with Edwin Honig that "allegory reveals a fundamental way of thinking about man and the universe," and that its "rhetorical, or figurative, language [expresses] a vital belief." In Honig's analysis of the relation between allegory and religious myth and ritual, and in Angus Fletcher's discussion of allegory as "the language of religion," closely related to magical thinking, modern criticism reaffirms the bond between allegory and faith in a spiritual, metaphysical reality. More recently, in an important article on the present state of criticism of medieval literature, Hans Robert Jauss, stressing the need to recognize the "alterity" of medieval texts, specifically recommends the definition of allegory as a "poetry of the invisible":

I see a far from exhausted perspective in the old basic definition of the allegorical *modus dicendi*, still used by Winckelmann, as making possible "the presentation of invisible, past, and future things." To my mind, this not only opens up a formal relationship between such heterogeneous literary genres and traditions as allegoresis, personification, allegorical fiction, typological visionary literature, psychomachia, bestiaries, and love-allegory. It also establishes a connection of content, against the background of that which H. Blumenburg once called the still unwritten "*Geistesgeschichte* of the invisible," that "world, afar and beyond, of the invisible, which for the Middle Ages was at once the sphere of religious authority." Since that sphere cannot be represented mimetically, but only allegorically, medieval allegory can be interpreted as the poetry of the invisible, and its history can be rewritten under this title. [19]

Because in the medieval view the invisible world engenders and determines phenomena in the visible world, a mimetic work cannot represent reality as completely as an allegory, and any approach to an allegorical work must at least begin in the faith that allegory can express this vision of reality. Moreover, as Jauss indicates, the definition of allegory as the poetry of the invisible provides a connection of both form and content between subgenres of allegory hitherto regarded as disparate. From this point of view the generic impurity of *Piers*, often taken as a sign of decay and confusion, suggests just the reverse: Langland's faith frees him to move about, not only between what we recognize as "realism" and "allegory," but also between typology and personification, dream vision and psychomachia. In his view of reality these are all connected. As Fletcher demonstrates in his chapter entitled "The Cosmic Image," the best allegory is generally mixed, whereas the "purer" works manifest the dull formalism and poverty of imagination characteristic of detachment and disbelief. When Muscatine describes Langland's sudden shifts from realism to personification to psychomachia as "surrealistic," he is suggesting that *Piers* represents a breakdown of the unified medieval world view in a way that is analogous to the sense of crisis and ideological breakdown evoked by modern surrealist art. But Fletcher describes this same temporal and spatial discontinuity as basic to allegory; allegory is "surreal" by virtue of its appeal to the invisible world of ideas rather than to the visible world alone, and herein lies its similarity to modern surrealism. [20]

Jauss particularly advises modern critics of medieval texts to make more use of *The Discarded Image*, C. S. Lewis's description of the medieval model of the universe and its classical, Neoplatonic, Christian, and barbarian sources. The model is a divinely ordered and plenitudinous system of hierarchies in which the visible and invisible worlds are bound together by divine love. The earthly region of mutability, with its demons, is connected with the nine immutable hierarchies of the planets, populated by nine hierarchies of angels. Beyond the fixed stars lies the perfect heavenly ether, a place where time and space do not exist, the seat of the Prime Mover who is also the Judeo-Christian Creator. The Creator has set the model in motion in a perfect harmony of correspondence between the celestial hierarchies of the macrocosm and the various earthly hierarchies of the microcosm: the Great Chain of Being, the church, the secular social order, the family, and each individual body and soul. These corresponding orders are also bound together by laws of cause and effect; for example, the discord in human souls can cause disruptions in the macrocosm. It is generally understood that Langland appeals to this model of the universe on certain occasions in the poem, such as Reason's sermon about the plagues and bad weather that result from human sin (V.13–20) and the arrival of "Kynde Conscience" from "out of þe planetes," bringing diseases to chastise the wicked (XX.80–87). For the most part, however, Langland takes for granted the physical model Lewis describes; he is not especially interested in redescribing the order of the cosmos for its own sake. But he is interested in analyzing humanity's place and duty within this order, and to do so he borrows many of the organizational rules and principles he perceives as governing God's creation.

The single most important of these rules is also the very rule by which the poet may imitate divine creation in his poem: the rule of universal symbolism. In his study of medieval symbolism Johan Chydenius demonstrates the pervasiveness of "[t]he idea that all created things are symbols of God."[21] Drawing from Augustine's definition of signs, in *De doctrina Christiana*, as things that impart knowledge of something beyond themselves, and from his teaching in *De Trinitate* that all created things, and especially human beings, are *vestigia Trinitatis*, Chydenius shows that "in the end it is only God who is *res*, everything else is *signum*." In Rom. 1:20 Augustine finds scriptural proof that all things signify God: "Ever since the creation of the world his invisible nature, namely, his eternal power and deity, has been clearly perceived in the things that have been made." And Chydenius discerns the doctrine "that visible things are images of invisible beauty" in the thought of both Pseudo-Dionysius and John Scot Eriugena; for them all things in nature and Scripture "have not been created for their own sake but in order to represent invisible beauty, to which God, through them, calls all men back." Chydenius also traces the doctrine of universal symbolism in the writings of the Victorine school, St. Bonaventure, St. Albert the Great, and St. Thomas Aquinas, citing especially Hugh of St. Victor's description, in his *Eruditio didascalica*, of divine creation as a book written by the hand of God. As Curtius shows, this image of divine creativity was a commonplace throughout the Middle Ages, used by theologians, philosophers, and poets alike. Chydenius cites the example of Alan de Lille:

> *Omnis mundi creatura*
> *Quasi liber et pictura*
> *Nobis est et speculum.*

> (Every creature in the world is, for us, like a book and a picture and a mirror as well.)[22]

Langland, too, is fond of using the mirror as an image for the world-as-image; his mirror images suggest that humanity, the church, Scripture, and the whole created world should be seen as reflecting their Creator (XI.9, XII.95, XII.152, XV.162, XV.527), and this is an image he shares also with Dante (*Paradiso* XXIX.144–45). But more important for our purposes is Langland's use of images of books and writing to show both that humanity is created in the image of God, as his signifier (IX.38–44), and that consequently not only Scripture but any human text may reflect God:

> Right as a lord sholde make lettres; [if] hym lakked parchemyn,
> Thouȝ he [wiste to] write neuer so wel, [and] he hadde [a]
>   penne,
> The lettre, for al þe lordshipe, I leue, were neuere ymaked.
> And so it semeþ by hym [þere he seide in þe bible
> *Faciamus hominem ad imaginem nostram*]
> He moste werche wiþ his word and his wit shewe.

> (IX.39–44)

Alþouȝ men made bokes [þe maister was god]
And seint Spirit þe Samplarie, & seide what men sholde write.
(XII.101–2)

Because human beings are God's "lettres"—his Word worked into a fleshly medium that preserves intact the image of that Word— human writing, too, may bear God's signature.[23]

As in divine creation, the most important rule in *Piers Plowman* is that every created thing bears the pattern of the Creator; everything in the cosmos signifies God. This is why God may be found in Scripture, in his traces in the material world, and in the human heart; it is also why people may know him to some extent, and why they may imitate him in their own books. In the cosmos Lewis describes, the hierarchies of creation are the gradations of increasing and diminishing similitude to God: the highest angels are most like God, the lowest inanimate objects are least like him; but all creation exhibits some degree of likeness to the Creator and is in a sense a metaphor or similitude for the Creator. In light of this model of the cosmos as a plenitudinous but closed hierarchical system of similitudes for God, Lewis suggests that the medieval poet's effort to create meaning must have been substantially different from the kind of creative effort a modern poet makes:

> [T]he man of genius then found himself in a situation very different from that of his modern successor. Such a man today often, perhaps usually, feels himself confronted with a reality whose significance he cannot know, or a reality that has no significance; or even a reality such that the very question whether it has a meaning is itself a meaningless question. It is for him, by his own imagination, to discover a meaning, or, out of his own subjectivity, to give a meaning—or at least a shape—to what in itself has neither. But the Model universe of our ancestors had a built-in significance. And that in two senses: as having "significant form" (it is an admirable design) and as a manifestation of the wisdom and goodness that created it. There was no question of waking it into beauty or life.[24]

There is certainly no such question for Langland; if anything, he relies too heavily on his readers' preunderstanding of the significance of the divine order to which his images allude. The most important thing modern readers should understand in order to enter Langland's poetic cosmos is that everything is significant; that nothing can fail to signify; that, indeed, there is no escaping significance.

But if people, their books, and creation at large are all similitudes for God, it is important to understand also that likeness is not sameness, and that similitude necessarily suggests nonsimilitude. Modern readers wishing to bridge the gap of alterity between their own and Langland's world must understand, as part of that world, the absolute alterity of God from everything in his creation—the gap of otherness between God and humanity transcended only by faith in Christ as the one man not merely similar to God but identical with God. The belief in the otherness of God is of central importance, not only to the Christian conception of reality but also to its conception of human language as a means of apprehending and expressing the truth. A common idea in medieval Christian thought is that God may be known only by *similitudo*—that is, by the signs of his existence and action in the material world—and that "[t]he ordinary language and the ordinary modes of knowledge in which we deal when we study created things therefore apply to the divine only in a transferred or specially adapted sense."[25] Pseudo-Dionysius responds to this problem by formulating both an affirmative and a negative approach to the apprehension of God. In the latter, the *via negativa*, words that define humans and the material world are used negatively to define God: if the world is mutable and finite, God is immutable and infinite.[26] Although negative theology and its emphasis on the transcendence of God are especially associated with Pseudo-Dionysius, the idea of God's unlikeness to humans and to human language is not peculiar to him but, as Margaret Ferguson shows, may be traced also in the writings of Augustine, and is to a great extent implicit in Christian doctrine. From Plato's distrust of the written word as lacking the "presence" of speech and thus vulnerable to misinterpretation, from Aristotle's requirement that good art be mimetic, and from Cicero's definition of metaphorical words as "those which are transferred and placed as it were, in an alien place," Ferguson infers the classical assumption that proper words, properly used, may really express an external and absolute reality. But if, as Christian faith posits, the ultimate reality is not the here and now

but a timeless and changeless deity who created the material world
as a system of mere similitudes to himself, then no human language
can hope to express reality except indirectly, through similitude and
nonsimilitude. Ferguson demonstrates this idea in her analysis of
Augustine's *Confessions:*

> For Augustine . . . all language is a metaphorical detour in the
> road to God because no sequence of words, even "proper" words,
> can adequately represent an atemporal and holistic significance.
> . . . Language as the representation of God is necessarily faulty;
> it is not only outside its source of significance but it is by nature
> unable to imitate an "inside" conceived as Divine Presence. Lan-
> guage is essentially inadequate because the concept of presence
> entails a notion of meaning as the immediate unveiling of a
> totality. Language is, in Derrida's phrase, a "figuration exilée"
> because its structural dissimilarity from its external referent is
> manifested by its inability to reveal except by a temporal pro-
> cess, not by an instantaneous unveiling. [27]

Human beings and their words are signifiers for a divine Signified,
but they are weak and partial signifiers, expressing both likeness and
difference; even the purest Christian can only reduce the nonsimilitude, never destroy it, and for Augustine, too, Ferguson concludes,
the only solution is Christ: "Christ is the only 'image' which can
bridge the absolute gap between sign and signified by allowing the
'image to coincide with the substance.' " Yet it is because humanity
exists in exile from God in a "region of unlikeness," and because
human language subsequently is itself only a "figuration exilée," an
inadequate signifier for something to which it is similar yet essentially dissimilar, that allegory is a valid way to express reality. Ferguson notes Augustine's frequent use of metaphors of exile and jour-
neying to describe the human quest for God, although this quest,
like God himself, is actually atemporal and nonspatial:

> Augustine's use of spatial metaphors in his own discourse is
> an emblem of his awareness that the very nature of language,
> which dictates an epistemology of measuring "spaces of time,"
> is radically "figural" with respect to God's atemporal truth. Now
> such an awareness that language is absolutely unlike the mean-

ing to which it refers is precisely the phenomenon which de Man defines as allegory, the mode in which language points "to a meaning which it does not itself constitute."[28]

If all words are only figural expressions of Truth, then figurative language, with its self-conscious insistence on the relationship between signifier and signified as a relationship only of likeness and unlikeness, is a more accurate representation of the Truth.

In his study of the "symbolist mentality" of the Middle Ages, M. D. Chenu describes metaphor and analogy as concealing, "in dialectical suspension between likeness and disparity, the intrinsic bond uniting the material and spiritual realms, here conjoined in a single stroke of thought."[29] "Dialectical suspension" does not imply the modern dialectic of opposition and synthesis; nor, Chenu argues, does it suggest the rationalism of medieval scholastic dialectic. Medieval writers adopted symbolism, "the subtle play of analogies drawn from the mysterious kinship between the physical world and the realm of the sacred," not as a means of rational, logical analysis of the nature of Truth, but as its own "method of inquiry and formulation." Chenu explains as follows:

> "A symbol," said Hugh of Saint-Victor, "is a juxtaposition, that is, a coaptation of visible forms brought forth to demonstrate some invisible matter." The play of this sort of reasoning did not constitute proof. Hugh's "demonstration" ought rather to be rendered as "display"; to think the opposite would be seriously to confuse two distinct modes of thought to the detriment of both. To bring symbolism into play was not to extend or supplement a previous act of reason; it was to give primary expression to a reality which reason could not attain and which reason, even afterwards, could not conceptualize.[30]

Symbolism is not a tool of logic, or of any mode of rational thinking: it is a formulation of Truth as paradox, as both "likeness" and "disparity" bound together "in a single stroke of thought." Symbolism is a way of describing the paradoxical nature of reality, and is "rooted in the 'dissimilar similitudes' of the hierarchical ladder" of creation itself.[31] Moreover, as the rhetorical solution to the problem of expressing the inexpressible, the symbol presents a paradox in which

—as in the paradox of Christ—the reader's faith is invoked as the means of bridging the gap between signifier and signified, flesh and spirit, human and divine. In the Middle Ages, to write symbolically was to imitate not only creation but Scripture, "which, by strange paradox, taught divine mysteries in a human language incapable of containing them."[32]

This same paradoxical, nonrational habit of thought is responsible for the allegory in *Piers Plowman*. Chenu makes a somewhat Coleridgean, rather disparaging distinction between symbolism and allegory:

> While metaphor or parable developed an *image* which, by its dissimilar similitude and in its entirety, initiated one to an understanding of the spiritual reality so figured, allegory was the analytical exploration of an *idea* which made use of details dissected and abstracted from an image, with each detail having specific meaning. It was no longer the Ark as a whole which was taken as a type or symbol of the church, but it was each detail of its construction that was explored in a new complex of meanings —its beams, its design, its length, and the like.

While Honig, Fletcher, and others have done much to rehabilitate allegory from this narrow perception, it is important to understand that whatever the technical distinction, Langland blends his methods indiscriminately. Piers as Everyman or the sower of the Word is a fine symbol of the man who imitates Christ; but Piers is also depicted as part of an allegory in which his oxen, seed, cart, and barn are carefully identified as the Gospels, cardinal virtues, Christendom, and the church. The tree of charity that grows in each heart is at first presented allegorically, with its roots of mercy, trunk of truth, leaves of Christian law, and blossoms of pure speech; but this tree is also associated with the tree of the knowledge of good and evil and with the Trinity because, as the tree of free will in every heart, it symbolizes the true kinship between all the children of Adam, each of whom is also the image of God. Edgar De Bruyne analyzes symbolism and allegory as they were defined in the Middle Ages, isolating an additional distinction between the medieval concept of allegory as something that "can refer only to real ob-

jects" and our own view of allegory as a mere rhetorical device—
what was known then as "parabolism."[33] De Bruyne acknowledges,
however, that in poetry such as the *Divina commedia* "we sometimes slip from profane parabolism into theological allegory."[34] This
is clearly also true of Langland's poem, where merely verbal resemblances (tree, Trinity, *arbor, Arbitrium*) evoke real resemblances between Everyman, Adam, and God. And the same slippage may be
seen, in *Piers*, between allegory and symbolism; Langland is not so
much concerned with the mechanics of signification as he is with
the paradoxical Truth that all symbolic modes reflect.

Then, too, as Chenu points out, there are many differences between Augustinian and Pseudo-Dionysian symbolism. The latter emphasized the inherent symbolism of all created things, "which, before
anything else and by their very nature, were so many representations, so many 'analogies' "; but for Augustine the sign had a more
subjective value:

> Augustine's "sign" belonged on the level of his psychology of
> knowledge and was developed with materials drawn from that
> psychology. It was conceived as the tool of man's spiritual ex-
> perience as this experience compassed the whole field of lan-
> guage, including the varieties of figurative expressions. It was
> consequently the knower himself who was the principle and rule
> of the "sign"; it was he who gave the "sign" its value, over and
> beyond any objective basis in the nature of things, always ex-
> trinsic to the soul. In any Christian conception of "sign," there-
> fore, the interior life of man, and above all faith, were primary.
> Without faith, understanding of the word of God was finished;
> without faith, a spiritual sense to sacred history could no longer
> exist; without faith, efficaciousness disappeared from the sacra-
> ments.[35]

This appears at first to be a great difference indeed: whether we
label Langland an Augustinian or a Pseudo-Dionysian thinker appears to determine whether we understand his poem to be merely
about words and ideas or about things themselves—what we regard
as objective reality. But in fact this distinction need not and cannot
be made. As we have seen, in his *De Trinitate* even Augustine subscribes to the idea that all created things truly bear the image of their

Creator, and Chenu cites the example of Hugh of St. Victor to show that "in the twelfth century and throughout the whole of the Middle Ages, the two strains were continually crossed and are difficult to distinguish."[36] If Langland understands the difference between the Augustinian and Pseudo-Dionysian conceptions of the sign, he makes no distinction in his poetry, which assimilates the psychological forms of dream vision and psychomachia with the "literal" allegory of typology and figuralism. In Langland's poetic cosmos, it is true that without faith in the truth of this significance, no one can achieve salvation. Humanity is created in God's image; but if people do not faithfully imitate Christ's life in their own, their inherent likeness alone will not save them.

It is because of this requirement that the proper interpretation of the nonsimilitude in Langland's allegory becomes vital to any understanding of the poem: the degree of nonsimilitude in an allegory is the measure of the vehicle's distance from its divine tenor; in the vehicle of humankind it is the measure of sin, of the failure to engage in active imitation of God. Nonsimilitude of course presupposes similitude; no matter how great a distance people put between themselves and God, no matter how they distort the image of God within them, they cannot erase that kinship to God which is their nature; they cannot escape their absolute and sole significance as beings in relation to God. The likeness is always there, but people must actively supply the faith in God, and by extension, in their own significance as the image of God, if they are to activate the saving power of symbols to unite spirit and flesh. And an imaginative version of the faith that invests the paradoxic symbol with the power to save is necessary also to our reading of Langland's allegory; we as modern readers must suspend our disbelief, must enter imaginatively into Langland's medieval Christian faith, in order to bind the tenor and vehicle of his allegory and to apprehend the significance of its nonsimilitude within the poem's cosmic structure. The folk's failure to perceive their divine significance in the Prologue is a sign of their fatal nonsimilitude to God; but if we, too, fail to interpret their actions in relation to Langland's Tower of Truth, then we, like the folk, will not have received the message of Truth that the poet's allegory seeks to convey.

The following chapters further define and examine the ordering principles that shape Langland's poetic cosmos into a faithful vision of wholeness, connectedness, and unity through multiplicity. Chapter 1 maps out the larger dimensions of this cosmos and its structural base in the medieval conception of time and space. Chapter 2 discusses the central importance of the Christian theory of human nature and understanding to *Piers* as the autobiography of Will. Chapter 3 explores the microcosms of Langland's allegorical imagery and their representation of the microcosm of human society, and chapter 4 attempts to reconstruct from evidence in the poem Langland's theory of a salvational poetic. This study owes some of its general conception, but very little of its actual approach, to the works of D. W. Robertson, Jr., and Robert Jordan, whose theories of medieval literature are based closely on the Christian-Neoplatonic model of the cosmos.[37] Ultimately, neither the methods of patristic exegesis advocated by Robertson nor the "quantitative procedures" Jordan derives from Neoplatonism provide the key that unlocks the closed cosmos of *Piers,* and this is partly because, for all their differences, both Robertson and Jordan stress "the central importance of the rational faculty in medieval art."[38] The new tradition of *Piers Plowman* criticism has brought to light once and for all the nonrational and paradoxical aspects of both theme and structure in Langland's poem. But paradox, far from being opposed to the medieval view of reality and its divinely ordered cosmic model, lies at its very center, at that impossible juncture where the visible and invisible worlds unite.

1
Creating the Cosmos
Space, Time, and Eternity
✦

Neither Will nor the reader must undergo an arduous journey to be granted a vision of the whole cosmic structure in *Piers Plowman*. Unlike Dante's pilgrim, who begins in darkness and whose vision progressively expands toward the climactic unfolding of the celestial rose, Will is at once presented with a simultaneous vision of heaven, hell, and middlearth:

> . . . as I biheeld into þe Eest, an heiȝ to þe sonne,
> I seiȝ a tour on a toft trieliche ymaked,
> A deep dale byneþe, a dongeon þerInne
> Wiþ depe diches and derke and dredfulle of siȝte.
> A fair feeld ful of folk fond I þer bitwene.
>
> (Pr. 13–17)

Despite its appearance in a dream, this order is presented as objective reality; it appears independently of Will's understanding or belief—he vaguely suspects it to be "of Fairye" (Pr. 6)—and its reality is re-asserted in the next passus by Holy Church. Langland's re-creation of the cosmic order in his poem is neither inductive nor progressive but begins, like its original, by fiat, and operates exclusively by deduction: divine order is the major premise, and we must not question it; instead the poet tells us what, given this order, we must do.

The few lines Langland devotes to the subject suggest that his cosmos is conceived as a divinely appointed system of hierarchies or circles designating degrees of likeness and unlikeness to God. Dame Holy Church explains the rebellion of the angels in this way, describ-

ing their fall as a change of likeness produced by a change in belief
and placing Lucifer, like Dante's Satan, at the very bottom of hell:

> "For þei leueden vpon [Lucifer] þat lyed in þis manere:
> *Ponam pedem in aquilone & similis ero altissimo.*
> And alle þat hoped it myȝte be so, noon heuene myȝte hem
>   holde,
> But fellen out in fendes liknesse [ful] nyne dayes togideres
> Til god in his goodnesse [garte þe heuene to stekie]
> And [stable and stynte] and stonden in quiete.
> Whan þise wikkede wenten out wonderwise þei fellen,
> Somme in Eyr, somme in erþe, somme in helle depe.
> Ac Lucifer lowest liþ of hem alle."

(I.118–26)

Imaginative later justifies God's ways to Will by invoking the circular hierarchies of heaven and hell in order to explain the salvation of
the pagan Troianus and the thief on the cross:

> "Ac þouȝ þat þeef hadde heuen he hadde noon heiȝ blisse,
> As Seint Iohan and oþere Seintes þat deserued hadde bettre. . . .
> And riȝt as Troianus þe trewe knyȝt [tilde] noȝt depe in helle
> That oure lord ne hadde hym liȝtly out, so leue I [by] þe þef in
>   heuene.
> For he is in þe loweste of heuene, if oure bileue be trewe,
> And wel lose[l]y he lolleþ þere by þe lawe of holy chirche."

(XII.196–97, 210–13)

To the little extent that he describes it, then, Langland's cosmos is
shaped like Dante's.

But Langland is not interested in charting these circles in spatial
detail; he is interested in heaven and hell primarily as the loci of
moral absolutes that are reflected in greater and lesser degrees by
human actions in this world. Dame Holy Church explains that Truth
and Wrong dwell in the tower and dungeon respectively, and adds
that those who are truthful in their daily lives bind themselves in
similitude to God:

> "[For] who is trewe of his tonge, telleþ noon ooþer,
> Dooþ þe werkes þerwiþ and wilneþ no man ille,

He is a god by þe gospel, a grounde and o lofte,
And [ek] ylik to oure lord by Seint Lukes wordes."

(1.88–91)

To embody truth is to imitate God, and it is most important to understand that in Langland's universe Truth is not merely an abstraction, a word on the tongue, but God himself:

"The tour on þe toft", quod she, "truþe is þerInne,
And wolde þat ye wrouȝte as his word techeþ.
For he is fader of feiþ, and formed yow alle
Boþe with fel and with face, and yaf yow fyue wittes
For to worshipe hym þerwiþ while ye ben here."

(1.12–16)

Absolute Truth has a real being in God; all earthly things, including people, are relative truths and possess only a secondary reality as imitations. The passage describes a reciprocal relationship between God and humanity: because God created people, they must re-create God in words and deeds that imitate his Word of Truth. If people do well, then, they are not following some intellectual moral abstraction of their own creation but are imitating Christ, the real Word of God. This is the meaning behind the deliberate duality of reference in words such as "Dowel" throughout the poem. At the end of the pardon scene, Langland warns people to do well in anticipation of judgment in the Court of Christ:

At þe dredful dome, whan dede shulle rise
And comen alle [bi]for crist acountes to yelde,
How þow laddest þi lif here and hi[s] law[e] keptest,
[What] þow didest day by day þe doom wole reherce.
A pokeful of pardon þere, ne prouincials lettres,
Theiȝ [þow] be founde in þe fraternite [among] þe four ordres
And haue Indulgences doublefold, but dowel [þee] helpe
I sette youre patentes and youre pardon at one pies hele.

(VII.193–200)

Having set up the image of sinners giving account of their deeds to Christ, Langland subtly shifts the meaning of Dowel to include Christ himself:

Forþi I counseille alle cristene to crie god mercy,
And Marie his moder be meene bitwene,
That god gyue vs grace er we go hennes
Swiche werkes to werche, while we ben here,
That, after oure deeþ day, dowel reherce
At þe day of dome we dide as he hiȝte.

(VII.201–6)

It is not simply that our good deeds will speak for us in the next life
(as in the morality play *Everyman*), but that good deeds demonstrate
obedience to the teachings of Christ: to do well is to imitate Dowel.
For Langland everything one may do on earth has significance only
in its relation to real, divine exemplars.

If humanity's whole significance is derived from its similitude to
God, it follows that the greater the sinner, the more the sinner signifies nonsimilitude to God. Langland's cosmos is structured on the
Neoplatonic and Augustinian definitions of good as absolute presence in God and evil as the absence of good resulting from the perversion of the individual will.[1] Dame Holy Church identifies sin as
Wrong or False, the mere negation of Truth, possessing no meaning
outside its nonexpression of Truth. This is why, for example, Lady
Meed and her family are depicted as parodies of the royal family of
heaven, borrowing its form but devoid of content. As Truth is the
"fader of feiþ," Wrong is "Fader of falshede" (I.64). Holy Church's
father is God (II.29), and her betrothed is called both Mercy (II.31)
and "Leautee" (II.21), for in Christ justice and mercy are united; thus
the church is both the daughter and the bride of Truth or God. Conversely, Lady Meed's father is False "þat haþ a fikel tonge" (II.25),
both the son of Wrong and Wrong himself, and her betrothed is False
Fickle-Tongue, later referred to simply as "Fals" (II.41, 66); so Meed
is both daughter and bride of Falsehood. The marriage deed Simony
and Civil Law read (II.72–114) has all the form of the Christian deed
of marriage ordained by God and the church, but lacks the content
of love:

"Witeþ and witnesseþ þat wonieþ vpon erþe
That Mede is ymaried moore for hire goodes

Than for any vertue or fairnesse or any free kynde.
Falsnesse is fayn of hire for he woot hire riche."

(II.75–78)

And finally Conscience reveals that this Meed, far from being a good
signifier of divine spiritual meed, expresses almost the opposite; so
great is human abuse of rewards that only the name of Meed remains
to mark the place where likeness should be:

"Ther are two manere of Medes, my lord, [bi] youre leue.
That oon god of his grace [gyueþ] in his blisse
To [hem] þat [werchen wel] while þei ben here. . . .
Ther is [a] Mede mesurelees þat maistres desireþ;
To mayntene mysdoers Mede þei take."

(III.231–33, 246–47)

Langland is not saying that there are two truths, one the ideal Truth
of divine revelation and one the material truth of human experience;
he shows Lady Meed to be a greatly dissimilar similitude for spiritual meed because material rewards, as people commonly bestow
them, signify more the absence of spiritual meaning than its presence. The source of the Meed allegory is Holy Church's quotation
of Jesus' answer to the Pharisees, in which Jesus draws an analogy
between spiritual and material debts, not to show that they are similar, or to justify material wealth as a truth in its own right, but to
emphasize the unlikeness between spiritual and material things and
to show that the two must not be confused:

"Go to þe gospel", quod she, "þat god seide hymseluen,
Tho þe poeple hym apposed wiþ a peny in þe temple
[If] þei sholde [worshipe þerwiþ Cesar þe kyng].
And [he] asked of h[em] of whom spak þe lettre,
And þe ymage [y]lik[e] þat þerInne stondeþ.
'Cesar[i]s', þei seiden, 'we seen wel echone.'
'Reddite Cesari', quod god, 'þat Cesari bifalleþ,
Et que sunt dei deo or ellis ye don ille.' "

(I.46–53)

Caesar is not to be worshiped, nor is divine love to be purchased with
money. In Langland's vision of things, to imitate Lady Meed's worldly

money-marriage would not be to make a concession to "reality" rather than following some lofty but impractical ideal of romantic attachment. Langland never opposes the ideal to the real in this way, because to him the ideal *is* the real, and the material a poor imitation at best. Anyone who chooses not to imitate God in Christian faith becomes, like Lady Meed, an extremely dissimilar similitude.

All this is to say that Langland is a realist in the medieval philosophical sense and not in the modern sense of naturalism and materialism. To him universals such as Truth are not merely words but the real ideas or Forms in the mind of God, of which material creation is an imitation.[2] People, like their words and like all creation, are limited signifiers for the divine reality of the Word. Certainly they may choose to make themselves into poorer signifiers—that is a matter of free will. But those who choose not to imitate God will still be signifiers in the same system of meaning. The universe is a closed system in which even efforts at nonmeaning do not escape divine meaning, as Will himself perceives of the Christian who wishes to deny his Christianity:

"For þouȝ a cristen man coueited his cristendom to reneye,
Riȝtfully to reneye no reson it wolde.
For may no cherl chartre make ne his c[h]atel selle
Wiþouten leue of his lord; no lawe wol it graunte.
Ac he may renne in arerage and rome from home,
As a reneyed caytif recchelesly rennen aboute.
A[c] reson shal rekene wiþ hym [and rebuken hym at þe laste,
And conscience acounte wiþ hym] and casten hym in arerage,
And putten hym after in prison in purgatorie to brenne."

(XI.125–33)

The Christian system of meaning governs the whole cosmos and everything in it; people may go into debt to their Lord, but they cannot change their identity as God's creatures. So when Langland imitates this system by creating an allegorical character such as Meed, whose actions are poor signifiers for the divine tenor of spiritual reward, he is not saying that material "reality" has betrayed humanity's imagined ideals; he is saying rather that people divorce themselves from the spiritual reality from which they derive their existence, their meaning, and their name as the children—the images—of God.

Lady Meed is a nonsimilitude for spiritual reward because, as her money-marriage indicates, she is devoid of love, and love is the divine glue that binds all the hierarchic similitudes of the universe. Divine love created the universe in space, and it also causes it to continue in time: as Dame Holy Church defines it, love binds not only the material hierarchies of the cosmos but also the sequences of history, making past, present, and future into a single, unified whole:

> "For truþe telleþ þat loue is triacle of heuene:
> May no synne be on hym seene þat vseþ þat spice,
> And alle hise werkes he wrouȝte with loue as hym liste;
> And lered it Moyses for þe leueste þyng and moost lik to
>   heuene,
> And [ek] þe pl[ante] of pees, moost precious of vertues.
> For heuene myȝte nat holden it, [so heuy it semed],
> Til it hadde of þe erþe [y]eten [hitselue].
> And whan it hadde of þis fold flessh and blood taken
> Was neuere leef vpon lynde lighter þerafter,
> And portatif and persaunt as þe point of a nedle
> That myȝte noon Armure it lette ne none heiȝe walles.
> Forþi is loue ledere of þe lordes folk of heuene
> And a meene, as þe Mair is, bitwene þe [commune] & þe
>   [kyng];
> Right so is loue a ledere and þe lawe shapeþ;
> Vpon man for his mysdedes þe mercyment he taxeþ."
>   (1.148–62)

As God is both the source of love and love itself, so Holy Church describes him as both tree and balm: as a tree he unites the branches of creation into a single living being, and as the balm of love he permeates creation. Moreover, the passage is clearly a description of Christ, but it does not describe his coming as a discrete event in time. Christ is always coming: he came when God created the universe ("And alle hise werkes he wrouȝte with loue"); he came to Moses; he is coming today to bind human societies, just as he binds "þe lordes folk of heuene"; his coming is the bond of love that continuously preserves creation. The image is of a love that binds all spaces and all times into unity, and this is not fanciful imagery for Langland but a way of describing a reality that is nonspatial and atemporal. Once again, what we are able to perceive only at the end of Dante's pilgrimage is presented here at the outset of Will's; when Dante the pilgrim gazes at last into the eternal light of God, he sees the entire universe, through which he has slowly ascended circle by circle, bound by love into a single, timeless whole, just as his own poem, created over the course of many years, is now at last a complete and timeless creation:

> Nel suo profondo vidi che s'interna,
>   legato con amore in un volume,
>   cio che per l'universo si squaderna:
> sustanze e accidenti e lor costume
>   quasi conflati insieme, per tal modo
>   che cio ch'i' dico e un semplice lume.
> La forma universal di questo nodo
>   credo ch'i' vidi, perche piu di largo,
>   dicendo questo, mi sento ch'i' godo.
> Un punto solo m'e maggior letargo
>   che venticinque secoli a la 'mpresa
>   che fe Nettuno ammirar l'ombra d'Argo.[3]

(In its depth I saw ingathered, bound by love in one single volume, that which is dispersed in leaves throughout the universe: substances and accidents and their relations, as though fused together in such a way that what I tell is but a simple light. The universal form of this now I believe that I saw, because, in telling this, I feel my joy increase.

A single moment makes for me greater oblivion than five and twenty centuries have wrought upon the enterprise that made Neptune wonder at the shadow of the Argo.)[4]

Both Dante and Langland are intent upon imitating divine reality in their allegories; each makes his poem a likeness of the created universe, which is itself a similitude for the divine reality upon which it is patterned. The poets are the gods of their fictive worlds, creating structures in which time and space are similitudes for a transcendent reality. Dante reveals in *Paradiso* that the circles of heaven through which Dante the pilgrim has appeared to be physically progressing are merely symbols designed to convey spiritual states to the fallen human mind:

Qui si mostraro, non perche sortita
  sia questa spera lor, ma per far segno
  de la celestial c'ha men salita.
Cosi parlar conviensi al vostro ingegno,
  pero che solo da sensato apprende
  cio che fa poscia d'intelletto degno.
Per questo la Scrittura condescende
  a vostra facultate, e piedi e mano
  attribuisce a Dio e altro intende. . . .[5]

(These showed themselves here, not because this sphere is al-
lotted to them, but to afford sign of the celestial grade that is
least exalted. It is needful to speak thus to your faculty, since
only through sense perception does it apprehend that which it
afterwards make fit for the intellect. For this reason Scripture
condescends to your capacity, and attributes hands and feet to
God, having other meaning. . . .)

Yet throughout his poem, Dante pays close attention to the strict
proprieties of time and space; he concedes the need for such representation and only at the very end attempts to envisage atemporal
reality through symbols of unity and paradox. Langland, on the other
hand, begins *Piers* with both a vision of the whole Christian universe and images suggesting the spaceless and timeless reality that it
signifies. Truth, Love, and Christ may reveal themselves to people at
selected moments in time, but they are not of time; on the contrary,
they are together the sole Creator and continuous Preserver of time.
    That Langland does not regard the temporal world as reality in any
final sense is important to both the theme and the structure of his
poem. The idea especially of the relative nature of time, of its contin-
gency on an atemporal Truth—the idea, in fact, of time as a weak and
repetitive similitude for atemporal reality—is central to Langland's
allegory. In "Time, Apocalypse, and the Plot of *Piers Plowman*,"
Mary Carruthers argues that "*Piers Plowman* is written within the
intellectual tradition of Christian eschatology, which values time
and temporality differently from neoclassically based aesthetics,"
and that as a result, "time is not something to be transcended but
to be embraced as the medium in which salvation occurs." I see several problems with this idea. First, although Langland obviously did

not follow neoclassical aesthetic rules for unity of time, place, and action, it is inaccurate to suggest that he did not seek to transcend time in *Piers*, for that he certainly did. Carruthers's own observations about time in the poem do not support a view of Langland as embracing time: she states that *Piers* does not follow a linear progression; that instead it endlessly repeats the same pattern of wandering, conversion, and pilgrimage; that it has no clear-cut beginning or end; and that it seems to circle eternally around the "midpoint" of the Resurrection. Such unconcern for the mimetic representation of time does not suggest that Langland valued time per se. Second, Carruthers supports her assertion that Langland's conception of time was not neoclassical by citing Oscar Cullmann's distinction between the linear, progressive time of primitive Christianity and the cyclic time of the Greeks; yet there is no reason Langland's time should be that of the primitive Christian, since, as Cullmann himself argues, "very early the Greek conception of time supplanted the Biblical one, so that down through the history of doctrine to the present day there can be traced a great misunderstanding, upon the basis of which that is claimed as 'Christian' which in reality is Greek." Cullmann attributes the essential difference between Greek and biblical time to differing attitudes toward the relationship between time and eternity. In Platonic Greek thought, he explains, time and eternity are qualitatively different, whereas to primitive Christians time was simply a part of the endless succession of ages that constituted eternity. "For Plato, eternity is not endlessly extended time, but something quite different; it is timelessness. Time in Plato's view is only the copy of eternity thus understood," and it is the Platonic Greek view that Christian theology has adapted to its use down through the ages.[6]

Although Augustine adapts Plato's ideas to accommodate the Christian sense of destiny, so that, as Herman Hausheer puts it, "time is not a perpetual revolving image of eternity, but is irreversibly moving in a definite direction," nevertheless Augustine's notion of time is chiefly Platonic in its insistence that "there is no time in God."[7] It is certainly the Platonic view of time that Augustine espouses in *The Confessions*, where he forestalls questions of what God did before he created the world by arguing that there was no "before," since there was no time before God created the world, and God is not in time.[8] Time for Augustine, as Margaret Ferguson shows, is a defining characteristic of the "region of unlikeness" (a term from Plato) in which we live in exile from the Eternal One. It is because Augustine sees a qualitative difference between time and eternity that he arrives at "a distinction of *essence* between God's 'Word' and human 'words,'" since words are necessarily "signs in time," expressing partially and sequentially a reality that is whole and simultaneous. Morton Bloomfield describes the medieval view of time as "ahistoric," a view in which a few vital moments in history are adapted to an "extra-historical reality," so that "Christ is sacrificed every minute of the day, and man continually falls." The idea does much to explain Dame Holy Church's definition of love. Bloomfield is referring to the medieval Christian figural view of history made familiar by Erich Auerbach, who explains that in this view "a connection is established between two events which are linked neither temporally nor causally—a connection which it is impossible to establish by reason in the horizontal dimension" and which is attributed instead to "Divine Providence." The result, as Auerbach explains, is that "[t]he horizontal, that is the temporal and causal, connection of occurrences is dissolved; the here and now is no longer a mere link in an earthly chain of events, it is simultaneously something which has always been. In the eyes of God, it is something eternal, something omni-temporal, something already consummated in the realm of fragmentary earthly event."[9] Georges Poulet complements the idea of a figural view of history in *Studies in Human Time*, where he points out that to the medieval mind there was no difference between divine creation and divine preservation of the temporal world:

> In one sense [men] were being created every moment; not that God was obliged each moment to create them anew, but rather that in all the range of their existence, by the same act of will, the Creator caused them to be and to endure. "Creation and pres-ervation are an indivisible action; thence the absolute unity of this action and the fact that its maintenance proceeds not by a succession nor by a continuation, strictly speaking, but rather by the permanency of a single indivisible action."[10]

Creation happens at every moment in time, the Creator being eter-nal and beyond time. Poulet also cites Thomas Aquinas's definition of time as a "defect in matter," quoting him and commenting as follows:

> "Succession in the formation of things is due to a defect in matter, which originally is not fitly disposed to receive form; but when it is so disposed, it receives form instantaneously." From this point of view, matter was nothing other than a resistance which, manifesting itself in the substance of a thing, hindered that thing from assuming instantly the fullness of being which its form would confer upon it; a resistance which introduced distance and tardiness, multiplicity and delay, where everything, it seemed, should have happened simultaneously and at once. *Tempus facit distare.* [11]

In imperfectly imitating the divine substance of the Word, then, matter produces a sort of cosmic stuttering called time; humanity's "region of unlikeness" to God is a time-space continuum that is essentially unlike divine presence. As spatial matter is an imperfect copy of divine forms, so time is an imperfect copy of divine simultaneity.

In trying to describe this divine reality, medieval writers often abandoned the hopelessly timebound processes of human logic and resorted to paradox. God, as Poulet shows in *The Metamorphoses of the Circle*, is commonly represented throughout the Middle Ages as "a sphere of which the center is everywhere and the circumference is nowhere." God is not in time or space, nor do all of time and space make up God, but God is entirely present in all times and all spaces. St. Bonaventure explains the paradoxical figure: "Because God is eternal and absolutely actual, He enfolds all durations and exists simultaneously in all their moments as their center and circumference. And because He is infinitely simple and infinitely great, He is wholly within all and without all; and it is for this reason that He is an intelligible sphere of which the center is everywhere and the circumference nowhere." [12] As Poulet shows, this figure for describing God was popular not only among philosophers and theologians but also among poets such as Dante, whose God of Love in the *Vita nuova* likens himself to "the center of a circle equidistant from all points on the circumference," and who describes his vision of God at the end of *Paradiso* as an infinite circle of light derived from a central ray:

E'si distende in circular figura,
   in tanto che la sua circunferenza
   sarebbe al sol troppo larga cintura.
Fassi di raggio tutta sua parvenza
   reflesso al sommo del mobile primo,
   che prende quindi vivere e potenza.[13]

(It spreads so wide a circle that the circumference would be too large a girdle for the sun. Its whole expanse is made by a ray reflected from the summit of the Primum Mobile, which therefrom takes its life and potency.)

Naturally, this figure is closely related to the paradox of the Trinity, which also describes a single, eternal God whose "parts" are not partial but whole, infinite, and simultaneously one. Jean de Meun, among others, combines these figures in a description of the incarnation of Christ:

C'est le cercles trianguliers,
C'est li triangles circuliers
Qui en la vierge s'ostela.

(This is the triangular circle,
This is the circular triangle
That within the Virgin found its home.)[14]

The reference to the Incarnation in this connection is vitally important, for Jean is here describing the greatest paradox of all, which is the point of intersection between linear, progressive time and the simultaneous wholeness of eternity, the point at which material space encloses infinite spirit.[15] Christ alone connects the two worlds, and Christ alone constitutes humanity's hope for escape from the exiled sequences of time and space to unity and simultaneity with God. As Ferguson explains, Christ is the only "word" for Augustine that "can bridge the absolute gap between sign and signified. . . . Christ is the only true 'similitudo' because His relation to God is one of genuine 'simultaneity.' "[16] Henri de Lubac traces the history of the concept of Christ as the "Verbum abbreviatum," the one Word that transcends time and space, signifying God at once and eternally.[17] And this, as we have seen, is the same vision of Christ's role as that presented by Dame Holy Church in her definition of love.

Adherents to the old tradition of *Piers* criticism have devoted much research to finding a logical progressive order in the many sequences of the poem, whereas critics in the new tradition, sensing the repetitive, nonprogressive tendencies of Langland's allegory, attribute them to the poet's frustration and disbelief. What the two traditions are observing, however, are the two halves of a paradox expressing a medieval Christian vision of Truth. The life of fallen humanity is filled with temporal processes, sequences, degrees, and hierarchies, and these Langland reproduces in his depiction of the world. But this world is governed by a divinity that is timeless, an absolute reality that confounds all temporal sequences in eternity. It is only through the perception of the paradox by which the human is permeated with the divine and time is intersected by eternity— it is only, in short, through faith in the paradox of Christ, and not through any sequence of human logic alone—that humanity is saved. This is the paradoxical truth that Langland strives to reproduce in his allegory in order to induce in both Will and the reader a vision of faith and unity. The way in which this paradoxical truth functions as a structure of Langland's universe may be seen in three sequences in the poem: Piers's pilgrimage in quest of Truth's pardon, the journey through Christian history to the advent of Christ in Passus XVI and XVII, and the sequence of the three Do's as they are variously defined throughout the poem.

We have already seen how Langland uses the Ten Commandments to reinvest the pilgrimage allegory with its originally intended significance. The common allegory of pilgrimage expresses a spiritual journey toward God through the similitude of a literal journey through time and space. Strangely, however, Piers's journey to Truth ends exactly where it began, with the acquisition of love for God and one's fellow humans. When asked by the folk how they may reach Truth, Piers explains that they must begin by demonstrating their love and faith through deeds of meekness and conscience:

> "Ye moten go þoruȝ mekenesse, boþe men and wyues,
> Til ye come into Conscience þat crist wite þe soþe,
> That ye louen oure lord god leuest of alle þynges.
> And þanne youre neȝebores next in none wise apeire
> Oþerwise þan þow woldest [men] wrouȝte to þiselue."
>
> (v.561–65)

Love of God and one's neighbor is of course Christ's abbreviated version of the Ten Commandments, so that the rest of the journey, describing obedience to the Ten Commandments, is simply another way of expressing the first requirements of love; those who love God and their neighbors will not swear or covet, steal or slay, lie or neglect the sabbath. The Castle of Truth toward which Piers directs the pilgrims is "Botrased wiþ bileef-so-or-þow-beest-noȝt-saued" (V.589), but faith is the foundation upon which the whole journey must be based from the start. Piers finally promises that if this journey is accomplished, Grace will grant the pilgrim a vision of Truth and charity—but the vision appears in the heart of the pilgrim and is nothing other than the loving faith with which the pilgrimage began:

"And if grace graunte þee to go in [in] þis wise
Thow shalt see in þiselue truþe [sitte] in þyn herte
In a cheyne of charite as þow a child were."
(v.605–7)

The pilgrimage ends where it starts, with the sinner's discovery and willing acceptance of faith and love within; the journey is accomplished the moment it begins.

This atemporal and nonspatial pilgrimage is also part of a larger sequence including the plowing of the half acre and the arrival of Truth's pardon. After describing to the folk the path to Truth, Piers agrees to lead them on their pilgrimage, but only if they will first help him to plow, sow, and harvest his field. The plowing scene becomes a discourse on the social contract, and instead of returning to the theme of pilgrimage, Langland has St. Truth send a general pardon to all those who work faithfully with Piers. In his article on the second vision, John Burrow notes that the sequence of sin, repentance, penance, and absolution would have been familiar to the medieval audience, but he argues that Langland's sequence is actually a series of "substitutions" demonstrating his anxiety concerning allegory's adequacy to express the Truth. Burrow sees the plowing scene as a substitution for a failed pilgrimage allegory, the pardon scene as another substitution for the failed plowing scene, and Will's quest in the *Vita* as yet another substitution for a failed pardon allegory.[18] But as we have seen, there is no sense in which the allegory fails to express its subject: it carefully demonstrates that salvation

resides not in literal pilgrimages but in willing and active obedience to God's law of love; indeed, its structure seems to imitate God
as the *Verbum abbreviatum*, expressing the spiritual "journey" as a
timeless instant in which the individual perceives and partakes of
divine love. There is no need, then, to substitute for it on the basis
of its failure to signify Truth. Moreover, it should be clear when
Piers is introduced to the folk as a plowman that the poet intends
to make use of him as such; the plowing scene is thus anticipated
before Piers's pilgrimage allegory begins. Nor are we meant to forget
the message of the pilgrimage allegory when we begin the plowing
scene, since during the latter Piers describes himself as God's "pil-
grym atte plow" and says, "My plow[pote] shal be my pi[k]" (VI.102,
103). A spiritual interpretation of the plowing scene is guaranteed by
the familiar pilgrimage allegory that precedes it and to which Piers
openly refers the significance of his plowing; after his description of
the way to St. Truth, no one can doubt that Piers represents no mere
plowman and that his act of plowing, too, has a higher meaning.
Piers is both Everyman the common laborer and Truth's own sower
of the Word; Langland shows that the honest plowman who works
out of love for God and his neighbor is just as much a teacher of
God's Word as the preacher who sows the Word.[19] The plowing scene
restates in a social context the message of the pilgrimage scene: that
salvation lies in acts expressing the love and faith within. What appears to be a sequence shifting from pilgrimage to plowing is actually
a single, unified statement about salvation. Piers says he will first
sow the half acre and then conduct the folk on their pilgrimage; but
this promised sequence of plowing to pilgrimage collapses into unity
as Piers dresses for both pilgrimage and plowing at once:

> "And I shal apparaille me", quod Perkyn, "in pilgrymes wise
> And wende wiþ yow [þe wey] til we fynde truþe."
> [He] caste on [hise] cloþes, yclouted and hole,
> [Hise] cokeres and [hise] coffes for cold of [hise] nailes,
> And [heng his] hoper at [his] hals in stede of a Scryppe:
> "A busshel of bredcorn brynge me þerInne,
> For I wol sowe it myself, and siþenes wol I wende
> To pilgrymage as palmeres doon pardon to haue."
>
> (VI.57–64)

The pilgrimage allegory is presented before the plowing allegory and promises to succeed it as an action; but in fact they exist simultaneously, each implicit in the other: the plowman tells of the pilgrimage, and his "pilgrymes wise" is a plowman's garb. It is not simply that each separate allegory says more or less the same thing as the other; rather, each has its whole meaning in conjunction with the other: the allegories of pilgrimage and plowing unite to show that true pilgrimage is what all people do in their daily labors when they do them out of love and faith, and that no other kind of action constitutes true penance.

Langland next presents the pardon scene, not as a substitution for the pilgrimage and plowing scenes, but as a conjoined extension of their ideas. The pardon is given to all people only upon the condition that they work, sowing the Word in the daily loving performance of their tasks; and this work is the spiritual pilgrimage upon which they must embark in order to receive their pardons:

> And alle þat holpen to erye or to sowe,
> Or any [maner] mestier þat myȝte Piers [helpe],
> Pardon wiþ Piers Plowman truþe haþ ygraunted.
>
> (VII.6–8)

The preceding scenes have already established that works of faith and love are required for salvation; when Hunger chastises those who refuse to help on Piers's half acre, he speaks of more than mere labor:

> "Kynde wit wolde þat ech wiȝt wroȝte,
> Or [wiþ tech]ynge or [tell]ynge or trauaillynge [of hondes],
> Contemplatif lif or Actif lif; crist wold [it als].
> The Sauter seiþ, in þe psalme of *Beati omnes*,
> The freke þat fedeþ hymself wiþ his feiþful labour
> He is blessed by þe book in body and in soule:
> *Labores manuum tuarum &c.*"
>
> (VI.247–52a)

"Feiþful labour" is required—not mere action but loving action that expresses faith. Nor has this requirement changed in any way when Piers resolves, upon reading the pardon, to change his ways:

> Of preieres and of penaunce my plouȝ shal ben herafter,
> And wepen whan I sholde [werche] þouȝ whete breed me faille.

The prophete his payn eet in penaunce and in sorwe
By þat þe Sauter [vs] seith, [and] so dide othere manye.
That loueþ god lelly his liflode is ful esy:
Fuerunt michi lacrime mee panes die ac nocte."

(VII.124–28a)

Piers may express himself here as though he has had a revelation, but he is only revealing the whole meaning of the earlier allegories: the point of the combined pilgrimage, plowing, and pardon allegories is that our daily bread should be penance and that therein lies our pardon. When Piers says, "My plow[pote] shal be my pi[k]" (VI.103), and then says, "Of preieres and of penaunce my plouȝ shal ben herafter" (VII.124), he is not trading definitions but explaining the whole meaning of his allegorical plow: in the first statement the plow is likened to a pikestaff in order both to borrow and to modify that instrument's traditional significance of penance; in the second statement the plow's full allegorical meaning is more directly expressed. Piers's decision to "cessen of my sowyng" and "swynke noȝt so hard" (VII.122) is not a recantation of the plowing scene, nor does it mean that the plowing scene is not to be read allegorically. Piers is only stating more directly what the plowing allegory means: that labor, whether it sows seeds or the Word of God in prayer, must be performed for love of God, not for "bely ioye" (VII.130), or the laborer will not be doing well. Finally, the pardon scene completes the idea —implicit throughout in Piers's name and dual role as laborer and spiritual guide—that every man must be his own pope and gain a pardon for himself through faithful works. But the identification between every man and the pope is also stated explicitly in the pilgrimage scene, where Piers advises each pilgrim to be able to say the following at the gate of Truth's castle:

"I parfourned þe penaunce þe preest me enioyned
And am sory for my synnes and so [shal I] euere
Whan I þynke þeron, þeiȝ I were a Pope."

(V.598–600)

Not even the pope is absolved of sin without true penance; therefore every man must look to the "cheyne of charite" in his own heart for salvation, and every man must be as much a Christ on earth as is the pope. Much later in the poem we again see the tree of charity in the human heart, and there, too, Piers is in the heart of every man, guarding this tree (XVI.1–17). But truth, charity, Christ, and the pope are all already shown to be enclosed in the human heart in this early sequence, where Piers is both the common laborer and the guide to Truth, the receiver of Truth's pardon and procurer of that pardon for all people. The image expands and is reexpressed later in the poem, but it does not really develop.

Thus Langland represents the path to salvation through the familiar linear process of pilgrimage, penance, and pardon. But this time-bound sequence signifies—as indeed should all human actions—the single, timeless message of love and faith. No mere sequence of rituals absolves people of sin; only a daily life of active love and obedience is true pilgrimage, true penance, and true pardon. Langland uses the traditional sequence as the literal level of a triune allegory that recognizes no partialness in its parts. Each unit in the sequence expresses the whole requirement of faithful action and the whole guarantee of salvation. At the bottom of this nonsequentiality lies the mystery of faith itself: what guarantees salvation at the end of the spiritual journey is not mere good deeds but the faith and love that initiate both the journey and the deeds. The end we seek is contained in the means of our seeking.

This paradoxical three-in-one structure is even more evident in the sequence depicting biblical history up to the advent of Christ: Langland faithfully outlines the historical progression from Old Testament law to New Testament grace, but he also views each event in this progression mystically, as a whole expression of the Truth of God that paradoxically exists whole in all of its parts. Each unique moment in time also partakes of timelessness.[20] It is "mydlenten sonday" (XVI.172), and Will encounters in succession Abraham/Faith, Moses/Hope, and the Samaritan/Charity who is also Christ. Abraham "seeks" Christ—that is, he knows himself to be a forerunner of the Savior—but he has also already met this Savior:

"[I] seke after a segge þat I seiʒ ones,
A ful bold bacheler; I knew hym by his blasen."
(XVI.178–79)

Abraham describes the man's blazon as "Thre leodes in oon," emphasizing also that each is "a persone by hymselue" (XVI.181, 185).

He tells Will that he met this man, who appeared to be "Thre men, to my siȝte" (XVI.227), and that he was tested by him (the sacrifice of Isaac) and made "foot of his feiþ, his folk for to saue" (XVI.245). But although Abraham represents faith—the first of the three Christian virtues and the foundation upon which biblical history must build toward the coming of Christ—his words emphasize the Trinity, and he discusses Christ as though Christ had already come. Abraham both describes God's creation of Christ in the past tense and includes himself among the "children of charite" created through the establishment of the church:

> "So god, þat gynnyng hadde neuere but þo hym good þouȝte,
> Sente forþ his sone as for seruaunt þat tyme
> To ocupie hym here til issue were spronge,
> That is children of charite, and holi chirche þe moder.
> Patriarkes and prophetes and Apostles were þe children,
> And Crist and cristendom and cristene holy chirche."
>
> (XVI.194–99)

Moreover, as a "part" of a trinity that cannot be divided, Abraham/ Faith also expresses in himself both the hope of salvation and the charity that rewards hope, for the Crucifixion is figured in his willingness to slay his son for God and in the rite of circumcision through which he and his heirs "[b]ledden blode for that lordes loue and hope to blisse the tyme" (XVI.237). Faith, then, expresses within itself the whole trinity of faith, hope, and charity.

Moses/Hope, in turn, explains that the "Knyght" he hopefully awaits is the one who gave him the laws on Sinai, which he already abbreviates to Christ's definition of *"Dilige Deum et proximum tuum"* (XVII.13). To Will's astonishment, Moses and Abraham agree that only Christ's abbreviated law of love has the power to save:

> *In hijs duobus mandatis tota lex pendet & prophet[e].*
> "[Is] here alle þi lordes lawes?" quod I; "ye, leue me", he seide.
> "Whoso wercheþ after þis writ, I wol vndertaken,
> Shal neuere deuel hym dere ne deeþ in soule greue;
> For, þouȝ I seye it myself, I haue saued with þis charme
> Of men and of wommen many score þousand."
> "[He seiþ] sooþ", seide þis heraud (Abraham).
>
> (XVII.16–22)

For reasons that will be discussed in the next chapter, Will does not understand how Abraham and Moses can agree. He sees faith and hope, not as necessary parts of the trinity with charity, but as two separate ways in which he may be saved:

"Youre wordes arn wonderfulle", quod I, "which of yow is
        trewest
And lelest to leue [on] for lif and for soule?"

(XVII.26–27)

Abraham, he complains, has told him that faith in the Trinity is enough for salvation, and now Moses says he must also love his neighbor if he hopes for salvation; consequently, he feels that he should make a choice between the two doctrines, and he does so:

"It is lighter to lewed men o lesson to knowe
Than for to techen hem two, and to hard to lerne þe leeste!
It is ful hard for any man on Abraham bileue
And wel awey worse ʒit for to loue a sherewe.
It is lighter to leeue in þre louely persones
Than for to louye and lene as well lorels as lele.
Go þi gate!" quod I to *Spes*, "so me god helpe,
Tho þat lernen þi lawe wol litel while vsen it."

(XVII.42–49)

But if Will really had faith in the unity of the Trinity, he would understand that faith and hope are part of the same single being, and that to have faith in God is also to love one's neighbor. He sees the movement from Abraham to Moses only as a progression through time, as a progressive piling up of laws and lessons, when both patriarchs describe themselves as part of a single, simultaneous whole.

The Samaritan/Charity meets with the other three at the spot where a man lies wounded by highwaymen. The fact that Abraham/Faith and Moses/Hope run away while the Samaritan/Charity (Christ) helps the man should not be disturbing; it is an allegorical expression of the fact that each virtue is distinct—as each person of the Trinity is distinct—and of the fact that salvation is only through charity, love, Christ. Nevertheless, the persons of the Trinity are one, and charity cannot exist without faith and hope any more than faith and hope can truly exist without charity. Will asks the Samaritan whether he should listen to the doctrine of Abraham or of Moses, and he is told that he should listen to both:

"A, swete sire", I seide þo, "wher I shal bileue,
As Feiþ and his felawe enformed me boþe,
In þre persones departable þat perpetuele were euere,
And alle þre but o god? þus Abraham me tauȝte;
And Hope afterward he bad me to louye
O god wiþ al my good, and alle gomes after
Louye hem lik myselue, ac oure lord abouen alle."
"After Abraham", quod he, "þat heraud of armes,
Sette [faste] þi feiþ and ferme bileue;
And as hope highte þee I hote þat þow louye
Thyn euenecristene eueremoore eueneforþ with þiselue."
(XVII.127–37)

By this allegory Langland asserts the unity of Christian faith and demonstrates the resolution of all oppositions in the paradox of Christ; charity unites faith and hope into a single, triune virtue. The Samaritan next explains the Trinity itself by analogy to the human hand and a lighted torch (XVII.140–298). His point in these analogies is twofold: he shows first that something may be both three and one, and second that charity is the most essential of the three since it alone binds the three into unity, as the Holy Spirit binds all people to God through Christ.

The sequence as a whole, then, demonstrates again the things we have already seen in Holy Church's definition of love and in the pilgrimage to St. Truth: that love binds all partial things, including time and space, into unity and simultaneity. Both the individual journey and Christian history are limited physical vehicles for a divine tenor that is already accomplished, complete, and timeless. This is why the poem not only begins with a complete vision of the Christian cosmos but also ends, as the culmination of the journey through biblical history, with another vision of the same contemporary Christian society as that depicted in the Prologue's field full of folk. It is as though, when all the historical sequences in the poem are completed, no time has really passed from the beginning to the end of Langland's poetic cosmos—as indeed time appears to be passing on earth, but does not exist for God.

This Christian truth is also reflected in the sequence of the three Do's, whose multiple definitions have suggested various hierarchic ordering principles to critics in the old tradition, and the loss of all ordering principle to those in the new. The former tend to focus exclusively on one of the sets of progressive attributes mentioned in the text, whereas the latter, noting that no one set of attributes seems to account for the entire meaning of the three Do's, tend to assume that if Langland could not settle on one definitive process for achieving salvation he must have doubted them all. Each of these perspectives sees only part of the whole truth about the three Do's. For example, D. W. Robertson, Jr., and Bernard Huppé's argument that throughout the poem the three Do's represent the active, contemplative, and prelatical orders of society leads them to assert that Piers the Plowman "represents God's ministry on earth in the *status prelatorum*" and that his plowing is symbolic "of the prelatical life." But as we have seen, the point of Langland's allegory of Piers and Truth's pardon is that all people in all walks of life must do well by acting as their own prelates, must save themselves and one another through loving actions that sow the Word. On the other hand, to point out that the three Do's signify many actions by many people is not to prove, as Mary Carruthers argues, that "Dowel is a word in search of a referent."[21] Langland's multiplicity of meaning leads to unity, not confusion; the many definitions of the three Do's reveal them to be a paradoxical trinity in which each part is both whole in itself and indissolubly linked in unity with the others.

Thought is the first to extend the definition of Dowel to the progressive hierarchy of Dowel, Dobet, and Dobest; he explains that Dowel is personal truthfulness and sobriety, Dobet is meekness and preaching to others, and Dobest is stopping wickedness and saving others from hell (VIII.78–99). This hierarchy of actions can also suggest the social hierarchy: Holy Church has already stated that in order only to do well every man must be "trewe of his tonge" and his "werkes," clerks must additionally "kenne it aboute," and kings must moreover "taken *transgressores* and tyen hem faste" (I.88, 89, 92, 96). Similarly, the image of Piers, who receives Truth's guarantee that all who do well will be saved, combines the honest laborer, the clerical sower of the Word, and the governing chastiser of gluttons and wasters. But other definitions of the three Do's make clear that social hierarchies are not to be automatically equated with the "þre fair vertues" themselves (VIII.79); such is Will's misunderstanding when he asks Clergy, " 'Thanne is dowel and dobet', quod I, 'dominus and knyȝthode?' " (X.336), and Scripture hastens to explain that knighthood and noble blood are of no use in the pilgrimage to Truth, and that riches are positive hindrances. When Thought likens the three Do's to the religious hierarchy of lay Christian, priest, and bishop, he is not saying that the lay Christian necessarily does well, the priest better, and the bishop best, but that the hierarchic social structure metaphorically expresses the triune nature of Dowel. Thought chooses the bishop as a metaphor for Dobest because of the symbolic value of the bishop's crosier:

> "Dobest is aboue boþe and bereþ a bisshopes crosse;
> Is hoked [at] þat oon ende to [holde men in good lif].
> A pik is [in] þat potente to [punge] adown þe wikked
> That waiten any wikkednesse dowel to tene."
>
> (VIII.96–99)

The three Do's are like social hierarchies in being articulated into parts that actually function only as a unity. The three Do's are unlike social hierarchies because material progress does not necessarily reflect spiritual progress and because, as we shall see, the spiritual states of Dowel, Dobet, and Dobest are not in every sense a progressive hierarchy.

Dame Study is angry at her husband Wit for teaching Will the three Do's:

> "And þo þat vseþ þise hauylons [for] to blende mennes wittes,
> What is dowel fro dobet, [now] deef mote he worþe,
> Siþþe he wilneþ to wite whiche þei ben [alle].
> But he lyue in þe [leeste degre] þat longeþ to dowel
> I dar ben his bolde borgh þat dobet wole he neuere,
> Theiȝ dobest drawe on hym day after ooþer."
>
> (X.134–39)

Dame Study is not simply saying that the life of Dowel is a good enough goal for the likes of Will; she is mocking the whole idea of making learned distinctions that divert the laity from perceiving the unity of God and of Christian faith. Her attitude toward the teaching of Dowel as three virtues is especially interesting in light of her earlier reference to people who make jests about the Trinity that "maken men in mys bileue" (X.118), and Anima later also complains of ignorant priests and friars who confuse the ignorant by preaching of the Trinity:

"Freres and fele oþere maistres þat to [þe] lewed [folk] prechen,
Ye moeuen materes vnmesurable to tellen of þe Trinite
That [lome] þe lewed peple of hir bileue doute."

(xv.70–72)

But Wit and the other visionary characters are not wrong to describe Dowel as a trinity. The conflict between these two authorities is resolved by Wit's immediate capitulation to Study, and by Study's subsequent acceptance of Will as a student; Study's real complaint is that study and logic cannot be allowed priority over faith and love:

"Ac Theologie haþ tened me ten score tymes;
The moore I muse þerinne þe mystier it semeþ,
And þe depper I deuyne[d] þe derker me [þouȝte].
It is no Science forsoþe for to sotile inne;
[Ne were þe loue þat liþ þerinne a wel lewed þyng it were].
Ac for it leteþ best bi loue I loue it þe bettre,
For þere þat loue is leder lakke[þ] neuere grace.
Loke þow loue lelly if þee likeþ dowel,
For dobet and dobest ben [drawen] of loues [scole]."

(x.185–93)

Once students concede the authority of faith over logic, they can accept the paradox of the trinity as a unity that is whole in all of its parts, a paradox that is evident in Wit's teachings and that students must accept in order to understand his teachings. One of Wit's definitions of the Dowel trinity, for example, is marriage, continence, and chastity, the traditional degrees of sexual purity; yet Wit also shows that all three Do's by their other definitions are contained in marriage itself:

"[Dowel in þis world is trewe wedded libbynge folk],
For þei mote werche and wynne and þe world sustene;
For of his kynde þei come þat Confessours ben nempned,

Kynges and knyȝtes, kaysers and [clerkes];
Maidenes and martires out of o man come.
The wif was maad þe w[y]e for to helpe werche,
And þus was wedlok ywroȝt wiþ a mene persone,
First by þe fadres wille and þe frendes conseille,
And siþenes by assent of hemself as þei two myȝte acorde;
And þus was wedlok ywroȝt and god hymself it made.
In erþe [þe] heuene [is]; himself [was þe] witness."

(IX.110–20)

Elsewhere Wit defines the three Do's in two sets of ways, so that Dowel is to obey the law and dread God, Dobet is to love one's neighbor and be patient, and Dobest is to help others and destroy evil. But within the institution of marriage lies the triune connection between God, one's neighbor and oneself, between law, love, and deeds, between Father, Son, and Holy Spirit; this is why true marriage contains in itself heaven on earth. Later, Abraham/Faith gives a similar definition of marriage, explaining that God created it as a representation both of faith, the first of the three virtues, and of the Trinity as well:

"In menynge þat man moste on o god bileue,
And þere hym likede and [he] louede, in þre persones hym
  shewede.
And þat it may be so and sooþ [sheweþ it manhode]:
Wedlok and widwehode wiþ virginite ynempned,
In tokenynge of þe Trinite, was [taken out of a man],
Adam, our aller fader. Eue was of hymselue,
And þe issue þat þei hadde it was of hem boþe,
And eiþer is oþeres ioye in þre sondry persones,
And in heuene and here oon singuler name.
And þus is mankynde and manhede of matrimoyne yspronge
And bitokneþ þe Trinite and trewe bileue."

(XVI.200–210)

A similar example of Dowel's paradoxical three-in-oneness and nonsequentiality may be seen in Wit's definition of the three Do's as the moral progression of obeying the law, loving one's neighbor, and helping others. The progression is logical; but Troianus, a pagan

saved by the pope's prayers because of his just judgments, firmly
asserts the primacy of love:

> "Lawe wiþouten loue", quod Troianus, "ley þer a bene!
> Or any Science vnder sonne, þe seuene artȝ and alle—
> But þei ben lerned for our lordes loue, lost is al þe tyme."
>
> (XI.171–73)

Troianus insists that justice alone did not save him, as it can save no
one without love.[22] This means, however, that by Wit's definition,
one must do better before one may do well. Wit and later characters
tend to associate Dobest with charity, but Troianus argues that no
one may do well without charity, either:

> "Whoso loueþ noȝt, he lyueþ in deeþ deyinge.
> And þat alle manere men, enemyes and frendes,
> Loue his eyþer ooþer, and lene hem as hemselue.
> Whoso leneþ noȝt he loueþ noȝt, [lord] woot þe soþe."
>
> (XI.177–80)

If Dowel is to obey laws, and yet mere obedience is worthless without love, then one must do better before one can do well. If Dobest
is charity, yet all love must manifest itself in charity toward others,
then one must do best before one can do better; or rather, all three
Do's are necessarily implicit in one another and cannot be separated.
In this sense there is no real progression: one either loves and has
faith, and therefore gives, or one does not.

Two more examples should suffice to prove the continuity of this
idea throughout the poem. Clergy defines Dowel as faith in the
"bileue" of the church, which, he specifies, must be faith in the Holy
Trinity as

> "Thre [propre] persones, ac noȝt in plurel nombre,
> For al is but oon god and ech is god hymselue."
>
> (X.245–46)

Imaginative extends this definition of Dowel as faith, including in
Dowel the entire trinity of virtues:

> "Poul in his pistle", quod he, "preueþ what is dowel:
> *Fides, spes, caritas, et maior horum &c.*

Feiþ, hope and Charite, and alle ben goode,
And sauen men sondry tymes, ac noon so soone as Charite."

(XII.28–31)

Although the superiority of charity implies a progression, Dowel
alone is all three virtues here. It is impossible to be truly charitable
without faith—to do best without first doing well—but it is equally
impossible to have true faith without being charitable—to do well
without also doing best. Augustine makes a similar observation on
the simultaneity of faith and charity and on their joint expression of
the human "journey" toward God: "Indeed, if faith staggers, charity
itself languishes. And if anyone should fall from faith, it follows that
he falls also from charity, for a man cannot love that which he does
not believe to exist. On the other hand, a man who both believes
and loves, by doing well and obeying the rules of good customs, may
bring it about that he may hope to arrive at that which he loves."[23]
In this sense faith, hope, and charity are not separate virtues but a
single state of being through which we "arrive at" unity.

This paradox of atemporal time, nonsequential sequence, and
simultaneous progression is at the heart of the scene in which Clergy
and Patience are asked to define Dowel. Both of their answers are riddles based on the paradoxical nature of *caritas* as the love that binds
heaven and earth, timelessness and time, into unity; but only Patience, who was schooled by Love herself, actually understands the
riddles. When asked for his definition, Clergy says with arid scholas-
ticism that he will not be able to answer until his sons, the seven
liberal arts, return from their studies at the castle of the Lord of Life
to report their findings. But he adds that in fact their findings may
already have been rendered moot:

"For oon Piers þe Plowman haþ impugned vs alle,
And set alle sciences at a sop saue loue one;
And no text ne takeþ to mayntene his cause
But *Dilige deum* and *Domine quis habitabit*
And [demeþ] þat dowel and dobet arn two Infinites,
Whiche Infinites wiþ a feiþ fynden out dobest,
Which shal saue mannes soule; þus seiþ Piers þe Plowman."

(XIII.124–30)

In her analysis of this passage, Anne Middleton makes two questionable assumptions: first, that Clergy himself is the source of the grammatical metaphor in lines 128 and 129, and second, that although
"infinite" may mean either lacking defined boundaries and therefore imperfect or all-inclusive and therefore perfect, the progressive
nature of the three Do's requires that it mean "imperfect" in this instance.[24] Once we see that the originator of the metaphor is actually
Piers, and that Clergy does not even pretend to understand it, we can
assume that Piers, who "set alle sciences at a sop," uses the grammatical terms with an ambivalence tinged with irony. In addition, he
has replaced the three Do's with "loue one," emphasizing the unity
of the Dowel trinity over its progressive aspect. The impossibility of
the riddle is Piers's point: equipped with only a limited intellect, the
fallen human mind learns only progressively; as Augustine shows,
human language itself is limited by its temporality, by its nature
as a sequence of differentiated and partial signifiers passing through
time.[25] But there can be no question of progress through time in the
world of absolutes, of divine simultaneous presence. Dowel, Dobet,
and Dobest are united in equal infiniteness; this is true both gram-
matically, since all three may be read as infinitive forms of the verb,
and semantically, since each signifies the whole in itself. If the trinity
of Dowel exists as a unity, how may humans, who learn only progressively, ever attain to Dowel? The answer, of course, is the thing
that cannot be learned: faith, the uniter of opposites, the paradoxical
resolver of impossible riddles. The answer is faith in Christ as the
incarnation of the timeless spirit of love into timebound flesh.

Patience's riddle is far more complex than Clergy's, and its intri-
cacies cannot fully be detailed here; but his message and his method
of expression are essentially the same, for the origin of his definition
of Dowel is Love herself, and her definition, too, is both progressive
and absolute, both divided and indivisible:

> "*Disce*", quod he, "*doce, dilige inimicos.*
> *Disce* and dowel, *doce* and dobet, *dilige* and dobest:
> [Th]us [lerede] me ones a lemman, loue was hir name.
> 'Wiþ wordes and werkes', quod she, 'and wil of þyn herte
> Thow loue leely þi soule al þi lif tyme.

And so þow lere þe to louye, for [þe] lordes loue of heuene,
Thyn enemy in alle wise eueneforþ wiþ þiselue.' "

(XIII.137–43)

The progression indicates logically that by learning we are enabled to teach, and by teaching we come to love. But the source of the learning and teaching here is Love herself; only love teaches patience, only love teaches the lesson one must learn in order to do well. There is no true learning or teaching without love; once again the end is in the beginning. Patience's subsequent riddle about having Dowel in a box (XIII.152) is indeed, as the gluttonous doctor labels it, "a dido" (XIII.172), since infinity can no more be enclosed than it can be divided into parts. But Patience uses another grammatical metaphor to show how, paradoxically, this enclosure may be accomplished *"ex vi transicionis"* (XIII.151). R. E. Kaske explains the Latin phrase as referring to the "power of transitivity by which a verb 'rules' its direct object in the accusative case."[26] As an infinitive, Dowel may be embodied in physical action by the divine power of transitivity: the transforming power that encloses the infinite godhead in the body of Christ also encloses the Host in its box. Love is the power of transitivity that incarnates infinitives; love is the mysterious union we seek with God, and paradoxically it is our only means of attaining it.

Like the material cosmos of time and space, then, the temporal and spatial structures of Langland's poetic world function as signifiers for the unity and timelessness of Truth. The structure of the poem imitates divine vision itself, depicting time and history not only from the progressive human point of view but also from the point of view of eternity, and showing that each moment of every human sequence is no less imbued with divine wholeness than is the sequence as a whole. Like the God who is both point and circumference, the poem is structured so that "the maximum is in the minimum." Like the Trinity, the poem's parts are an interconnected series of "infinites." Lawrence Clopper has argued that the Trinity is the structural model for the poem, pointing to Langland's emphasis on the Trinity's paradoxical three-in-oneness in the Samaritan's allegories of the hand and the taper. Clopper comes close to articulating a poetic structure founded on paradox; yet he ends by emphasizing threeness over oneness and mapping out additional progressive structures in the poem, suggesting, for example, that the *Visio* is the Father, the *Vita de Dowel* the Son, Dobet the Holy Spirit, and Dobest the three as a unity. His focus on progressive and linear sequence partially distorts his perception of *Piers*, especially concerning the wholeness of the poem's early visions. In stressing the gradual development in the visionary characters' teachings, he argues that Dame Holy Church's instruction is limited and reductive because she "insists that the Dreamer need only know the basic tenets of the church in order to be saved."[27] But Holy Church requires of Will everything that will ever be required of him in the poem: Dobest is generally defined as charity in the later passus, and in Passus I Holy Church repeatedly insists that "chastite wiþouten charite worþ cheyned in helle" (I.188, 194). Her vision of Dowel, like the Samaritan's vision of Dobest, centers upon the love of Christ that binds the Trinity, binds human time, and binds people to God and to one another. Kind's final advice to Will in Passus XX—"Lerne to loue" (XX.208)—is the same advice Will receives from Dame Holy Church in Passus I:

> "For þouȝ ye be trewe of your tonge and treweliche wynne,
> And as chaste as a child þat in chirche wepeþ,
> But if ye louen lelly and lene þe pouere,
> [Of] swich good as god sent goodliche parteþ,
> Ye ne haue na moore merite in masse n[e] in houres
> Than Malkyn of hire maydenhede þat no man desireþ."
>
> (I.179–84)

And it is the same advice he receives from Dame Study in Passus X:

> "Loke þow loue lelly if þee likeþ dowel,
> For dobet and dobest ben [drawen] of loues [scole]."
>
> (X.192–93)

Clopper argues correctly that the poem's structural basis in the Trinity is made clearest in the later passus, where the search for Dowel becomes a search for the Trinity itself; but it is important to understand that the trinitarian vision of each part as an expression of the whole underlies every allegory in the poem from beginning to end.[28]

For this reason any analysis of *Piers* that details only linear growth, progress, or development is bound to misrepresent the poem. It is not, indeed, that the poem never reflects or imitates sequences: the surface of *Piers* is covered with sequences imitating the traditional stages of individual pilgrimage and biblical history and superimposing other sequential patterns in the structural divisions of passus, *Visio*, and *Vitae*. But these sequences remain, in a sense, on the surface of the poem; they are signifiers resisting the simultaneous unity of their signifieds, as time is material resistance to eternity. To read the poem only as a linear progression is to take the signifier for the truth it shadows.[29] Such readings generally assume that to Langland the material world of time and space was "reality" in an absolute sense: Elizabeth Kirk, who judges that a correct view of the poem "depends on seeing it linearly," does so on the supposition that Langland is at heart a nominalist, portraying the "conflict between the ideal and the actual" and espousing a doctrine of "double truth."[30] Kirk argues that tension is produced when Langland establishes "the 'reality' of actual human experience" and "superimposes on it a second and authoritative 'reality'" of divine revelation; "[t]hus man lives in the presence of two kinds of realities."[31] Charles Muscatine arrives at a similar conclusion when, after surveying and discounting the many structural models proposed for *Piers* by earlier critics, he concludes resignedly that "Langland's sense of the present reality rends the curtain of allegory." But *Piers* is not, as Muscatine suggests, "a quest that has many beginnings, no middle, and an ambiguous end"; it is a quest whose end is in its beginning, and vice versa.[32] Anne Middleton is right to observe that "attempts to recount the whole narration of this journey as a developing succession of acts and events tend to emphasize discontinuity rather than progression," and that the poem is better explained "in episodic units whose arrangement seems somehow reiterative rather than progressive."[33] But she identifies this episodic unit as the debate or contest; describes the Meed, Wit and Study, and Abraham-Moses-Samaritan episodes as demonstrations of the "mutual incompatibilities or gaps" between various power-hungry authorities; and concludes that these debates "end in discord and irresolution."[34] She agrees with Kirk that the poem describes "two truths"—revealed truth versus cognitive learning, authority versus experience—and asserts that "the central intellectual and spiritual concerns of the poem are shadowed at every point by a self-referential doubt about the cultural, moral, and spiritual standing of the poem."[35] We are presented with a choice between progressive discontinuity and reiterative discontinuity, when an awareness that for Langland time and sequence are metaphors for an eternal reality should free us altogether from the tyranny of the "two truths."

John Ganim begins his study of Middle English narrative by pointing out that "the perception of the world by means of sequential and linear understanding was generally held to be an imperfect apprehension of a universal order that could only be appreciated from the perspective of eternity." Yet, he argues, "all narratives must finally respect the limits of time and space," and his study is directed toward medieval narrative romances and their poets' ways of handling the "contradiction of imaging truths that exist beyond time within narratives that center increasingly on the sophisticated representation of mundane and fleeting experience."[36] Granted that a certain amount of tension must be implicit in the medieval poet's creation of any temporal narrative, it nevertheless follows from this requirement that allegory, as opposed to representation, must least involve the medieval poet in tension, since it narrates "fleeting experience" as a sign for eternal truth. In Langland's allegory, what appear at first to be only linear narrative sequences are self-contained allegories that support one another in signifying the same thing. It is as though Langland were imitating no merely human rhetoric, no merely temporal narrative order, but the divine expository style of Jesus himself, who describes the kingdom of heaven in a series of discrete parables that employ related imagery: "A sower went out to sow. And as he sowed, some seeds fell along the path . . ."; "the kingdom of heaven may be compared to a man who sowed good seed in his field . . ."; "the kingdom of heaven is like a grain of mustard seed which a man took and sowed in his field . . ."; "the kingdom of heaven is like leaven which a woman took and hid in three measures of flour . . ."; "the kingdom of heaven is like treasure hidden in a field . . ."; "the kingdom of heaven is like a merchant in search of fine pearls . . ."; "the kingdom of heaven is like a net which was thrown into the sea . . ." (Matthew 13).[37] Each parable describes the same thing using similar images whose exact significance shifts kaleidescopically if the parables are read as a sequence: seed is first the Word of God, then the human soul, and then the kingdom of heaven.

Throughout *Piers* Langland borrows heavily from many of these parable images: they are the source of his sowing scenes (Passus VI and XIX), of the harvesting and gathering of souls into the barn of Unity Holy Church (XIX), of the tree of charity sown in the human heart and its fruit snatched away by "the evil one" (XV), of the tree of Christ (I) that grows and spreads into the tree of the church (XV), and of spiritual treasure (I–IV). Like Jesus, Langland is eternally speaking in parables: "indeed, he said nothing to them without a parable" (Matt. 13:34); and like the disciples, Langland's critics continue to complain, "Why do you speak in parables?" (Matt. 13:10) Jesus' answer is Langland's answer, too, and it expresses one of the central paradoxes upon which Langland builds his poem: "To you it has been given to know the secrets of the kingdom of heaven, but to them it has not been given. For to him who has will more be given, and he will have abundance; but from him who has not, even what he has will be taken away. This is why I speak to them in parables, because seeing they do not see, and hearing they do not hear, nor do they understand" (Matt. 13:11–13).

It is not that Jesus speaks in parables to prevent the faithless from understanding; rather, it is because they are faithless that they do not understand his parables. Understanding, here, is conceived as being communicated not through any sequence of human words or lessons alone but by divine grace, which paradoxically both activates and is activated by the individual will. In this conception, faith cannot be obtained simply through a gradual external process of cognition; understanding must instead be gained through faith arising from within. Langland appears to have this meaning in mind when, in the middle of his plowing scene, he recalls another parable from Matthew:

> Mathew wiþ mannes face mouþe[þ] þise wordes:
> *Seruus nequam* hadde a Mnam and for he [n]olde [it vse]
> He hadde maugree of his maister eueremoore after,
> And bynam hym his Mnam for he [n]old werche
> And yaf [it hym in haste þat hadde ten bifore];

And [siþen] he seide—[hise seruauntȝ] it herde—
"He þat haþ shal haue and helpe þere [nede is]
And he þat noȝt haþ shal noȝt haue and no man hym helpe,
And þat he weneþ wel to haue I wole it hym bireue."

(vi.238–46)

The allegory, like the parable, is designed not to teach faith to the
faithless but to awaken readers to the gift of faith that already lies
within them and that, once awakened, will enable them to read the
allegory with understanding.[38] Readers who expect only a linear, progressive unfolding of ideas will be frustrated by the poet's habit of
"explaining" one allegory with another allegory and of suggesting
that a relationship of text to gloss exists between various parts of the
poem, when in fact it does not. Such is the case with the divisions
of *Visio* and *Vita*, where the latter seems to promise a down-to-earth
moral interpretation of the mysterious allegories of the *Visio* but is
actually another series of allegories that, although related to those
in the *Visio*, are related only obliquely, as though everything in the
Visio were already self-apparent.[39] The same relationship of text to
gloss is promised of the Prologue and Passus I when the latter begins
with the narrator's assurances:

What þ[e] Mountaigne bymeneþ and þe merke dale
And þe feld of folk I shal yow fair shewe.

(i.1–2)

But in the subsequent conversation between Will and Dame Holy
Church, very little of the vision in the Prologue is directly mentioned, and although much of what Dame Holy Church says in
her allegories is similar to what has been shown in the allegories
of the Prologue, we are unlikely to see the connection unless we
have already understood the Prologue. Like Jesus' explanations of the
kingdom of heaven, Langland's explanations of his allegories, paradoxically, cannot help us unless we somehow already understand.

In a brief reference to *Piers*, Ganim suggests that Langland confounds narrative sequence and blurs distinctions in style, syntax,
and image, not, like Lydgate and other late medieval poets, out of
"anxiety about legitimacy and order," but "to make us question the
validity of logical inquiry unaccompanied by a constant conscious-

ness of the unity and vision necessary to faith."[40] Faith is the key
to both style and theme in *Piers*. Because Langland does not believe
faith can be taught through any logical sequence of events or ideas
alone, he presents within each part of each sequence the whole paradoxical vision of faith, on the supposition that at some point readers
will be awakened both to faith and to an understanding of the poem.
Like Will, we as modern readers try in vain to unlock the poem's
meaning logically without suspending our disbelief in the Christian
paradoxes on which the poem is based. Like Will, we begin *Piers* in
the expectation of a logically progressive pilgrimage toward Truth,
Dowel, Charity, Unity, God; and our expectation of sequential development leads us to assume that we will understand more, say, in
Passus XV than we did in Passus V, that Passus XV will actually be
closer to Truth than Passus V. And our assumption is valid for the
vehicle of the allegory, which traces Will's temporal life and education from youth to great age, and charts his spiritual progress from
wandering to pilgrimage to unity; but the sequence of Will's life, like
the lesser sequence leading to Truth's pardon, and like the pilgrimage to Truth's castle within that sequence, is also a temporal vehicle
for an atemporal tenor: as we shall see, there is a sense in which
Will's pilgrimage makes no real progress until the moment of faith
that brings him instantly into Unity. The whole poem is in this sense
a pilgrimage only allegorically, expressing through the vehicles of
time and space a Truth that is outside time and space. For modern
readers as for Will, the only escape from time into Unity, the only
bridge over the gap between tenor and vehicle, is the leap of faith; we
must either enter imaginatively into the medieval Christian faith or
resist this faith in paradox and wander through Langland's allegories
in endless noncomprehension.

In arguing for a strictly linear reading of *Piers,* Elizabeth Kirk
writes as follows:

> Perhaps the ideal commentator on *Piers Plowman* would bring
> to the poem total, simultaneous awareness of the timeless struc-
> ture that is Christian theology. But he would be drawn by the
> poem, not into contemplation of this simultaneity, but into re-
> discovery through order. He, like every other reader, will be
> made to see some things first and others later, to understand the

later in terms of what the first looked like, and to reinterpret the first in terms of the later. He will find arguments that begin by confronting one issue and not others, in a process which cannot advance to new issues until a perspective on the first has been achieved, either through intellectual lucidity or through despair.[41]

The assumptions here are certainly logical; but it is a telling suggestion that efforts to appraise the poem purely intellectually may end in despair. On the other hand, what if Langland does not believe that Truth is to be found in human logic? What if the entire poem is based on Kind's paradoxical statement, "Learn to love"? In turning to the next chapter, which discusses Langland's theory of human understanding as shown in the education of Will, we should recall that Love herself defines Dowel in the poem as *"Disce, doce, dilige inimicos"* (XIII.137), and that Love is thus both the source and the goal, the beginning and the end of all learning.

2
Creating Humankind
Human Understanding and the
Life of Will

✦

All the nonsequential sequences identified in chapter 1 are in turn part of the larger sequence of Will's life and pilgrimage to Unity, describing the process of Will's physical aging and spiritual growth toward true understanding. But although the poem's framing structure suggests the traditional allegory of the journey of life in which youthful ignorance gradually gives way to aged wisdom, Langland actually takes little care to reproduce the temporal chronology of human physical existence. In fact, a quick overview of the poem's time frame shows Langland's account of Will's life to be so achronistic, so circular and antiprogressive, that one might almost as accurately describe the poem as a single, timeless moment in the life of Will.

Will's age at the poem's beginning is not specified, but we assume he is a young man because he appears to be setting out for the first time to encounter the "wondres" (Pr. 4) of this world. He seems to have had no schooling in either religion or the reading of allegory, since his quest is worldly and he does not understand the spiritual significance of the vision he encounters in the Prologue. Thus in Passus I he asks Holy Church not only to tell him what the vision means (" 'mercy, madame, what [may] þis [by] meene?' " [I.11]) but also to identify herself. But Holy Church's answer to the latter question, while it seems to satisfy Will, presents a logical problem for the reader:

"Holi chirche I am", quod she: "þow ouȝtest me to knowe.
I vnderfeng þee first and þ[i] feiþ [þee] tauȝte.

[Thow] brou3test me borwes my biddyng to [werche],
To·louen me leely while þi lif dureþ."

(1.75–78)

In the plot sequence of the poem Will is meeting Holy Church for the first time, and he clearly does not recognize her; yet she tells him he has known her all his life, that she has been his teacher and guide since childhood. The chronology of the allegory does not coincide with the chronology of the ideas it represents.

Will awakens at the end of the Meed vision but falls asleep again immediately, "er I hadde faren a furlong" (V.5). In the subsequent vision Will repents with the other sinful folk and sees the pardon sent by Truth; he awakens as the sun is setting (VII.146) and concludes, after having thought about these visions "[m]any tyme" (VII.149), that Dowel is the only true pardon. The entire *Visio*, then, occupies one day, and after an undetermined period, Will sets out "[a]l a somer seson for to seke dowel" (VIII.2), which may or may not be the same "somer seson" in which he began his first journey (Pr. 1). During an unspecified period Will roams the countryside, and after asking a pair of friars for directions, he again falls asleep, and again meets someone apparently for the first time:

A muche man me þou3te, lik to myselue,
Cam and called me by my kynde name.
"What art [þ]ow", quod I þo, "þat my name knowest?"
"That þow woost wel", quod he, "and no wi3t bettre."
"Woot I?" [quod I; "who art þow]?" "þou3t", seid he þanne.
"I haue sued þee seuen yeer; seye þow me no raþer?"

(VIII.70–75)

Of course Will's thoughts are always with him, and it would be awkward, to say the least, if Langland felt obliged to depict all the psychological personifications as following Will throughout the poem. But as in the scene with Holy Church, Langland deliberately stresses the incongruity between his allegory and temporal chronology. Will could simply have recognized Holy Church and Thought as his old friends; instead, Langland emphasizes the nonsequentiality of his poetic sequence.

After talking with Thought for "þre daies" (VIII.117), Will meets Wit and, immediately thereafter, Dame Study. Dame Study in turn directs Will to Clergy and Scripture, through a landscape as non-spatial and atemporal as that of Piers's pilgrimage route to Truth. Will sets out immediately and can "neuere stynte" until he arrives there (X.226). But after a single conversation with these two, he angrily rejects all intellectual and spiritual pursuits and falls into a dream within his dream in which he lives a life of worldly vanity for "fourty wynter and a fifte moore" (XI.47), and finally "for[yede] youþe and yarn into Elde" (XI.60). Here at the center of the poem Langland describes Will's entire adult life, repeating the worldly beginning of his journey "wondres to here" (Pr. 4) in Fortune's presentation of the "[m]irour þat hiȝte middelerþe" and her promise that "here myȝtow se wondres" (XI.9, 10), and depicting the arrival of Elde, who will come to Will again in Passus XX. The temptation to dismiss this miniature account of Will's life as a dream leads us to recall that the rest of the poem, including the second coming of Elde, is also merely a dream; moreover, any neat distinction between inner and outer dreams dissolves when Will, awakening back into the outer dream, encounters Imaginative, who claims to have followed and instructed Will "[þ]ise fyue and fourty wynter" (XII.3), a period of time that seems to correspond with that of the inner dream. Will also does not recognize Imaginative, and for a third time we are reminded that the sequence of events in the poem's presentation of Will's life corresponds in no literal way to any temporal sequence of events.

Nor can we find our chronological bearings by examining the passage of time during Will's rare waking moments. True, upon awakening from his dream of Imaginative he claims to wander "[i]n manere of a mendynaunt many yer after" (XIII.3), and following his vision of the Samaritan he describes himself as a pilgrim nearing the end of life:

> Wolleward and weetshoed wente I forþ after
> As a recchelees renk þat [reccheþ of no wo],
> And yede forþ lik a lorel al my lif tyme
> Til I weex wery of þe world and wilned eft to slepe.
>
> (xviii.1–4)

This description seems to justify the assumption that by Passus XX Will really is an old man. But a closer look at Will's waking time suggests that it is actually no less allegorical than his dreams: if here and elsewhere he claims to spend his waking life as a mendicant, when he awakens from his vision of the Resurrection at the end of Passus XVIII Will describes himself as a homebody and family man:

> . . . and riþt wiþ þat I wakede
> And callede kytte my wif and Calote my doghter:
> "[Ariseþ] and reuerence[þ] goddes resurexion,
> And crepe[þ] to þe cros on knees and kisse[þ] it for a Iuwel."
>
> (XVIII.425–28)

We recall with some surprise that Will's life has been a journey only metaphorically, and his pilgrimage to Dowel is now confined to a symbolic procession on his knees through the stations of the cross in church. Then, too, as critics have often noted, the distinction between sleeping and waking events in the poem is blurred by the intrusion of allegorical figures such as Need into Will's waking life (XX.4–50), and, one might add, by less obvious intrusions such as the "real" friars' perfect willingness to discuss the whereabouts of Dowel in the same allegorical language as is used in the dream visions (VIII.8–61). Finally, after seeming to spend his entire life, both in and out of dreams, roaming the world in pilgrimage, Will both begins and ends his journey toward Unity in one moment in Passus XX:

> And [I] by conseil of kynde comsed to rome
> Thoruȝ Contricion and Confession til I cam to vnitee.
>
> (XX.212–13)

We have already seen Will repent and receive absolution with the other folk in the *Visio* (V.60–61, 186–87), and afterward we saw him undertake his pilgrimage in the *Vita*. But here in Passus XX the entire pilgrimage toward Unity—presumably the subject of the whole poem —is undertaken and completed in two short lines. Like Piers's pilgrimage to Truth, then, and like the larger sequence from confession to pardon of which Piers's pilgrimage is part, Will's pilgrimage of life is also an allegory for an event outside time and space. In the autobiography of Will, as in the lesser sequences of the poem, Langland uses time and space as lesser, redundant analogies for a transcendent reality, thereby imitating divine creation.

The structure of Will's life suggests something about Langland's attitude toward human nature, and especially toward learning and the means of attaining faith. For it appears that neither Will nor the reader is expected to gain faith and spiritual understanding through any purely temporal process or linear sequence in the poem. If the chronological flow of events on earth is not the true medium through which people come to learn Truth, then there must be some vertical connection between God and humankind instilling knowledge of eternal truths from within. Augustine's theory of divine illumination posits just such a connection; in his view it is not the teacher who teaches but "the inner light of truth" in each soul: "[W]e do not listen to anyone speaking and making sounds outside ourselves. We listen to Truth which presides over our minds within us, though of course we may be bidden to listen by someone using words. Our real Teacher is he who is so listened to, who is said to dwell in the inner man, namely Christ, that is, the unchangeable power and eternal wisdom of God."[1] Knowledge for Augustine is obtained not by the mere transmission of words but by these words' illumination of the preexisting truth within. The theory presupposes humanity's creation in the image of God; Augustine gives the source of all illumination as the Christ that inheres within the self.

But certainly to know many things is not to know Christ, and intellect alone cannot save the soul. Even granting that all knowledge comes from within, there must be some distinction between learning facts and attaining faith. In *The Confessions* Augustine discusses his scholastic education in detail, charting the progress of his ideas about God and the cosmos; but in no sense does this growth of knowledge lead him to faith. Instead he describes his conversion as a direct and instantaneous enlightenment by divine grace: "No further would I read, nor did I need, for instantly, as the sentence ended, —by a light, as it were, of security into my heart, —all the gloom of doubt vanished away." Augustine specifies that his conversion to faith, rather than coming through learning or his own power of mind, came through a mysterious turning of his will to acceptance of Christ: "And this was the result, that I willed not to do what I willed, and willed to do what Thou willest. But where, during all those years, and out of what deep and secret retreat was my free will summoned forth in a moment, whereby I gave my neck to Thy 'easy yoke,' and my shoulders to Thy 'light burden,' O Christ Jesus?"[2] All knowledge is attributable to the Christ within; reason is the human faculty that constitutes God's image. But faith—the perception of Christ himself in the soul—is the only redemptive knowledge, and is not to be obtained through the fallen processes of human learning alone.

For this reason critics who analyze only the process of Will's intellectual education overlook an important part of Langland's paradoxical theme. Margaret Goldsmith, for example, usefully analyzes the progress of Will's studies in medieval Christianity but is not entirely correct in describing it as "the gradual process of his conversion"; for the moment of conversion is as different from the years of education as divine timelessness is different from human time. Goldsmith acknowledges this distinction in a different context at the end of her article: "Will's question to Holy Church 'How may I save my soul?' is answered by Langland through the voices of the apostles and the great monastic teachers of the past: and they give but one answer: 'From your own resources, you cannot.' There has to be an infusion of the Holy Spirit into the questing soul."[3] Will's education does indeed progress from one idea to the next; and the direction of his education is inward, from the intellectual processes of Thought, Wit, and Study toward the deeper spiritual perception of the Christ within. But this final perception is itself the gift of faith, not the last inevitable step in a human process of logic. Moreover, since the gift of faith is the perception of absolute divine presence, there is a sense in which it is an absolute gift, whole and complete in itself; and for this reason, critics who discern in Langland's allegory the medieval hierarchic degrees of spiritual perfection are also seeing only part of Langland's paradoxical representation of Truth.[4] From the human perspective there are indeed many degrees in the spiritual life of faith; but from the divine perspective that Langland imitates in the paradoxical structures of his poem, simply to have faith is to enter into unity, to enter into an absolute state of grace that recognizes no degrees or distinctions among its members. This is the significance of Jesus' parable of the vineyard, and another Middle English allegorist has also made poetic use of the paradox. The *Pearl* poet, who shares Langland's interest in parables, retells the parable of the vineyard to show that human conceptions of degree are confounded by the spiritual insight that to participate at all in divine love is to participate wholly and equally. Like the thickheaded Will in *Piers,* the dreamer in *Pearl* is skeptical of paradox, saying to his beatified daughter, "Me thynk thy tale unresonable"; yet the *Pearl* child conveys the poet's paradoxical theme:

> "Of more and lasse in Godes ryche,"
> That gentyl sayde, "lys no joparde,
> For ther is uch mon payed inlyche,
> Whether lyttel other much be hys rewarde."[5]

This is what it means, in an absolute sense, to enter into unity with God and humankind, and the attainment of this state is not dependent on the amount of physical or temporal labor invested toward achieving it.

Within his allegory of Will's education, Langland is careful to preserve the distinction between human learning and the divine gift of understanding by faith: as Imaginative explains to Will, Christian scholastic study (Clergy) and the study of God through his traces in the natural world (Kind Wit), though related to the knowledge of Christ by faith, are no substitute for it and do not by themselves lead to salvation:

> "Clergie and kynde wit comeþ of siȝte and techyng
> As þe book bereþ witnesse to burnes þat kan rede:
> *Quod scimus loquimur, quod vidimus testamur.*
> Of *quod scimus* comeþ Clergie, [a] konnynge of heuene,
> And of *quod vidimus* comeþ kynde wit, of siȝte of diuerse
>   peple.
> Ac grace is a gifte of god and of greet loue spryngeþ;
> Knew neuere clerk how it comeþ forþ, ne kynde wit þe weyes:
> *Nescit aliquis vnde venit aut quo vadit &c.*
> Ac yet is Clergie to comende and kynde wit boþe,
> And namely Clergie for cristes loue, þat of Clergie is roote. . . .
> Forþi I counseille þee for cristes sake clergie þat þow louye;
> For kynde wit is of his kyn and neiȝe Cosynes boþe
> To oure lord, leue me; forþi loue hem, I rede."

$$(\text{XII.}64\text{–}71, 92\text{–}94)$$

Earthly learning and knowledge by faith in Christ are "kin"—that is, the Christ within the soul is the "root" of both kinds of knowledge—but they are not to be confused; only the latter saves the soul. Marcia Colish summarizes the medieval theory of knowledge in similar terms:

> The Aristotelian certainty that sensory data lead to a knowledge of prior and non-sensible realities was paralleled by the scriptural assertions that God can be known through His creation, which He is believed to resemble. Yet, the kind of knowledge of God which the Christian regarded as normative in this life was faith. Knowledge by faith was firm and certain, but partial. It could be acquired only by an infusion of God's grace in the mind of the subject, and it involved his moral conversion as well as his intellectual assent.

If, as Augustine argues, the teacher does not actually teach anything, but only recalls to the mind of the student the truth already within, the teacher must be especially helpless in attempting to inform faith; since divine grace alone can awaken the knowledge of Christ, there can be no linear, developmental course of instruction at the climax of which this awakening can be guaranteed. Colish explains the spiritual teachers' predicament: "Neither their logical rigor nor their verbal precision or eloquence could encompass the mystery of the Godhead. The hearer's intellectual entry into the life of the Trinity would be initiated and accomplished by God, through grace. This notion was a matter of faith."[6] "Initiated and accomplished"—that is, the whole "process" of "learning" faith is simultaneously begun and ended in the moment of the soul's recognition of the Christ within. Hence Piers's pilgrimage to St. Truth, which both begins and ends in the perception of Charity, Love, and Truth in the heart. If all knowledge, to the medieval mind, is to some extent divorced from the earthly contingencies of time, space, and words, knowledge by faith is more certainly so.

Mary Carruthers rightly argues that *Piers* is an epistemological poem; as the autobiography of Will, the poem traces the protagonist's search for certain knowledge of Christ.[7] But given the medieval theory of knowledge, it should come as no surprise that *Piers* is an epistemological poem in which the answer sought is known from the beginning, and in which Will discerns it, not through the temporal process of his studies and experience, but in a single moment of perception. The structure of Will's autobiography is as repetitive and circular as it is progressive and developmental. It is intimately connected with Langland's understanding of time as a secondary, contingent reality caused by a "defect in matter"; Will's repeated failure to perceive the image of God within himself is the primary cause of the poem's continuation, just as the resistance of matter to divine form causes the repetition that is time and space. Thomas Aquinas's statement that once matter is disposed to receive divine form "it receives form instantaneously,"[8] is also true of Will, whose knowledge by faith is awakened in the instant he ceases to resist the will of God and perceives God's image within him. In addition to following the linear progression of his earthly education, Will's autobiography continuously circles, both thematically and structurally, around the central paradox of faith, a paradox by which one comes to know what cannot be learned. Finally, the distinction between faith and learning, despite their shared source in the Christ within, is especially important to Langland's analysis of Will's life, for the poet uses conventional learning as a metaphor for knowledge by faith, a metaphor that achieves its meaning more through nonsimilitude than similitude.

Langland subscribes to the general theory of divine illumination, but he does so in his own idiosyncratic and poetic way. It is not difficult to find the theory reflected in his idea of "kynde knowyng" as an innate human knowledge of kinship with God, or "Kynde." But it is perhaps less easy to see that Langland's concept of Dowel is also rooted in this theory. When Will asks Wit to teach him about Dowel he receives the following answer:

"Sire Dowel dwelleþ", quod Wit, "noȝt a day hennes
In a Castel þat kynde made of foure kynnes þynges.
Of erþe and Eyr [it is] maad, medled togideres,
Wiþ wynde and wiþ water witt[i]ly enioyned.
Kynde haþ closed þerInne, craftily wiþalle,
A lemman þat he loueþ lik to hymselue.
Anima she hatte; [to her haþ enuye]
A proud prikere of Fraunce, *Princeps huius mundi*,
And wolde wynne hire awey wiþ wiles [if] he myȝte.

Ac kynde knoweþ þis wel and kepeþ hire þe bettre,
And [haþ] doo[n] hire wiþ sire dowel, duc of þise Marches."

(IX.1–11)

God has created in each individual a certain knowledge of the good
to protect the soul from sin; Dowel as the knowledge of how to do
well is apparently an intuitive, God-given faculty. The allegory of
the scene works on two levels at once: as Everyman, Will foolishly
seeks to learn from others what he already must know but refuses
to acknowledge, while as the human will, he ignores what his own
wit intuitively tells him—Wit's ability to define Dowel being proof
that Dowel is innate. Wit takes advantage of Will's inquiry about
Kind to explain that part of God's image in human beings is their
endowment with the ability to do well; Dowel is the image of God
in human nature:

"Kynde", quod [he], "is creatour of alle kynnes [beestes],
Fader and formour, [þe first of alle þynges].
And þat is þe grete god þat gynnyng hadde neuere,
Lord of lif and of liȝt, of lisse and of peyne.
Aungeles and alle þyng arn at his wille
Ac man is hym moost lik of marc and of [shape].
For þoruȝ þe word þat he [warp] woxen forþ beestes,
[And al at his wil was wrouȝt wiþ a speche],
Dixit & facta sunt,
[Saue man þat he made ymage] to hymself,
And Eue of his ryb bon wiþouten any mene.
For he was synguler hymself and seide *faciamus*
As who seiþ, "moore moot herto þan my word oone;
My myȝt moot helpe forþ wiþ my speche".
Right as a lord sholde make lettres; [if] hym lakked parchemyn,
Thouȝ he [wiste to] write neuer so wel, [and] he hadde [a]
        penne,
The lettre, for al þe lordshipe, I leue, were neuere ymaked.
And so it semeþ by hym [þere he seide in þe bible
Faciamus hominem ad imaginem nostram]
He moste werche wiþ his word and his wit shewe."

(IX.26–44)

People can do well in imitation of God because God used not only his Word but his good work in creating them. The verb *faciamus* is plural, although God is singular, because in making humanity God needed both these components, whereas he needed only his Word to create animals. Wit twice repeats that God used both Word and works in this special act of creation.

> "And in þis manere was man maad þoruȝ myȝt of god almyȝty,
> Wiþ his word and werkmanshipe and wiþ lif to laste. . . ."
> "[Th]at he wroȝte wiþ werk and wiþ word boþe;
> Thorgh myȝt of þe mageste man was ymaked."
>
> (IX.45–46, 52–53)

Knowledge of Dowel, then, preexists in everyone; it comes from within rather than through any purely temporal process of learning, whether authoritative or experiential. The will is free to accept or reject this knowledge, of course; but it is there just the same.

If all people are innately endowed with a knowledge of Dowel, it might seem that non-Christians, too, may be saved through good works. But as we have seen, Dowel is both good deeds and Christ; to do well in the poem is specifically to imitate the life of Christ, whose deeds were performed for love of God and humankind. This does not contradict Langland's notion that Dowel is innate, for he conceives of Christ as God's perfect creation of humankind in his own image; it is because Christ is the perfect human expression of Dowel in man that he has the power to save, for he reconnects the likeness between God and humanity that was defaced in the Fall. Thus Repentance's absolution through Christ emphasizes the connection between Christ's creation and humankind's:

> "I shal biseche for alle synfulle oure Saueour of grace
> To amenden vs of oure mysdedes: do mercy to vs alle,
> God, þat of þi goodnesse [g]onne þe world make,
> And of nauȝt madest auȝt and man moost lik to þiselue,
> And siþen suffredest [hym] to synne, a siknesse to vs alle,
> And for þe beste as I bileue whateuere þe book telleþ:
> *O felix culpa, o necessarium peccatum Ade &c.*
> For þoruȝ þat synne þi sone sent was to erþe
> And bicam man of a maide mankynde to saue,

And madest þiself wiþ þi sone vs synfulle yliche:
Faciamus hominem ad ymaginem [et similitudinem] nostram;
Et alibi, Qui manet in caritate in deo manet & deus in eo."

(v.478–86a)

If Christ is the only perfect image of God in humankind, then the Dowel that is a lesser image of God in each human being is specifically that likeness to Christ in the human heart which enables people to do well in imitation of Christ. To do well is not merely to perform good works but to perform them through love and faith in Christ. Because a certain knowledge of Dowel and of Christ is conceived as built into the soul, and because God's grace is infinite, Langland accepts the possibility of salvation in special cases where non-Christians have done extremely well (Troianus); but generally there is no guarantee of pardon through good deeds without Christian faith. As Clergy and Imaginative explain (X.238–50, XII.29–32), Dowel is faith in the Christian God as well as good works, as *caritas* by definition includes both good works and Christian love.

If Dowel is not merely good works but the intuitive faith in Christ that generates good works, then the whole discussion of Dowel is another way of discussing "kynde knowyng." There has been some debate about the significance of this phrase: R. W. Frank translates it as "natural knowledge," which seems right enough in the sense that it is a knowledge that is natural to humankind. But it should be added that Kind in Wit's definition above is not merely the goddess Natura, now operating under the aegis of a Christian God, but God the Creator himself, whose image is stamped upon humanity as a kind knowing of kinship to God and an ability to do well in imitation of Christ. Kind knowing is a natural knowledge of one's relationship to the supernatural God: it is a spiritual knowledge of realities beyond the natural world. Edward Vasta defines the phrase more accurately as wisdom derived from a direct, personal, experiential knowledge of divine love, which he believes Will finally achieves in Passus XVIII with his vision of Christ. But Mary Davlin rightly observes that Will is still seeking kind knowing in Passus XX, although she interprets Kind's final injunction, "Lerne to loue," as proof that kind knowing is the fruit of a cognitive process through which Will grows in the course of the poem until he at last gains "experiential wisdom." That this is not an entirely satisfactory explanation is made clear by Britton Harwood, who points out that one does not attain faith by learning to be good, but that to become good one must first have faith. Here Harwood places his finger on the paradoxical pulse of Langland's allegory; but immediately he attempts to explain the problem logically. He argues that the kind knowing Will seeks is the equivalent of Ockham's *notitia intuitiva*, a term in which intuition "means nothing instinctive or mysterious" but "simply derives from *intueri*, 'to gaze at, pay attention to'"; a kind knowing of Christ, then, would be knowledge of him as "an existing singular object known immediately *as* existing."[9] But if Will is to be a strict logician throughout the poem, he can never obtain a kind knowing of Christ, since Harwood and Ockham agree that "[b]y natural means in this life man apparently cannot have intuitive knowledge of God," and that "[p]ropositions like *'deus est incarnabilis'* cannot be evidently known."[10]

Harwood draws no conclusion about whether Will ever achieves kind knowing; but significantly, in suggesting how Will might achieve it he subverts his own attempt to define the phrase logically: although the prospect for an evident knowledge of God looks bleak, he proposes that such a knowledge "may nevertheless be given to Will when that seedy vagabond looks into himself, as 'in a Mirour'" (XV.162), implying that kind knowing must somehow be within Will but not at first perceived. Harwood's phrase "be given" further suggests that this knowledge may be a gift of grace, a possibility that he mentions in a footnote, remarking that "both Scotus and Ockham agreed that *notitia intuitiva* might be supernaturally provided."[11] If after all kind knowing must preexist in people and be awakened supernaturally by grace, then we are back to the original paradox of faith's priority to learning, a paradox that logic can obviously do little to resolve. And this of course is the point: faith cannot be obtained through the logical, rational process of human thought and learning alone. Kind knowing in *Piers* is both instinctive and mysterious; it is within people, as Dowel is within them, because God created it in them. Dowel and kind knowing are essentially the same thing: they are the image of God in humanity by which faith is made possible; and, once awakened, they are faith itself.

But Will repeatedly insists that he has no kind knowing of Dowel, and that for this reason he must ask others. The statement is self-contradicting, since it asks for intuitive understanding from an outside source. But because kind knowing and Dowel are two formulations for the same knowledge by faith, the statement is also indicative of the paradoxical circularity that informs the whole poem: one must have faith to achieve faith, have kind knowing to understand kind knowing. Will rejects the various definitions of Dowel until he can have a kind knowing, but Dowel is the very kind knowing he seeks. One does not progress from good deeds to faith, or from faith to good deeds; the two are dual manifestations of a single awakening by grace. The same circularity characterizes the exchange between Will and Dame Holy Church concerning kind knowing in Passus I. She first explains that people may be faithful because God created them as such:

> "The tour on þe toft", quod she, "truþe is þerInne,
> And wolde þat ye wrouȝte as his word techeþ.
> For he is fader of feiþ, and formed yow alle
> Boþe with fel and with face, and yaf yow fyue wittes
> For to worshipe hym þerwiþ while ye ben here."
>
> (1.12–16)

Then, having shown that God is Truth, she explains that people who are truthful are "ylik to oure lord" (I.91). But Will perversely responds that this truth, this faith, is not in him:

> "Yet haue I no kynde knowyng", quod I, "ye mote kenne me bettre
> By what craft in my cors it comseþ, and where."
>
> (1.138–39)

On the one hand he insists that he does not have kind knowing, and asks Holy Church to teach it to him as if it were a matter of dogma; on the other hand he implies that if he knew logically how kind knowing gets in his body, he would have it. But kind knowing is itself the human perception of God as Creator, so that even as Will asks to be taught, he rejects the only true teacher as unproved; in waiting for a rational proof of grace, he cuts it off at its source. If there is any philosophical logic of the kind Harwood describes in the poem, it is in Will's wrongheaded attempts to analyze faith logically. Kind knowing is by definition self-evident and inexplicable, but only the faithful can perceive this truth, and no logic alone will bring Will to faith. Holy Church's exasperated response, a circular definition of kind knowing as "a kynde knowyng þat kenneth in þyn herte / For to louen þi lord leuere þan þiselue" (I.142–43), is the only definition possible, and if Will refuses to acknowledge kind knowing, he cannot possibly understand this definition. [12]

Learning, then—not memorization or logical quibbling but true spiritual understanding—is for Langland not a merely rational, linear process but a paradoxical mystery resolvable only by faith: the paradox of faith, like that of Christ, is a problem to those without faith but is the resolution of the problem to those who have it. But Langland's conception of learning is not as alien to modern notions as one might suppose. The circular, nonprogressive, and simultaneous nature, not only of Holy Church's definition of kind knowing as kind knowing, but also of the poem's nonsequential sequences and its structure as a whole, offers parallels to the modern concept of the hermeneutical circle, which Richard Palmer explains as follows:

> Understanding is a basically referential operation; we understand something by comparing it to something we already know. What we understand forms itself into systematic unities, or circles made up of parts. The circle as a whole defines the individual part, and the parts together form the circle. . . . [A]n individual concept derives its meaning from a context or horizon within which it stands; yet the horizon is made up of the very elements to which it gives meaning. By dialectical interaction between the whole and the part, each gives the other meaning; understanding is circular, then. Because within this "circle" the meaning comes to stand, we call this the "hermeneutical circle."

Will cannot piece together his faith in God through a series of given facts; he must accept the whole Truth of God before he can assess the truth of any other facts. This is true also for us as readers of the poem: we cannot gradually learn that "the parts together form the circle" of the poem but must also first understand that the "circle as a whole defines the individual part"—in this case to such an extent that the part reexpresses the whole circle. Palmer sums up the dilemma nicely when he asks, "How can a text be understood, when the condition for its understanding is already to have understood what it is about?"[13] In a sense the hermeneutical circle is a modern expression of the kind of mystery Langland isolates in his description of knowledge by faith. Both attitudes toward understanding are illogical, and both offer a solution that transcends logic. Palmer explains:

> Of course the concept of the hermeneutical circle involves a logical contradiction; for, if we must grasp the whole before we understand the parts, then we shall never understand anything. . . . Is the concept of the hermeneutical circle therefore invalid? No; rather, we must say that logic cannot fully account for the workings of understanding. Somehow, a kind of "leap" into the hermeneutical circle occurs and we understand the whole and the parts together.

This leap, for Langland, in which all is suddenly understood at once, is the leap of faith; it is the awakening by grace of the kind knowing within the heart. The kind knowing of faith can be seen as a medieval equivalent of another modern hermeneutical term: "Explanatory interpretation makes us aware that explanation is contextual, is 'horizontal.' It must be made within a horizon of already granted meanings and intentions. In hermeneutics, this area of assumed understanding is called preunderstanding."[14] Will cannot understand Holy Church's words because he rejects as unproved the very preunderstanding that would make her words meaningful to him. The kind knowing of faith is Will's God-given preunderstanding—the direct, intuitive apprehension of a divine system of significance without which no understanding can take place.

From Langland's conception of true understanding as preexisting within the self and awakened directly by divine grace, we may derive two central facts about *Piers* as the autobiography of Will. First, it should be clear that Will's quest for knowledge must also be a quest for self-knowledge, since the wisdom he seeks is already a part of himself; hence, for example, Scripture's scornful words, *"Multi multa sciunt et seipsos nesciunt"* (XI.3). Second, we can predict that the form of this quest will not be simply a linear development through time. The idea of an autobiography that describes the attainment of both faith and self-knowledge in a single moment that could perhaps have happened at any time seems strange to modern readers; the narrative process of recounting one's life would seem in itself to presuppose only a gradual development through time and space. But as we have seen, when Augustine wrote *The Confessions* —the formal paradigm for Christian autobiography—he made no such assumptions about learning through time. In a recent analysis of *The Confessions*, in a chapter appropriately entitled "The Formal Paradigm," William Spengemann isolates three distinct stages in the structuring of Augustine's autobiography, shifting from "historical self-recollection" (books I–IX) to "philosophical self-exploration" (X–XII), and finally to "poetic self-expression" (XIII). He argues that subsequent autobiographers from Dante to Dickens invariably use one of these three structural paradigms, and moreover that "the sequence of forms in *The Confessions* and the reasons behind its formal modulations from history to philosophy to poetry rehearse the entire development of the genre from the Middle Ages to the modern era."[15] Although he does not mention Langland, Spengemann's discussion of autobiography is revealing in connection with *Piers*, which, though an allegorical poem containing elements of both philosophical self-exploration and poetic self-expression, generally supports Spengemann's evolutionary theory in being primarily an autobiography of historical self-recollection. This form, in *Piers* as well as in *The Confessions*, suggests both that faith and self-knowledge are one and that they are granted by grace rather than through time and experience alone.

Spengemann shows that the "I" of the first-person narrative in books I through IX of *The Confessions* actually refers to two Augustines: the faithless protagonist whose life is the subject of analysis, and the faithful Christian narrator who analyzes these events from a godlike position of omniscience. "To dramatize the importance of conversion, Augustine draws a sharp distinction between the old, unregenerate self, who could see his life only from an ever-shifting perspective within it, and his new converted self, who sees that life as an eternally complete moral design with all its parts existing simultaneously in timeless space." After the conversion the divided self disappears; Augustine is whole. This dichotomy between protagonist and narrator suggests more than that an older, wiser Augustine is looking back on a younger self, for the omniscient narrator is the representative of the divine truth that is always present, always available to the young Augustine. In a sense, the narrator is an already existing part of Augustine that the young, self-ignorant protagonist is free to discover at any time:

> [T]he converted narrator, who embodies . . . truth, exists complete throughout the narrative, standing alongside the fallen self as the voice of the eternally present truth to which the fallen self must awaken. . . . [N]arrator and protagonist are separated primarily by faith, not by time. Although the narrator is obviously older than the protagonist, his knowledge is not attributed to his age or his past experience, to wisdom achieved in time, but to the faith which he could have embraced at any time.

Augustine presents himself as a divided consciousness, an unintegrated psyche that can achieve integration only in the moment of conversion to faith. The portrayal of faithlessness as self-alienation, and of the truth the protagonist seeks as simultaneously possessed by the narrating self, attests to Augustine's dual assumption that the knowledge he seeks is within him, waiting to be activated by grace, and that time and experience are not the means through which faith is achieved. Spengemann summarizes Augustine's analysis:

> Time does not lead to the truth, only to vanity and sorrow. . . . Lust does not lead to satiety and from there to continence. Lust leads only to more lust; continence alone will produce continence, and that requires faith. Learning does not lead to faith, as his mother wrongly believes. Faith alone brings wisdom, and his learning does him far more harm than good. . . .
> Conversion, then, is an awakening to the truth that has been present from the beginning—doctrinally in the ambient spirit of God's eternal truth and formally in the *persona* of the narrator. It is not an arrival at some wisdom that has been waiting for him down the path of his life in time. [16]

Once again understanding is conceived as mysteriously circular: one cannot grow from ignorance to wisdom, from faithlessness to faith; one must paradoxically begin with the faith and the wisdom that are sought. And once again, the solution is the divinely inspired awakening of a preexisting wisdom, which allows admittance into the eternal circle of faith and understanding in one instantaneous leap.

In his autobiography, too, Langland uses the "I" to signify both the omniscient narrator and a character within the narrative. There is a difference between this usage and the more commonly discussed use of the "I" to represent a character who is also identified as the poet: like Chaucer the pilgrim in *The Canterbury Tales*, Will is playfully identified with the poet from time to time, and these moments of play will be discussed in chapter IV. But Chaucer's narrator is the same as Chaucer the unreliable pilgrim, stating his agreement with the Monk's venal philosophy as readily as his approval of the virtuous Parson. Langland's "I," however, refers to two distinct voices, one willful and fallible and one divinely authoritative; nor can the wise narrator be explained as an older Will, for as in Augustine's spiritual autobiography, Langland's godlike narrator and errant protagonist are separated not only by time but by faith: Langland's narrator is a voice completely removed from the world of time and human error, a representative of divine truth whose word may not be doubted within the cosmos of the poem. Whereas Will speaks in the past tense, his perceptions bound by the confines of time and space, the narrator speaks in the timeless present, judging the action of the poem from a point outside the action. Our failure to distinguish between these two voices, or our failure, like Will's, to accept the visions the narrator presents as absolute Truth, can lead to serious misunderstanding of the poem. Mary Carruthers, for example, supports her interpretation of *Piers* as a poem of anxiety by arguing that Will contradicts himself in the opening of Passus I, when in fact she is dealing with two different voices. The first is that of the omniscient, timeless narrator:

What þ[e] Mountaigne bymeneþ and þe merke dale
And þe feld ful of folk I shal yow faire shewe.

(1.1–2)

But the second voice, which addresses Holy Church, is clearly Will's, speaking within the narrative frame:

I was afered of hire face þei3 she fair weere
And seide, "mercy, madame, what [may] þis [by]meene?"

(1.10–11)

Carruthers argues that in the first lines it is Will who is confident of his interpretive powers and that "when Lady Holy Church approaches him, his confidence dissolves into a question about the very things he had been so sure of nine lines earlier." Barbara Nolan recognizes "Will's double voice . . . in the prologue—as sleepy wanderer and doomsday preacher reviling the evil of the world"—and distinguishes between temporal and timeless perspectives in the poem, but does not equate this "preacher" voice with that of the omniscient narrator, assuming instead that Langland's "poetic voice represents a decisive, irreversible shift in perspective from the sureness of a soul *in aevo* to the linear uncertainties of a spirit *in medias res.*" Priscilla Martin sees Will as representing both the author and allegorized *voluntas*, yet does not distinguish between authoritative and unreliable voices, arguing that "[i]nstead of being a god-like creator, in control of his work, the author reduces himself to a humiliated creature within it."[17] More confusing still, other critics have posited, in addition to Will, a "Dreamer" who is responsible for the visions of the poem and whose visions may be the product of "the Dreamer's own confused mind."[18] Reference to this elusive Dreamer has become accepted practice in the criticism, and its effect is usually to call into question the validity of the dreams by attributing them to a human and fallible source. But Langland's reason for using the dream vision convention is to make spiritual truths accessible and undeniable; if, in imitation of Will's disbelief, we doubt that the poem's visions are intended as divine expressions of reality presented through grace and kind knowing, then we deprive ourselves of the only objective standard for judging the poem's events, and can read the poem only as an expression of doubt and confusion. Certainly we must often doubt Will's words, since Will is the willful fool against whom we are invited to contrast our greater wisdom in interpreting visions; but we must have faith in the narrator if we are to understand the world of the poem, for the narrator is the divine authority of that world. There is only one moment of union between Will and the narrator in *Piers*, and that is the moment when Will finally accepts faith and ceases to be willful. At this instant, as in the instant of Augustine's conversion, the two voices become one; as soon as Will enters into Unity Holy Church "by conseil of kynde" (XX.212), he disappears as a separate voice, entering into unity with his other self, the self who has presented the visions of Truth all along, the wise and faithful narrator.[19]

Langland's psychomachic allegory supports the equation between faithlessness and lack of self-knowledge and attests to the preexistence of wisdom within the protagonist. As we have already seen in the confrontation between Wit, who understands and acknowledges kind knowing, and Will, who refuses it, the protagonist's psyche is frequently depicted in conflict, and Will consistently fails to recognize or understand these other elements of his own self. The fact that Thought, Wit, Imaginative, and Anima all bear witness to God as Creator, Savior, and Holy Spirit is evidence that knowledge by faith is a kind knowing for Will as Everyman—evidence that only Will as the obstinate will persists in rejecting. Moreover, the dream vision itself attests to Will's split personality by making the entire poem an ongoing dialogue between a sort of subconscious, which sends out the dream visions from the wholeness of its perception, and a repressive consciousness that distorts and misinterprets that message. The whole function of Langland's dream vision is psychic integration: the repressed part of the self knows something that is concealed from the conscious Will, and the dream is an attempt at self-communication. Again, the visions themselves become proof of Will's inherent kind knowing.

Keeping in mind Langland's theory of human understanding and the ways in which it shapes his poem, let us examine in more detail the allegorical life of Will. In the Prologue the distinction between Will and the narrator is immediately made apparent. The ambivalence of Will's opening self-description is puzzling, and if we think of this Will as the generator of the dream, we might mistakenly assume the veracity of the visions to be questionable. But Langland is careful to incorporate distance not only between Will and the dream but also between Will and the reader, by inserting the trustworthy narrator between them. The poet stresses Will's worldliness at the outset: Will is dressed "as an heremite, vnholy of werkes," in order to learn of the "wondres" of "þis world" (Pr. 3, 4). His travels at first have no clearly spiritual intent, nor, when he begins to see the vision, does he at first recognize it as having a spiritual significance: to him it is "a ferly," possibly "of Fairye" (Pr. 6). The voice that provides the interpretive description of the field full of folk is not this Will's but the narrator's, for the voice understands the religious nature of the dream and sees into the hearts of its characters, judging them with godlike powers of perception. Langland does not have Will say, "It seemed to me that these plowmen were good, but those proud-looking men seemed wicked"; instead, the voice shifts from Will's confusion to the narrator's absolute assurance:

> Some putten hem to plouʒ, pleiden ful selde,
> In settynge and sowynge swonken ful harde;
> Wonnen þat [þise] wastours with glotonye destruyeþ.
> And somme putten hem to pride, apparailed hem þerafter,
> In contenaunce of cloþynge comen d[is]gised.
>
> (Pr. 20-24)

We may instinctively doubt the virtue of Will as he is introduced, but the judgments of the narrator, breaking into the scene from without and piercing all human disguises, cannot be doubted. The narrator's judgment falls even on Will indirectly, as he contrasts evil, disguised men and false hermits who wander about the countryside with honest hermits who "holden hem in hire selles" (Pr. 28). It is the narrator who exercises his angry wit on the social injustices he describes in the Prologue, implicating even his audience in the general decadence:

> Thus [ye] gyuen [youre] gold glotons to [helpe]
> And leneþ it Losels [þat] leccherie haunten.
>
> (Pr. 76–77)

And it is still the narrator who addresses the reader at the beginning of Passus I, promising an explanation of the Prologue (on which he has already commented heavily) through the vision of Dame Holy Church. Will, however, neither understands the significance of the Prologue vision nor even recognizes Holy Church; his nonrecognition of the agency that "vnderfeng þee first and þ[i] feiþ [þee] tauʒte" (I.76) is an allegory for his failure of faith, and in turn, his lack of faith is the cause of his failure to recognize Holy Church and understand her teachings. Although Holy Church has taught him the doctrines of Christian faith, faith itself cannot be taught, and without it no spiritual understanding is possible.

In the course of the *Visio* Will sees sin, confesses, is shriven, and acknowledges that the only true pardon is Dowel; if this were enough to save him, Will would be saved at the end of Passus VII, and the poem would be finished. But knowledge by experience alone does not bring faith, and the distinction between Will's tentative voice and the narrator's authoritative tone at the end of Passus VII should make it clear that Will has in no way gained faith or understanding at this point. After debating with himself whether or not he should take dreams seriously at all, Will finally draws a timid conclusion:

> Al þis makeþ me on metels to þynke,
> And how þe preest preued no pardon to dowel
> And demed þat dowel Indulgences passe[þ],
> Biennals and triennals and Bisshopes lettres.
> Dowel at þe day of dome is digneliche vnderfongen;
> [He] passeþ al þe pardon of Seint Petres cherche.
>
> (VII.173–78)

Will has decided, after much debate and inner turmoil, that Dowel is better than a paper pardon; the next words spoken in Will's voice follow directly from this statement and begin the *Vita:*

> Thus, yrobed in russet, I romed aboute
> Al a somer seson for to seke dowel.
>
> (VIII.1–2)

Now that he thinks Dowel is better, he is resolved to pursue it. But in between these two statements, in the last twenty-five lines of the *Visio,* another voice takes over. At first it seems to be a human voice, bound in contemporary time but better educated than Will and surer of its opinion:

> Now haþ þe pope power pardon to graunte
> [Th]e peple wiþouten penaunce to passen [to ioye]?
> This is [a leef of] oure bileue, as lettred men vs techeþ:
> *Quod cumque ligaueris super terram erit ligatum & in
> celis &c.*
> And so I leue leely, lor[d] forb[e]de ellis,
> That pardon and penaunce and preieres doon saue
> Soules þat haue synned seuen siþes dedly.
> Ac to truste [on] þise triennals, trewely, me þynkeþ
> [It] is noȝt so siker for þe soule, certes, as is dowel.
>
> (VII.179–86)

Finally, the voice escapes the earth and time altogether, and the *Visio* ends in the confident tones of the narrator, the angry God who both presents and condemns the corrupt world of the poem, and who knows the whole truth about each human destiny:

Forþi I rede yow renkes þat riche ben on erþe
Vpon trust of youre tresor triennals to haue,
Be [þow] neuer þe bolder to breke þe x hestes,
And namely ye maistres, Meires and Iugges,
That haue þe welþe of þis world and wise men ben holden
To purchace pardon and þe popes bulles.
At þe dredful dome, whan dede shulle rise
And comen alle [bi]fore crist acountes to yelde,
How þow laddest þi lif here and hi[s] lawe keptest,
[What] þow didest day by day þe doom wole reherce.
A pokeful of pardon þere, ne prouincials lettres,
Thei3 [þow] be founde in þe fraternite [among] þe foure ordres
And haue Indulgences doublefold, but dowel [þee] helpe
I sette youre patentes and youre pardon at one pies hele.
                                                                (VII.187–200)

This is very different from the transitional voice, with its cautious "trewely, me þynkeþ / [It] is no3t so siker for þe soule, certes, as is dowel," and even further removed from Will's labored decision "þat dowel Indulgences passe[þ]." And if it were Will who is speaking in the last paragraph of the *Visio*, there would be little need for the *Vita*, since the speaker understands that Dowel is both Christ and the image of Christ within that enables people to do well:

Forþi I counseille alle cristene to crie god mercy,
And Marie his moder be meene bitwene,
That god gyue vs grace er we go hennes
Swiche werkes to werche, while we been here,
That, after oure deeþ day, dowel reherce
At þe day of dome we dide as he hi3te.
                                                                (VII.201–6)

The tone is gentler, even human again, including the speaker in the general need for grace; but it is still the voice of a narrator who understands Dowel, as Will, setting off "to seke dowel," does not. The dual

"I" is less evident in the *Vita*, the narrator's role being taken over more completely by the visionary teachers, who also constitute unacknowledged aspects of Will's own psyche. But in the final passus of the poem, where the vision of Unity Holy Church is unmediated by teachers, the narrator's voice is strong again; and it is here that Will finally turns to God, merges with this narrator, and attains unity.

Will's failure to achieve knowledge by faith is confirmed by his first encounter in the *Vita*, in which two friars explain that Dowel exists among sinners because God gave them free will to protect their souls from mortal sin by doing well:

> "For he 3af þee [to] yeres3yue to yeme wel þiselue
> Wit and free wil, to euery wi3t a porcion,
> To fleynge foweles, to fisshes and to beestes.
> Ac man haþ moost þerof and moost is to blame
> But if he werche wel þerwiþ as dowel hym techeþ."
> "I haue no kynde knowyng", quod I, "to conceyuen [þi] wordes
> Ac if I may lyue and loke I shal go lerne bettre."
>
> (VIII.52–58)

Dowel is Christ, whose teachings all should follow, but it lives among people because of the "yeres3yue" of knowledge and free will placed within them by God. Will responds as he did to Holy Church, that he has no such gift for recognizing and following Dowel, and that experience and education will supply it. But the friar's teachings, and Will's failure to learn by them, suggest just the contrary— that Dowel cannot be learned in this way.

Will next meets Thought but, in failing to recognize him, demonstrates that his lack of faith is a lack of self-knowledge.[20] When Thought tries to explain to Will the triune nature of Dowel, Will refuses to believe him, and does so, ironically, in the name of the inner knowledge that Thought both represents and attempts to impart:

> I þonked þo3t þo þat he me [so] tau3te.
> "Ac yet sauoreþ me no3t þi seying, [so me god helpe!
> More kynde knowynge] I coueite to lerne,
> How dowel, dobet and dobest doon among þe peple."
>
> (VIII.111–14)

Will is asking not simply what kinds of good works people do but how it is that they can do them; again, he refuses to listen on the grounds that he has no kind knowing, only to ask how such knowledge comes to be in people. Thought's response that no one can tell him if not his own wits is as circular as Holy Church's definition of kind knowing:

> "But wit konne wisse þee", quod þoȝt, "where þo þre dwelle
> Ellis [n]oot [no man] þat now is alyue."
>
> (VIII.115–16)

Wit in turn describes the trinity of Dowel in his Castle of Caro allegory. But this time Will has no chance to respond, for Wit's wife, Dame Study, angrily steps in to make sure that Will is not abusing Wit. If Wit teaches the Trinity, the perverse Will can use logic to twist this teaching into falsehood:

> "Than telleþ þei of þe Trinite [how two slowe þe þridde],
> And bryngen forþ a balled reson, taken Bernard to witness,
> And puten forþ presumpcion to preue þe soþe."
>
> (X.54–56)

A faithless will can distort the true message of his wit; although Wit's teaching is true, Dame Study chastises him because Will might take it wrongly. She sees that Will seeks knowledge because he has no faith, and conversely that because he has no faith, he cannot possibly understand what Wit has to tell him; hence her repeated insistence that one should not "will to wit" (X.121, 127, 129, 136) but should have faith.[21] The pursuit of knowledge through study is an abuse of wit if performed by a faithless will. This is why Study sends Will off to Clergy and Scripture when he asks her to "kenne me kyndely to knowe what is dowel" (X.151).

Clergy defines Dowel as "a commune lyf . . . on holy chirche to bileue / Wiþ alle þe articles of þe feiþ þat falleþ to be knowe" (X.238–39), adding specifically that one must have faith in the Trinity in order to do well. But Will flatly equates Dowel and Dobet with "*dominus* and knyȝthode" (X.336), and when Scripture patiently corrects him he throws a tantrum, illustrating the dangers of a faithless education:

"This is a long lesson", quod I, "and litel am I þe wiser;
Where dowel is or dobet derkliche ye shewen.
Manye tales ye tellen þat Theologie lerneþ."

(x.377–79)

We recall Study's criticisms of Theology, whose musings become
"derker" the deeper one studies them unless the study is founded
on faith and love. Will's complaint against learning both describes
and exemplifies the abuse of learning by the faithless, for in making
his argument he misuses much of what Study, Clergy, and Scripture
have just taught him: they explained the dangers of faithless learning
and bad preaching in order to convince Will of faith's primacy, but
Will perversely uses these lessons as excuses not to believe. When
Will quotes Augustine to support his decision to abandon Study,
Clergy, and Scripture, he does not notice that Augustine's insistence
on faith before study is the same lesson his teachers have been trying
to teach:

"... Austyn þe olde, and heiȝest of þe foure,
Seide þus in a sermon—I seigh it writen ones—
'Ecce ipsi ydiot[e] rapiunt celum vbi nos sapientes in inferno
    mergimur'.
And is to mene to [Englissh] men, moore ne lesse,
Arn none raþer yrauysshed fro þe riȝte bileue
Than are þise [kete] clerkes þat konne manye bokes,
Ne none sonner saued, ne sadder of bileue,
Than Plowmen and pastours and [pouere] commune laborers,
Souteres and shepherdes; [swiche] lewed Iuttes
Percen wiþ a Paternoster þe paleys of heuene
And passen Purgatorie penauncelees at hir hennes partyng
Into þe [parfit] blisse of Paradis for hir pure bileue."

(x.459–70)

In attempting to use Augustine's words as logical proofs rather than
as exhortations to faith, Will does not perceive that he is one of "þise
[kete] clerkes" who quote godly texts to their own damnation. He
turns against Study, Clergy, and Scripture because he does not understand their message, and he does not understand because he lacks the
faith that is the message they wish to teach him. What Will is really

rejecting in abandoning his teachers is not intellectual learning, as he insists, but their repeated message of a faith that must be found in the self before it can be supported by study. For all his learning in the first ten passus, he has not learned the one thing that can effect a real change in him; enticed from his pilgrimage by Fortune's promise to show him worldly "wondres" (XI.10), Will is here exactly where he began in the Prologue when he set out "wondres to here."

Through contemplating the question of his salvation, with the help of Scripture and others, Will gradually finds the correct answers to his earlier complaints against Clergy and Scripture. At one point Will seems to be making such progress that Kind himself appears to him and presents middlearth, not as a mirror in which Will's own fleshly nature is reflected, but as an image through which to perceive and love the Creator (XI.322–26). Kind's effort to teach Will to love is reenacted later in Passus XX. But here Will does not "learn to love"; instead, he is rebuked by Reason for faithlessly questioning the ways of God (XI.369–78). It seems illogical to Will that of all God's creatures humankind alone should refuse to be ruled by reason; but Reason has just shown him that this is so, and in thus questioning Reason, Will is committing the sin he complains of, and blaming God for it. The circularity of this process is emphasized by Imaginative when he points out that Will "aresonedest Reson" (XII.218). Instead of trusting his Creator Will demonstrates his lack of faith, and the vision is taken from him.

Despite the teachings of Imaginative and Patience, Will admits at the beginning of Passus XV that he still understands neither Dowel nor kind knowing:

Ac after my wakynge it was wonder longe
Er I koude kyndely knowe what was dowel.
(XV.1–2)

Will's next teacher, Anima, has so many names that it seems as though he, the latest part of Will's psyche to appear, is actually composed of all the others; he is *animus, mens, memoria, racio, sensus,* wit, wisdom, conscience, *amor,* and *spiritus* (XV.23–37). In a general way we may see in Anima all the earlier psychomachic characters, and this is perhaps why each part of Will's psyche has told him essentially the same thing. Even Will is included in Anima ("whan I wilne and wolde *animus* ich hatte" [XV.24]); yet as always Will does not recognize him, and in seeking to comprehend Anima intellectually he betrays his failure to understand what all the earlier visionary characters have tried to teach him. First he lightly quips that Anima has as many names as bishops have, but Anima sees the willful skepticism behind Will's levity:

> "That is sooþ", seide he; "now I se þe wille.
> Thow woldest knowe and konne þe cause of alle [hire] names,
> And of [myne] if þow myȝtest, me þynkeþ by þi speche."
> "Ye, sire!" I seide, "by so no man were greued
> Alle þe sciences vnder sonne and alle þe sotile craftes
> I wolde I knewe and kouþe kyndely in myn herte."
> "Thanne artow inparfit", quod he, "and oon of prides knyȝtes."
>
> (xv.44–50)

Anima explains that Will's quest for intellectual understanding alone is contrary to the ways of kind knowing:

> "It were ayeins kynde", quod he, "and alle kynnes reson
> That any creature sholde konne al except crist oone.
> . . . .
> That man þat muche hony eteþ his mawe it engleymeþ,
> And þe moore þat a man of good matere hereþ,
> But he do þerafter, it dooþ hym double scaþe.
> . . . .
> And riþt as hony is yuel to defie and engleymeþ þe mawe,
> Right so þat þoruȝ reson wolde þe roote knowe
> Of god and of his grete myȝtes, hise graces it letteþ."
>
> (xv.52–53, 57–59, 64–66)

The devouring of mere knowledge, far from nourishing the soul, effectively cuts it off from God's grace, the one true source of knowledge by faith.

When Will asks Anima to define charity, Anima calls it "a fre liberal wille" (XV.150). Will's response, ironically, shows his disbelief even as it proves that he is created in God's image and is therefore capable of faith:

"I seiȝ neuere swich a man, so me god helpe,
That he ne wolde aske after his, and ouþerwhile coueite
Thynge þat neded hym noȝt and nyme it if he myȝte.
Clerkes kenne me þat crist is in alle places
Ac I seiȝ hym neuere sooþly but as myself in a Mirour:
[Hic] in enigmate, tunc facie ad faciem."

(xv.158–62a)

Instead of faithfully perceiving Christ through his earthly reflection
in his own heart, Will uses this reflection to complain that Christ
and Charity are not here. Anima responds that until Will has faith
in Christ, he cannot perceive the pure Charity that is Christ:

"Wiþouten help of Piers Plowman", quod he, "his persone
    sestow neuere."
"Wheiþer clerkes knowen hym", quod I, "þat kepen holi
    kirke?"
"Clerkes haue no knowyng", quod he, "but by werkes and
    wordes.
Ac Piers þe Plowman parceyueþ moore depper
What is þe wille and wherfore þat many wight suffreþ:
Et vidit deus cogitaciones eorum. . . .
Therefore by colour ne by clergie knowe shaltow [hym] neuere,
Neiþer þoruȝ wordes ne werkes, but þoruȝ wil oone,
And þat knoweþ no clerk ne creature on erþe
But Piers þe Plowman, Petrus id est christus."

(xv.196–200a, 209–12)

As Dowel signifies both Christ and the image of God in humanity,
so Piers is both the Christ who perceives the charitable will in the
human soul and the charity in people that enables them to perceive
Christ. In essence, Anima is telling Will that he must have charity
to perceive charity, love Christ to know Christ, have grace to receive
grace. Will thanks Anima, but still has no idea what he means: "Ac
ȝit I am in a weer what charite is to mene" (XVI.3). In the subsequent
allegory of the tree of charity Will's plucking of an apple reenacts the
Fall: as Anima has explained, Will's hunger, like Adam's, is for the
wrong kind of knowledge.
    In the next vision, the Samaritan attempts to teach Will about the

Trinity by analogy to the hand, whose fist, palm, and fingers work together as a single entity. But he also demonstrates by this allegory the paradoxical nature of Will's own dilemma of faithlessness. For if the Father is the fist, the Son the fingers expressing the fist in action, and the Holy Spirit the palm that unites fist and fingers, then the one unforgivable sin, the sin against the Holy Spirit, may be likened to a palm that is pierced and thus unable to "grasp" God. By this image Langland links faithlessness, the failure to "receive" the Trinity within one's heart, with the killing of Christ, and therefore with the defacement of the image of God in the heart:

> "[Ac who is hurte in þe hand], euene in þe myddes,
> He may receyue riȝt noȝt; reson it sheweþ.
> For þe fyngers þat folde sholde and þe fust make,
> For peyne of þe pawme power hem failleþ
> To clucche or to clawe, to clippe or to holde.
> Were þe myddel of myn hand ymaymed or yperissed
> I sholde receyue riȝt noȝt of þat I reche myghte.
> · ·
> By þis skile", [he seide], "I se an euidence
> That whoso synneþ in þe Seint Spirit assoilled worþ he neuere,
> Neiþer here ne elliswhere, as I herde telle:
> Qui peccat in spiritu[m] sanct[um] &c,
> For he prikeþ god as in þe pawme þat peccat in spiritu[m]
>   sanct[um]."

(XVII.187–93, 198–201)

Faithlessness, lovelessness, is an unforgivable sin because by its nature it destroys the only means of forgiveness, keeping the faithless in a never-ending circle of damnation. If they do not love, they cannot "receive" God, nor can God "receive" them. It is Christ himself who is speaking here of being "pricked" and "pierced" in the palm by each faithless person, and the punning connection between "prikeþ" and "peccat" emphasizes their real relatedness. Faithlessness, then, wounds the Christ that preexists in the heart, and the Samaritan repeats that such a sin is "vnkynde" (XVII.254, 259, 260, 264): it is unlike one's true nature, a denial of the real self, a lack of kind knowing. Will suspects that he might possibly be guilty of such a sin, and he asks if there is still help for such a sinner:

"I pose I hadde synned so and sholde [nouþe] deye,
And now am sory þat I so þe Seint Spirit agulte,
Confesse me and crye his grace, [crist] þat al made,
And myldeliche his mercy aske; mighte I noȝt be saued?"

(XVII.299–302)

Of course, this is exactly Will's sin, and the hypothetical wording of his question reveals the same resistance to faith that has made all his pilgrimages seem so futile. But even now, the Samaritan assures him, there is hope that God's mercy may help to activate the dormant love and faith in Will's heart and to realign the will toward God (XVII.350–54).

In the heavenly debate over the human soul that Will witnesses in his next vision, Peace argues in humanity's defense by placing the problem of learning at the center of the issue of salvation. She claims that human sin may be excused because by nature people learn only through differences and oppositions:

"For hadde þei wist of no wo, wele hadde þei noȝt knowen;
For no wight woot what wele is þat neuere wo suffrede,
Ne what is hoot hunger þat hadde neuere defaute.
If no nyȝt ne weere, no man as I leeue
Sholde wite witterly what day is to meene.
Sholde neuere riȝt riche man þat lyueþ in reste and ese
Wite what wo is, ne were þe deeþ of kynde."

(XVIII.205–11)

Peace argues that mercy should be shown humankind for the very reason they sin: because they cannot understand except through the timebound processes of logic and experience. This is not to say that people can come to faith and salvation through temporal education and experience, for there is no salvation through human understanding alone, and Christ's mercy is needed to redeem humankind from the deadly cycle of fallen learning, with its inexorable movement from ignorance to sin to death. In a single image, Peace shows both the dilemma of human understanding and Christ's resolution of the problem:

"Sholde neuere riȝt riche man þat lyueþ in reste and ese
Wite what wo is, ne were þe deeþ of kynde.

So god þat bigan al of his goode wille
Bicam man of a mayde mankynde to saue
And suffrede to be sold to se þe sorwe of deying."
                                                (XVIII.210–14)

By a surprising twist, the death of kind is transformed into the death
of Kind: Christ came not only because people sin and die but also
because, like a rich man, he had to "learn" sorrow. Of course Langland does not literally mean that God had to learn anything, since
his point is that people need mercy because they cannot understand
absolutes as God does. It is a very different kind of understanding
through which Christ reunites God and humankind. This is a kind
knowing, a resurrection of the image of God in humanity that makes
knowledge by faith both possible and salvational. And it is this kinship, this genuine relation between the self and God, that Jesus emphasizes in his dispute with Lucifer:

"A[c] to be merciable to man þanne my kynde [it] askeþ
For we beþ breþeren of blood, [ac] noȝt in baptisme alle.
Ac alle þat beþ myne hole breþeren, in blood and in baptisme,
Shul noȝt be dempned to þe deeþ þat [dureþ] wiþouten
    ende. . . .
For I were an vnkynde kyng but I my kynde helpe. . . ."
                                                (XVIII.375–78, 398)

After the Resurrection the argument between Mercy and Justice,
Peace and Truth, is ended, their opposing claims resolved in the paradox of Christ.

The last two passus document the establishment by Grace of
Christian society under the auspices of Unity Holy Church, and its
subsequent decay under the onslaught of Pride and Antichrist. Will's
final vision in Passus XX of Unity Holy Church as a castle under
siege collapses all of Christian history, from the founding of the
church, to its present state, to the attack of Antichrist in the last
days, into a single unified timeless vision. In the same way, Will's
last actions are also his first actions; they are the beginning and end
of his pilgrimage to Unity, accomplished in a single moment. Conscience, the leader of the forces of Unity Holy Church, calls out to
Kind for help, and Kind responds by sending pestilence, old age, and

death to chastise the people, an action that condenses the aftermath of the Fall and the contemporary age of plague with the future disasters of the Apocalypse. Elde particularly afflicts poor Will, who is comically made both bald and impotent at a stroke. But at this odd moment of levity and self-mockery—or perhaps not so odd, since the entire autobiography of Will chronicles the life of a fool—Will finally awakens to kind knowing, in the moment of his direct perception of Kind and submission to Kind's will; at this moment he suddenly "learns" Dowel. In fear of death he cries out to Kind to grant him salvation—and significantly it is the first time we have seen Will pray:

> And as I seet in þis sorwe I sauȝ how kynde passede
> And deeþ drogh neiȝ me; for drede gan I quake,
> And cryde to kynde: "out of care me brynge!
> Lo! Elde þe hoore haþ me biseye.
> Awreke me if youre wille be for I wolde ben hennes."
>
> (xx.199–203)

After all his questions and complaints, Will simply prays to Kind to save him if it is Kind's will; at last Will is ready to align his will with God's. Kind tells him he will be saved if he enters "into vnitee" (XX.204) and learns "som craft" (XX.206) that he can do there; that is, he tells Will to enter into the faith of the church and to do well. But of course Will has never been able to understand Dowel; he asks Kind "what craft is best to lerne?" (XX.207). Kind's response is the same answer Will has been hearing all along: no particular action or study or knowledge will save him; he must simply "[l]erne to loue . . . and leef alle oþere" (XX.208). When Will asks Kind, "How shal I come to catel so to cloþe me and to feede?" (XX.209), Kind tells him what he has already been told, but only now hears:

> "And þow loue lelly lakke shal þee neuere
> [Weede] ne worldly [mete] while þi lif lasteþ."
>
> (xx.210–11)

This was also the answer given in Piers's decision not to worry about "bely ioye" at the end of the *Visio*. Will did not understand it then; but now, hearing it at last from Kind as a kind knowing, he understands. And suddenly, in two lines, the thing toward which he has all along been trying unsuccessfully to progress is accomplished:

> And [I] by conseil of kynde comsed to rome
> Thoruȝ Contricion and Confession til I cam to vnitee.
>
> (XX.212–13)

Two lines encompass Will's entire pilgrimage to Truth, from beginning to end. When he enters into Unity, Will is entering not only into the church in faith and love but also into inner unity, the spiritual kingdom of heaven: he is no longer willful, and thus there is no longer a separate Will. For the rest of the poem there is only the narrator, angrily describing the contemporary Christian society that so obviously fails to imitate this spiritual kingdom, from the same omniscient viewpoint as in the Prologue. Will has united with his faithful self; he has perceived the kind knowing that has been in him all along and that has produced the visions of the poem.

By phrasing Will's final question about how to achieve salvation in terms of learning a craft, Langland is not implying that faith is something one learns, like carpentry; nor is Kind's final response, "Learn to love," meant to be taken literally. Daniel Murtaugh suggests that the idea of learning in the poem, "if not the cause of grace, is yet a figure or symbol of it," and that "the activities of the mind in the service of learning differ from the workings of grace in our progress to salvation only as an image differs from a likeness."[22] Because Murtaugh takes salvation to involve progress, his emphasis here is on Langland's supposed tendency to link learning with faith. Certainly the use of progressive, temporal learning as a metaphor for instantaneous knowledge by faith is a favorite device throughout the poem, and Langland sees learning by study and experience as important supports to faith. But in the world view represented by Langland's allegory, the two kinds of learning are crucially different. All creation reflects God to greater and lesser degrees, and learning is naturally a lesser reflection of divine knowledge by faith; but as the poet invokes earthly treasure to distinguish it from the divine treasure of Truth in Passus I through IV, and as he uses time and space themselves as analogies for a timeless reality, so he uses learning primarily as a nonsimilitude for kind knowing. Dowel is to be found not in logical analysis but in love, and Dame Study concludes her tirade against the murky intellectualism of theology with an ironic twist:

"Loke þow loue lelly if þee likeþ dowel,
For dobet and dobest ben [drawen] of loues [scole]."
(x.192–93)

It is characteristic of Langland's style that he plays on the nonsimilitude between the tenor and vehicle of this metaphor just where the central point of his discussion is that kind knowing and Dowel cannot be learned. Piers himself offers the same nonsimilitude upon first entering the poem: the well-traveled pilgrim has never found St. Truth, but Piers can guide the folk to Truth because "I knowe hym as kyndely as clerc doþ hise bokes" (V.538). It is natural that a clerk should know his books and, in a different sense, natural that a person should know Truth. But the thrust of the allegory opposing Piers to the pilgrim is that experience of the world does not teach Truth, and the thrust of the metaphor is that books do not teach it either: to know books is not necessarily to know God. The nonsimilitude is evoked again in Piers's definition of Dowel and Dobet as "two Infinites, / Which Infinites wiþ a feiþ fynden out dobest" (XIII.128–29). Since Piers has "set alle sciences at a sop saue loue one" (XIII.125), his apparent reference here to grammatical terminology seems more to contrast the two kinds of knowledge than to compare them. Will's treatment of kind knowing as a lesson he must learn is indicative of his whole problem, a problem he has not yet resolved when Kind finally reaches him in Passus XX. But suddenly, at Kind's command, Will is capable of reading the metaphor, "Learn to love"; suddenly he does not ask any more questions, does not defer faith until some later time in hopes that it may be logically demonstrated through more learning. He does not "learn" to love; he simply knows it.

At the beginning of the poem, Holy Church angrily responds to Will's insistence that he lacks kind knowing by criticizing his education in Latin:

"Thow doted daffe!" quod she, "dulle are þi wittes.
To litel latyn þow lernedest, leode, in þi youþe:
Heu Michi quia sterilem duxi vitam Iuvenilem.

It is a kynde knowyng þat kenneþ in þyn herte
For to louen þi lord leuere þan þiselue."

(1.140–43)

When Will later rebels against Study's, Clergy's, and Scripture's
teachings, arguing perversely that many clerks "han corsed þe tyme /
That euere þe[i] kouþe [konne on book] moore þan *Credo in deum
patrem*" (X.472–73), Scripture denounces him with yet another Latin
lesson:

Thanne Scripture scorned me and a skile tolde,
And lakked me in latyn and liȝt by me sette,
And seide "*Multi multa sciunt et seipsos nesciunt.*"

(XI.1–3)

Obviously it is valuable to learn Latin, but not because learning Latin
will bring about self-knowledge and the kind knowing of faith; for
the message contained in these very lessons is that no external lessons, but only an internal awakening, can give Will the knowledge
he seeks: knowledge of many things does not lead to knowledge of
the self. Scripture and Holy Church are in the awkward position of
all medieval teachers: they cannot teach the one thing necessary to
make all their teachings meaningful to their pupil: faith must be preunderstood. Instead they express themselves in analogies that cannot
be properly understood unless the pupil suddenly "learns" faith. And
this of course is Langland's position as teacher/poet; he does not
expect to teach faith through a developmental series of lessons. Instead, he hopes to awaken the faith within his readers by repeatedly
presenting them with the paradoxical circularity of faith itself. To
understand his allegory is to imitate that faith.

3
Creating Society
Allegorical Imagery and the
Social Microcosm

✦

We have seen that the general shaping principles Langland employs in *Piers Plowman* are the very principles of contingent time and space that in his view shape the cosmos; we have also seen that the frame allegory of Will's dream/life reflects the poet's vision of humanity as created in God's image, so that faith and understanding preexist within each person and are not achieved merely by a process of learning through time. But the relationships between people, and between the various hierarchies of medieval Christian society, are also important in the poem; in fact, Langland is often regarded primarily as a sociopolitical theorist and satirist. Although Langland confines his social commentary within the larger framework of his orthodox representations of time and the human relationship to God, he nevertheless devotes most of his local imagery to the subject of human society and its function within this framework. There seems even to be an intrinsic connection, for Langland, between the poetic device of imagery and the idea of human society: Langland's perception of the bond of divine love in even the most mundane examples of social intercourse generates his most successful poetic fusions of matter and spirit, creating miniature allegorical systems of meaning. Critics often see Langland as a subversive revolutionary whose millennial or apocalyptic visions are limited entirely to this world, either advocating material social reform or prophesying the fall of the medieval Christian social order. But a close look at Langland's social imagery reveals just the opposite—that he conceives Christian society to be a true imitation of divine love patterned by and upon Christ its Creator, and that this divine pattern of love, though it can be either maintained or corrupted by human individuals, can be neither perfected nor destroyed except by God himself. Langland's poetry is indeed subversive of the social status quo; but it is subversive as Jesus' preaching was subversive: it embodies the subversiveness of spiritual faith.

Langland depicts time and space, and the earthly progress of individuals, not as self-contained, self-significant realities, but as divinely created metaphors for a timeless, transcendent reality; similarly, his allegorical imagery reflects his vision of the cosmos as constructed metaphorically, so that the vehicle generally designates something that is both materially real and dependent on the tenor for its whole, spiritual significance. Like Dante, Langland does not ask that the literal level of his allegory be discarded as an empty shell enclosing the kernel of spiritual meaning; he intends the reader to understand that the material world exists in real relation to the spiritual, as a physical symbol for spiritual realities. It is this view for which D. W. Robertson, Jr., argues when he demonstrates that to the medieval mind the physical and spiritual are not dialectically opposed but are hierarchically ordered as lesser and greater reflections of God.[1] Robertson's theory is especially interesting in light of his usual practice—exemplified in his criticism on *Piers*—of ignoring the literal level almost completely.[2] R. W. Frank, on the other hand, reads *Piers* strictly "as a literal rather than an allegorical poem." The reader is wise to remember that in the Middle Ages, as Rosemond Tuve points out, "[t]here is no question of a substitution of figurative for literal meaning; all doctrine touching allegory, varied and irreconcilably different in some other respects, is unanimous in claiming the validity of both the literal historical event and its allegorical significance." At the same time, Tuve reminds us that allegory need not always assign the same allegorical significance, or any allegorical meaning at all, to every figure that appears on the literal level; instead, the literal level may be "intermittently allegorically significant," indicating "the greater or less penetration of details of an incident with metaphorical meaning."[3] The precise allegorical meaning of a figure may shift, and a scene may be allegorical even though certain of its characters or actions have no specific allegorical significance.

Tuve's emphasis on the "literal historical event," however, seems to move us theoretically away from allegory and toward figuralism; indeed, if Dante's advice for reading his allegory is to be applied to Langland's poem, we must also recall Auerbach's view that the *Commedia* itself embodies a figural view of reality, which Auerbach is careful to distinguish from allegory:

> [A] figural schema permits both its poles—the figure and its fulfillment—to retain the characteristics of concrete histori-cal reality, in contradistinction to what obtains with symbolic or allegorical personifications, so that figure and fulfillment —although the one "signifies" the other—have a significance which is not incompatible with their being real. . . . Medieval symbolism and allegorism are often, as we know, excessively ab-stract, and many traces of this are to be found in the *Comedy* itself. But far more prevalent is the figural realism which can be observed in full bloom in sermons, the plastic arts, and mys-tery plays . . . ; and it is this figural realism which dominates Dante's view.

Following Auerbach's lead, Elizabeth Salter argues that in *Piers* there is less evidence for Robertson's fourfold allegorical system than for a figural view; she sees the poem as "an imitation of history, a con-struction of literal, historical truth, which can be accepted in its own right, like the literal, historical truth of the Scriptures." She concedes that it may be possible to reconcile figuralism and allegory in prac-tice, although she does not pursue the point. David Aers, however, takes up the gauntlet, suggesting that the two viewpoints, though theoretically at war, may coexist peacefully in poetic practice:

> In fact, "hellenistic" conceptions of the relations between image and idea were prevalent—prevalent enough to draw adverse criti-cism from modern theologians for encouraging medieval exe-gesis to dissolve the historical engagement of Biblical *figura*. The tendency to assume that sacred history contains allegorical meaning in the same way as the unhistorical images of nature, implies that the unique Christian allegory (typology) may not be any different in practice from other kinds of allegory. We can hardly be amazed if nothing in medieval practice corresponds

neatly to that "rigorous distinction" between Hebraic-Christian typology and hellenistic-Philonic allegory.[4]

The poet, after all, may be more interested in poetic assimilation than in a strict adherence to theological or philosophical distinctions. Then, too, if the Bible offered the medieval poet a figural view of reality, it also offered allegory in the parables of Jesus, the words of God himself. That Langland assimilates and fuses the two should be clear from his use of the parables of the sower and the minas in Passus VI: Piers's function as a guide to Truth in the preceding pilgrimage allegory establishes him in a priestly capacity, so that his work on the half acre is clearly intended to reproduce Christ's parable of the sower of the Word; yet the half-acre scene is also an allegory of the social contract, which is seen as organized according to this Word of love and brotherhood. Because Piers's work on the half acre signifies both literal plowing and the cultivation of God's Word, the half-acre scene should be understood to advocate all honest human labor, physical or spiritual. In the same way, Hunger uses the parable of the minas, not just to advocate the spreading of the Word, but quite literally to insist that people perform physical or spiritual labor in this world: "Contemplatif lif or Actif lif; crist wolde men wroughte" (VI.249).[5] The threat of hunger is quite literally intended, although a spiritual failing—human sin—is assigned as its cause. Langland's point in his figuralization of Jesus' parables is that any labor becomes a true signifier of the Word if it is performed in Christian love. Grace's distribution of crafts in Passus XIX shows that all good labor reflects divine grace because of the historical sacrifice of Christ and his subsequent establishment of the church and Christian society in a state of grace. In this sense even common laborers daily take part in the figural repetition of Christian history, and in doing so they actually contribute to both the physical and the spiritual nourishment of their fellow Christians: physically by their produce, and spiritually by their example.

Because we tend to see the physical and spiritual as opposed, modern readers frequently characterize Langland's allegory as being in a state of degeneration into representation, as though the literal or representational level of meaning could not coexist with the allegorical. This attitude persists throughout twentieth-century criticism of *Piers,* from Dorothy Owen's view of the poem as an attempt at the novel to Priscilla Martin's argument that Langland's allegorical efforts are "frustrated" by his impulse toward realism.[6] The effect of these assumptions, if not absolutely to divorce tenor from vehicle in Langland's allegory, is to proscribe severely the ways in which the two may be seen to relate to one another, and to destroy both the powerful ambivalence of which his allegory is capable and the overarching unity and harmony of the world vision in which this ambivalence is given play.

One of the allegorical scenes often described as degenerating into realism is the scene in which the Seven Deadly Sins confess and are shriven by Repentance (V.60–505).[7] The vision begins with Reason's sermon to the field of folk, in which he emphasizes their responsibility for appearances of disorder in the cosmos: there is a connection, he explains, between the material manifestations of plagues and astrological disturbances, and the spiritual disease of sin in the microcosm of the human soul (V.13–20). He shows how individual sins also disorder the social hierarchies of family, church, and state (V.30–56). The world Reason describes exists in a delicate balance of mutual interconnection between spiritual and material causes and effects. Reason concludes that the folk must repent and confess to be saved, and, logically, a confession scene follows the sermon. Rather than beginning with allegory and degenerating into representation, however, Langland begins this scene with the general idea of depicting the confessions of individuals from among the folk: he briefly describes the repentance of "Pernele proud-herte" and a "Lechour" (V.62, 71), not Pride and Lechery. It is mere representation, and not allegory, that soon strikes him as inadequate, and though his Envy, Wrath, Covetous, Sloth, and Glutton constantly shift between personification and representation, Langland stresses the many different human forms each sin may take, rather than representing each as a distinct individual. Covetous, for example, is portrayed as an apprentice, a peddler, a draper, a weaver, a spinner, a brewer, a thief, and a usurer, and he is also shown to spread into the actions of lords and ladies, knights and nobility:

> "I haue lent lords loued me neuere after,
> And haue ymaad many a knyȝt boþe Mercer and draper
> That payed neuere for his prentishode noȝt a peire gloues."
>
> (v.251–53)

In one sense, the knight learns greed from a swindling merchant; in another, greed is a sin common to all people but aptly symbolized by dishonest merchants, so that everyone is "boþe Mercer and draper." The stress is on both specificity and universality, which is the dual vision of allegory itself. Langland's treatment here is not a degeneration but a regeneration of the timeworn allegory of the Seven Deadly Sins: instead of people who confess that they are sinners, he presents sins who confess that they are people—that they are embodied every day in all classes of human society. The allegory is intended to express both the individuality and the universality of sin: sin is not something only certain people do, nor is it merely an amusing pageant of abstractions. It is a spiritual state of unlikeness to God that pervades society.

Langland's allegory is meant to be read both literally and figuratively; it describes a world in which the divine and profane, the spiritual and material, are profoundly interrelated. A closer look at one of the Sins' confessions may help to suggest the nature of this relationship. The poet presents Wrath's self-description as a gardener in a friary, not in order to shift from allegory into representation, but to introduce a particular allegorical image to express the growth of wrath among Christians:

> "I am wraþe", quod he, "I was som tyme a frere,
> And þe Couentes Gardyner for to graffen Impes.
> On lymitours and listres lesynges I ymped
> Til þei beere leues of lowe speche lordes to plese,
> And siþen þei blosmede abrood in boure to here shriftes.
> And now is fallen þerof a fruyt þat folk han wel leuere
> Shewen hire shriftes to hem þan shryue hem to hir persons.
> And now persons han parceyued þat freres parte wiþ hem
> Thise possessioners preche and depraue freres;
> And freres fyndeþ hem in defaute, as folk bereþ witnesse,
> That whan þei preche þe peple in many places aboute
> I, wraþe, walke wiþ hem and wisse hem of my bokes."
>
> (v.137–48)

Some of what Wrath says is intended quite literally: that dishonest friars cause trouble, that people dishonestly go to friars for confession, and that priests and friars angrily denounce one another. But

Wrath himself is more than just a troublemaking friar; he is also an external force that somehow both "grafts" lies upon the friars and acts as their teacher and adviser. In addition, Langland illustrates the development of wrath between friars and priests by way of a similitude between gardening and the "cultivation" of lies, in which the trees are the friars themselves, the "Impes" are lies, the blossoms are the friars' setting themselves up as confessors, and the fruit is the laity's preference of friars to priests. As an external agency, Wrath causes friars to lie, but the effects of their lying are shown to spread wrath throughout society in realistic ways: in the improper shriving of lords and folk and in the enmity between priests and friars. The result of this enmity, in turn, is to reinforce the magical hold Wrath has on the friars, thus perpetuating the circle of sin Wrath began. In the allegorical image of the tree—a symbol of natural growth and hence, in a sense, of causation—the unnatural element of the grafted branch is introduced, and as a result a foreign disease spreads throughout the other branches and into the blossoms and fruit. Like the tree, both the human body and human society are unities made up of many parts bound together in natural processes of cause and effect; but once sin is introduced by the mysterious agency outside these natural systems, the sin is necessarily propagated throughout the systems in an endless chain of growth. In the similitude of the tree of wrath Langland combines the allegorical action of Wrath with a naturalistic representation of the spread of wrath among people, and establishes a correspondence between the closed biological system of the tree, disrupted by the friar's graft, and the closed systems of the human body and society, infected by sin. As the microcosm of the growing tree is affected by the larger world of humans, so the human microcosms, both individual and social, are affected by forces from the macrocosm of the spiritual world. The image of Wrath, then, is not mere representation, or personification, or analogy; it depicts a series of closed systems related to one another by both vertical causation, where the invisible or superior controls the visible or inferior, and horizontal causation, where every action within each system produces a chain reaction.

That Langland's allegorical imagery embodies not only connections of similarity—what the modern reader regards as mere rhetoric —but also connections of contiguity and causation should suggest that allegory as a genre is more than extended metaphor. If, as Roman Jakobson theorizes, metaphoric thought dominates Romantic and symbolist poetry, whereas "metonymy . . . underlies and actually predetermines the so-called 'realistic' trend" in modern literature, then it should be clear that Langland's allegory, simultaneously metaphoric and metonymic, expresses a radically different conception of reality. In his chapter entitled "Allegorical Causation," Angus Fletcher reorients Jakobson's study of metaphoric and metonymic thought and language, arguing that allegory is rooted in two kinds of magical thinking: imitative magic, which presupposes the "causal efficacy of the parallel," and contagious magic, in which "the bond is contiguity, not similarity," so that "[w]hatever 'goes with' the object of the spell will suffice to bring that object under magical control."[8] Imitative magical thinking underlies all concepts of the relation between macrocosm and microcosm, and in this sense "the language of cosmic correspondence is an inherently magical language"; God's material creation imitates divine Forms in varying degrees that also then imitate one another, and by imitating Christ people may partake in the power of this divinely ordered system of correspondences. Contagious magical thinking pervades all psychomachic allegories, "rendered most frequently as the struggle between two warring armies of moral germs, the good and bad viruses."[9] Fletcher argues that "[c]ontagion is the primary symbol of Christian allegory since that allegory is chiefly concerned with sin and redemption"; Wrath is a disease which afflicts people causing them to act wrathfully, and the specific of Patience is required for their cure. By pointing out the causal connections between tenor and vehicle in allegory, Fletcher demonstrates anew that realistic detail in an allegory must not be read as undermining its allegorical intention:

> [T]he criterion of realism is wasted on the theory of allegory. There is no important difference between a very real, human, semiabstraction (Moloch, Belial, or the like) and a very unreal, nonhuman abstraction (a Gluttony, a Fever, or the like), since as long as they take part in total forms that are ritualized or symmetrically ordered, the ritual *form of the whole* will determine the final effect of each agent. The apparent surface realism of an allegorical agent will recede in importance, as soon as he is

felt to take part in a magical plot, as soon as his causal relations to others in that plot are seen to be magically based. This is an important point because there has often been confusion as to the function of the naturalistic detail of so much allegory. In the terms I have been outlining, this detail now appears not to have a journalistic function; it is more than mere record of observed facts. It serves instead the purposes of magical containment, since the more the allegorist can circumscribe the attributes, metonymic and synecdochic, of his personae, the better he can shape their fictional destiny. Naturalist detail is "cosmic," universalizing, not accidental as it would be in straight journalism. [10]

We should not mistake Wrath's self-identification as a friar for an attempt at journalistic realism; nor should we worry about the extent to which Wrath is conceived as a real diabolical entity, like Satan. Langland uses Wrath and his image of tree grafting to express the imitative and contiguous causal connections that he believes bind the physical and spiritual realms of the cosmos. Whether such belief is to be called magical or religious is a matter of individual preference.

As an example of contagious magic Fletcher quotes from Passus XX of *Piers*, where Conscience prays to Kind to send down plagues and death upon people for their sins, the same scenario Reason describes in his sermon at the beginning of the confession scene. Because plague is conceived as the physical effect of a spiritual state, Fletcher shows that Langland "is portraying a physical reality as well as a metaphysical belief." But sin is also a contagious disease infecting the whole human race, and this is why the scene in Passus XX is also a psychomachia describing Conscience's response to the body's invasion. As a result, Fletcher concludes, "Plague here is both the cause and the effect of sin, both a human failing and a divine retribution." In this sense the disease of wrath in the passage quoted above is the same as the plague—wrath is both cause and effect in a closed system of operation between spiritual and material planes. But Wrath's tree image also reveals a good deal of imitative magical thinking: the likeness Langland discovers between the naturalistic details of gardening and a spiritual malignancy of supernatural origin presupposes a cosmos that has been deliberately created and ordered in a system of correspondences. Fletcher is careful to remind the reader that "the two classes [of magical thinking] do merge with each other in many cases," and this is certainly true of the allegorical imagery of *Piers*.[11] The causal bonds underlying relationships of similarity and contiguity in Langland's imagery combine to re-create the entire cosmos in small; specifically, relationships of similarity re-create the system of vertical causation that binds God to humanity, and relationships of contiguity re-create the system of horizontal causation that binds people to one another. In addition, the system of horizontal, contiguous causation is itself caused vertically by God: the diseased social order, in which sin spreads by contagion, is still God's creation, bearing his image in similitude. In Langland's description of the foundation of Christian society, the newly risen Christ appoints Grace to ordain the social hierarchies and to divide grace equally among the various crafts, with the closing injunction that everyone must love and help one another:

> "Forþi", quod grace, "er I go I wol gyue yow tresor
> And wepne to fighte wiþ whan Anticrist yow assailleþ."
> And gaf ech man a grace to gide wiþ hymseluen
> That ydelnesse encombre hym noȝt, enuye ne pride. . . .
> And alle he lered to be lele, and ech a craft loue ooþer,
> [Ne no boost ne] debat [be] among hem [alle].
> "Thouȝ some be clenner þan some, ye se wel", quod Grace,
> "[That al craft and konnyng come] of my ȝifte.
> Lokeþ þat no[on] lakke ooþer, but loueþ as breþeren;
> And who þat moost maistries kan be myldest of berynge."
>
> (XIX.225–28, 250–55)

The grace Grace distributes is not only the knowledge of a particular craft but also the divine grace of love that restores the image of God in all people. As vertical or imitative cause, Grace is both the creator of society and the pattern of love upon which society is created. As horizontal or contiguous cause, grace is the image of this pattern in human society, both the love and the labor that cement the social hierarchies.

Langland's blend of allegory and figuralism, and his fusion of imitative and contiguous causation in his allegorical imagery, relate to his conception of time and causation in the poem as a whole. For time and space themselves are conceived to be caused vertically throughout the poem: they are weak and repetitive imitations of atemporal and nonspatial reality. As each moment of time owes its being directly to God, so each event in human history is shaped, not simply by previous events, but by the hand of God himself. This is why each moment of every Christian life, like every important event in Christian history, is a figural repetition of earlier events: God is continually reexpressing the same divine Truth through his temporal reflections. The idea of vertical causation is by no means unique to Langland in the Middle Ages. In his analysis of medieval modes of perception, William Brandt observes that some clerical chroniclers tend to break up the temporal movement of history and to formulate each event individually, weakening the sense of horizontal causation between events so that each seems to be caused independently by some single, unique thing—a comet, a dream, the will of God. Morton Bloomfield likewise distinguishes between "horizontal motivation" in medieval epic, in which one episode logically causes the next, and the "vertical motivation" that dominates medieval romance, in which "the motive is a mystery and comes from a divine force." Individual episodes in romance tend to be juxtaposed in unrealistic, illogical ways, and Bloomfield suggests that this vertical causation is directly related to the greater frequency and more extensive development of allegory in romance than in epic: "Because of its attitude toward the unknown, romance is more open to allegory and symbolism than epic. . . . Man is more naked and exposed in the romances than in the epic; he is in a liminal situation where the unknown hovers threateningly over him. He is in need of Christianity and of the merciful powers. He cannot rely on his own strength or on the rationality of the world as the epic hero can. Romance then is more naturally allegoric than the epic."[12] It seems safe to assume, on the basis of Fletcher's observations about allegory, that the connection here is not only between vertical causation and romance but between vertical causation and allegory; whether the medieval allegorical view is expressed in a romance or in a more overtly didactic religious poem, it still assumes that the material world is both affected by and an effect of the invisible.

If certain clerical chronicles and the allegorical romance share a weakened sense of temporal causation, in a similar manner Lang-

land's allegorical imagery in *Piers* tends not to develop in any logically progressive way. A number of critics have discussed the question of development in Langland's allegorical imagery, especially
with regard to the figure of Piers; John Lawlor, for example, argues
that Piers and the entire plowing scene in Passus VI have only literal
significance, and that the allegorical meaning of Langland's figures
develops only gradually. But much earlier, Greta Hort had already
perceived "rather a gradual unfolding of the meaning . . . than any
evolution in the idea"; she suggested that "[w]hat was the hidden
meaning in the earlier part of the poem becomes explicit in the
latter part." More recently, Stephen Barney's analysis of agricultural
imagery in *Piers* has led him to a similar conclusion: he sees Piers
as always having allegorical significance, though this significance is
perhaps expressed more elaborately at some times than at others.
In his study of bread imagery in the poem, A. C. Spearing counters
the reading D. W. Robertson and Bernard Huppé offer in their *Piers
Plowman and Scriptural Tradition*, which Spearing argues "would
arbitrarily make the 'higher' meaning of images totally present at
any point," with his own theory of these images' sharing a "sense
of the pregnancy of Biblical images," so that the later development
of an image is implicit but unfulfilled in the early imagery of the
poem.[13] All of these critics are responding to the sense of wholeness and conceptual completion that Langland's allegorical imagery
evokes from the very beginning of *Piers*; yet they also share the assumption that the meaning of the images must gradually unfold over
the course of the poem. This is fairly close to what happens, but it
is not exact. Langland's imagery offers a series of varying reflections
of a perfect, whole Truth that is never revealed in the course of the
poem; rather than gradually building on an initially simple allegorical image, the poet seems to regard each complex image as somehow
preexisting the world of the poem in its complete and unchangeable
form, as the Forms preexist in the mind of God. In the Prologue he
may refer to an image that is not explained until much later, but
the meaning of which must be understood before the Prologue itself
can be fully explained. Later, although he may present the image in
a number of more complete formulations, they will not develop out
of one another in any logical way, nor will the poet relate them to

one another directly. The various likenesses exist in isolation in the "history" of the poem, each reexpressing the poetic exemplar in its own way, and each re-creating in microcosm the closed system of meaning and causation that shapes the cosmos.

A look at Langland's tree imagery, one instance of which we have already seen in the tree of Wrath, will help to demonstrate the non-development of his imagery. Wrath's use of tree imagery to describe his method of infecting people and spreading from one to another presupposes a cosmic order already bound together; and the original bond, which wrath corrupts, is love, "þe pl[ante] of pees." It is love that unites heaven and earth, the spiritual and material worlds, and it is love that spreads throughout the earth to bind all people in kinship:

"For truþe telleþ þat loue is triacle of heuene:
May no synne be on hym seene þat vseþ þat spice,
And alle hise werkes he wrouȝte with loue as hym liste;
And lered it Moyses for þe leueste þyng and moost lik to
    heuene,
And [ek] þe pl[ante] of pees, moost precious of vertues.
For heuene myȝte nat holden it, [so heuy it semed],
Til it hadde of þe erþe [y]eten [hitselue].
And whan it hadde of þis fold flessh and blood taken
Was neuere leef vpon lynde lighter þerafter,
And portatif and persaunt as þe point of a nedle
That myȝte noon Armure it lette ne none heiȝe walles.
Forþi is loue ledere of þe lordes folk of heuene
And a meene, as þe Mair is, bitwene þe [commune] & þe
    [kyng]."

(1.148–60)

Dame Holy Church's definition of love describes the whole cosmic order, not only figurally—the burning bush of Moses and the cross of Christ are two figures for the single "tree" of Christ's unifying love —but also allegorically—as a tree spreads out in a unity of branches, so Christ's love spreads throughout the cosmos uniting heaven and earth, and so Christian love binds the hierarchies in the microcosm of society. That neither armor nor walls can stop it demonstrates the

absolute necessity of human connection through love; and because
the connection is inescapable, any one sin that distorts or corrupts
love is necessarily communicated throughout the branches of society. This is what happens in Wrath's "ymping" of sins on friars, who
then pass the sin to the laity and priests; and "ymping" is used later
by Wit to express the way in which the sins of the fathers are visited
upon the sons in a figural repetition of original sin:

> "Ac I fynde, if þe fader be fals and a sherewe,
> That somdel þe sone shal haue þe sires tacches.
> Impe on an Ellere, and if þyn appul be swete
> Muchel merueille me þynkeþ; and moore of a sherewe
> That bryngeþ forþ any barn but if he be þe same
> And haue a Sauour after þe sire; selde sestow ooþer:
> *Numquam collig[unt] de spinis uva[s] nec de tribulis ficus.*
> And þus þoruȝ cursed Caym cam care vpon erþe."
>
> (IX.150–57)

But there is no stated connection between any of the various tree
images in the poem, nor do the later images develop out of the earlier
in any clear or direct way; we must assemble them ourselves to approach a fuller view of the whole cosmic image Langland has in
mind, an image that each of these lesser images illuminates only
in part, even as each expresses in a different way the same divine
pattern of connection by allegorical causation.

Given Dame Holy Church's use of the tree as an image for divine
love, one might easily deduce that the church itself must preserve
such an image on earth; and it does, as Anima's later description of
the church shows:

> "I shal tellen it for truþes sake; take hede whoso likeþ.
> As holynesse and honeste out of holy chirche [spryngeþ]
> Thoruȝ lele libbynge men þat goddes lawe techen,
> Right so out of holi chirche all yueles [spredeþ]
> There inparfit preesthode is, prechours and techeris.
> [And] se it by ensaumple in somer tyme on trowes:
> Ther some bowes ben leued and some bereþ none
> There is a meschief in þe more of swiche manere [stokkes].
> Right so persons and preestes and prechours of holi chirche

[Is þe] roote of þe right feiþ to rule þe peple;
A[c] þer þe roote is roten, reson woot þe soþe,
Shal neuere flour ne fruyt [wexe] ne fair leef be grene."

(xv.91–102)

This tree is clearly allegorical, there being no literal or historical
connection between the church and trees, as there is between Adam
and the tree of knowledge, Christ and the cross, or friars and gardening; nor does it develop organically from the earlier tree imagery. It
is borrowed wholesale from pseudo-Chrysostom, as Anima admits
(XV.117). Yet it takes on figural resonance if the reader links it to the
other tree images, for then the church is not just similar to a tree
but a real reflection, an image of Christ's love, the divine exemplar
of which is best reflected on earth by the cross. And this is Anima's
point: that the church retains the image of God by nature but distorts it when it ordains bad priests, who in turn spread their sin until
the entire tree of Christianity is diseased.

Just as the microcosm of the church is presented as a true but diseased likeness of divine love, so the lesser microcosm of the soul is
presented as a garden in which grows the tree of charity, a tree that,
though it by nature resembles the tree of Christ, is also the source
of all sin[14]—hence Will's wish to taste the fruit of the tree of charity
in Passus XVI, by which he reproduces the sin of Adam and causes
the fall of all human beings, who then become the falling fruit as the
tree regains its symbolism of the contagion and transmission of sin
from generation to generation. Importantly, Langland's image of the
tree of charity employs both figuralism—linking the tree of knowledge with the tree of salvation—and allegory—likening the human
heart to a tree that, being the image of Christ, makes people capable
of saving or damning themselves. The usual effect of figuralism is to
deemphasize chronological history even as it reaffirms the historical
reality of Christian symbolism; and this is its effect in Langland's
poem, where the tree images are linked not by temporal development or even by direct reference to one another but by their mutual
reference to a complete system of meaning outside the text. When
Anima describes the tree of charity as having "leues" of "lele wordes,
þe lawe of holy chirche" and "blosmes" of "buxome speche" (XVI.6–
7), nothing in the text save the resemblance itself links this tree to

Wrath's tree, which was formed when he "ymped" lies on friars "Til þei beere leues of lowe speche" and "blosmede abrood in boure to here shriftes" (V.140–41). Many critics have noticed the similarity without the poet's calling it to their attention, but it is doubtful that they did so on the first reading; the earlier image presupposes our understanding of the later, and all the tree images taken together still do not add up to the divine poetic exemplar upon which each is patterned. Perhaps the best way to describe the nondevelopmental relationship between Langland's allegorical images is by analogy to Jesus' parable sequence. Each parable reuses one of a very few basic images to describe the kingdom of heaven, in such a way that, though the parables are related, they do not actually develop from a lesser to a greater expression of the whole Truth. Instead, each re-tells that Truth in a subtly different way that has its own integrity and wholeness as an image.

A second important point to be drawn from Langland's union of allegory and figuralism, and of imitative and contiguous causation in each allegorical image, concerns the way in which nonsimilitude between tenor and vehicle should be read. Langland presents a social order in which people not only are individual physical signifiers for God but also exist in material and spiritual connection to one another through their mutual likeness to and causation by God. It is impossible, in Langland's view, to disconnect people from one another, as it is impossible utterly to destroy the image of God in the human soul. But it is possible, through sin, to distort God's likeness, in both human and Christian society; For sin, the failure to perceive and act according to the real connection between oneself and others through God both distorts the image of God in the sinner and necessarily spreads this distortion to others by virtue of their connectedness. We recall Wrath's social tree, which continued to grow when the unnatural vice was "grafted," but which in growing naturally spread the disease, ultimately reinforcing the power of wrath. This closed system of diseased connectedness is expressed in a different way in allegorical imagery that emphasizes nonsimilitude, where the earthly vehicle's unlikeness to its divine tenor is a measure, not of the failure of allegory to depict reality, but of people's sinning failure to see reality as allegorical and of society's resulting failure to remain a good signifier of love and unity. The unified social order shown to be founded by Grace in Passus XX is also depicted at work in the Prologue; but here, people's very connectedness has caused the widespread sin that distorts the likeness to God in the face of human society, making it more unlike than like its divine pattern. The Prologue describes a vast network of sin, a unity of corruption; and in his social imagery throughout the poem Langland frequently employs nonsimilitude to express, not a vision of growing disconnection between people in a failing Christian social order, but a vision of an inescapable diseased connectedness that by its nature still reflects, and must always reflect, the hand of its Creator.

The Prologue introduces Langland's three favorite images for describing the state of diseased connectedness in contemporary Christian society: the court, money, and especially food and feasting. It is easy to see why Langland should have chosen these things, since they offer visible proof that such connection exists in everyday life; they are tangible evidence of people's genuine kinship, of their political, economical, and physical dependence upon one another. In the Prologue these images combine to create a detailed picture of the closed system of Christian society, which is recognizably patterned upon divine exemplars of love and unity but corrupted as a vehicle into great nonsimilitude to its tenor. And throughout the poem, Langland reuses these central social images in various combinations to represent the diseased social microcosm.

Langland's description of the field full of folk in the Prologue establishes what initially appears to be a merely verbal connection created through a play on words:

> Somme putten hem to plou3, pleiden ful selde,
> In settynge and sowynge swonken ful harde;
> Wonnen þat [þise] wastours with glotonye destruyeþ.
> And somme putten hem to pride, apparailed hem þerafter,
> In contenaunce of cloþynge comen d[is]gised.
> In preieres and penaunc[e] putten hem manye,
> Al for loue of oure lord lyueden [wel] streyte
> In hope [for] to haue heuenriche blisse.
> As Ancres and heremites þat holden hem in hire selles,
> Coueiten no3t in contree to [cairen] aboute.
>
> (Pr. 20–29)

The poet begins by opposing honest plowmen who work to feed others to gluttons and wasters who consume others' food without laboring. He develops the opposition by connecting this pair of physical opposites with a pair of spiritual opposites: proud wanderers and humble hermits who keep to their cells. The zeugmatic repetition of "putten hem" links the pairs, especially in the ironic connection between the honest physical laborers and the proud folk who "putten hem" to no labor at all, but to spiritual dishonesty. Through this unexpected chiastic linking of opposites from sequential pairs, we are implicitly invited to see the similitude between physical gluttons and spiritually false, proud people: each abuses one of God's vital material gifts of food, drink, and clothing (see Dame Holy Church's speech, I.7–26). More explicitly we are invited to connect the plowmen with the honest hermits, who "putten hem" to physical and spiritual labors and who "pleiden ful selde" and "lyueden [wel] streyte." The poet begins, then, by establishing the analogical nature of virtues and vices: all virtuous actions express themselves in similitude to one another, and all vicious actions, by expressing nonsimilitude to divine exemplars of love and charity, are also similitudes for one another.

As the opening association between laboring plowmen and praying hermits suggests, Langland connects the proper use and distribution of food with that of God's Word throughout *Piers*: words—and especially the Word—are a divine gift to be used to nourish people spiritually. The sins of gluttony and word abuse are frequently connected in the poem as well: verbal gluttons use words for their own pleasure or gain and deliberately misrepresent the Word, starving others of spiritual life. Although each act of word abuse distorts the word from its true referent and distorts the image of God in the soul of the speaker, the act naturally binds itself in meaningful correspondence to other sins and binds the sinner to other sinners, even causing others to sin. Throughout the Prologue, word abuse is shown to bind in similitude the most disparate of sins: beggars "risen [vp] wiþ ribaudie" (Pr. 44); pilgrims' "tonge was tempred to lye" (51); friars "[g]losed þe gospel as hem good liked" (60); the pardoner "preched . . . as he a preest were," promising to absolve sinners "of Auowes ybroken" (68, 71); priests "syngen for symonie" instead of preaching the Word (86); and bishops who should "[p]rechen and praye for hem, and þe pouere fede," instead "seruen þe kyng and his siluer tellen" (90, 92)—the pun on "tellen" is certainly intentional. But these sins, which are similar as abuses of divine gifts, also cause one another. The "[b]idders and beggeres" (Pr. 40) use their words to obtain more food than they need, and their physical gluttony in turn leads to the verbal and spiritual gluttony of ribaldry:

> In glotonye, god woot, go þei to bedde,
> And risen [vp] wiþ ribaudie [as] Roberdes knaues.
>
> (Pr. 43–44)

Pilgrims who lie about the virtue of their travels commit two sins that are more than mere metaphors for one another:

> Pilgrymes and Palmeres pliȝten hem togidere
> For to seken Seint Iame and Seintes at Rome;
> Wenten forþ in hire wey wiþ many wise tales,
> And hadden leue to lyen al hire life after.
> I seiȝ somme þat seiden þei hadde ysouȝt Seintes;
> To ech a tale þat þei tolde hire tonge was tempred to lye
> Moore þan to seye sooþ, it semed bi hire speche.
>
> (Pr. 46–52)

Both the pilgrimages and the lies distort the image of what they were created to signify. But it is because the pilgrimages are false that the pilgrims must lie; indeed, the pilgrims feel that the mere appearance of virtuous pilgrimage gives them "leue to lyen al hire lif after," as though the ritual frees them of any further duties to God. Given the causal connections within Langland's allegories, the whole significance of the abuse of words becomes clear. Words are the primary means of communication among people, given by God to promote social unity. True words of faith save both the speaker and the listener, indicating the binding, reciprocal, and proliferating nature of virtue. But in Langland's vision of universal connectedness, the abuse of words is also of a reciprocal and proliferating nature: abusers of words not only destroy themselves but also rob others of faith as gluttons rob the hungry of food. And as all sins equally distort the Word of God, so no sin is isolated: to sin is also to encourage sin in others, which invariably returns to support the original sinner in further crime. The friar who misinterprets the gospel acts as confessor to the wealthy merchant, who pays the friar rather than truly repenting, thereby contributing to the friar's habits of greed, gluttony, and word abuse (Pr. 58–67). The pardoner can dupe ignorant people because priests who should have taught the laity better are in London singing for souls (Pr. 68–82). Those who pay the pardoner not only fail to gain true absolution for their sins but also "gyuen [youre] gold glotons to [helpe]" (Pr. 76); the pardoners, of course, are gluttonous in two senses, for they starve the people spiritually in order to fill their own bellies. The bishop, who should keep pardoners from preying upon the ignorant, knows nothing about it because he is busy counting the king's silver. Money is repeatedly emphasized in this causal series: instead of using the Word to promote love, people abuse it to gain money, or to "buy" God's grace. Society is still bound in inescapable interconnection, but now it is bound by lies and money rather than by the true Word of love.

In the second half of the Prologue, Langland narrows his focus to comment on two analogically ordered systems within the social system: the papal court and the king's court. The poet's thoughts appear to shift associatively from the bishop who works in the king's court, to the Court of Christ that will finally judge him, to the papal court where cardinals judge unjustly; but in fact the connection goes beyond verbal association:

> Bisshopes and Bachelers, boþe maistres and doctours,
> That han cure vnder crist, and crownynge in tokene
> And signe þat þei sholden shryuen hire parisshens,
> Prechen and praye for hem, and þe pouere fede,
> Liggen at Londoun in Lenten and ellis.
> Somme seruen þe kyng and his siluer tellen,
> In Cheker and in Chauncelrie chalangen his dettes
> Of wardes and of wardemotes, weyues and streyues.
> And somme seruen as seruauntȝ lordes and ladies,
> And in stede of Stywardes sitten and demen.
> Hire messe & hire matyns and many of hire houres
> Arn doon vndeuoutliche; drede is at þe laste
> Lest crist in Consistorie acorse ful manye.
>
> (Pr. 87–99)

These bishops bear the crown and seal of the Court of God but have deliberately chosen a lesser master in the courts of earthly kings; instead of tending to their parishioners' spiritual debts to Christ (described as debts throughout the poem in the repeated phrase *redde quod debes*), they have chosen to collect and discharge the king's monetary debts. Bishops who "sitten and demen" in the king's court of law will themselves be judged by the higher Court of Christ to which they owe their allegiance. The analogy between Christ's and the king's court is part of the real similitude of the cosmos, but here Langland focuses on the similitude to point out the nonsimilitude: the ironic contrast between the bishops' real duties and their chosen positions makes the "signe" of their service to Christ point instead to their failure to imitate him, rendering them distorted signifiers of the Word and earning them just punishment in Christ's Court.

After mentioning the Court of Christ, Langland shifts into a discussion of the papal court, which, even more than the king's, is organized upon the model of the divine system of government and justice:

> I parceyued of þe power þat Peter hadde to kepe,
> To bynden and vnbynden as þe book telleþ,
> How he it lefte wiþ loue as oure lord hiȝte
> Amonges foure vertues, [most vertuous of alle],
> That Cardinals ben called and closynge yates
> There [crist is in] kyngdom, to close and to shette,
> And to opene it to hem and heuene blisse shewe.
> Ac of þe Cardinals at court þat kauȝte of þat name,
> And power presumed in hem a pope to make
> To han [þe] power þat Peter hadde—impugnen I nelle—
> For in loue and lettrure þe eleccion bilongeþ;
> Forþi I kan & kan nauȝt of court speke moore.
>
> (Pr. 100–111)

Christ created the papal court as an earthly imitation of his own court, with similar powers of saving and damning. But the pun by which cardinal virtues become cardinals also describes the way in which cardinals have arrogated to themselves the power of salvation that is actually attainable only through virtue. In the additional pun on *cardo* as "hinge," Langland shows that human salvation truly hinges upon observance of the cardinal virtues, which may close or open the gates of heaven; but salvation should not hinge on the approval of cardinals unless the latter truly signify the virtues for which they are named. The "eleccion" Langland means in this passage is not only the cardinals' assumed power to elect popes but the whole corrupt papal court's assumed power to choose Christ's elect. Both elections must be based "in loue and lettrure": if the cardinals are not virtuous and learned in the Word, they cannot elect the right pope, and if the pope grants pardons to those who are neither loving nor wise, the sin spreads from the papal court to society at large. Like the secularized bishops, the unvirtuous cardinals distort the true likeness to ideal virtue given them by Christ; they possess the name of virtue only, and Langland's description of the papal court stresses its nonsimilitude to the Court of Christ over its similitude.

Langland promises to speak no more of courts, but in fact he begins a new discussion of the court of state and its government of nobility and commons. Interestingly, although he insists that the king should rule his subjects in imitation of Christ, benevolently tempering justice with mercy, Langland does not see kingship as a divinely ordained office, but only as a part of the divinely ordained social contract:

> Thanne kam þer a kyng; knyȝthod hym ladde;
> Might of þe communes made hym to regne.
>
> (Pr. 112–13)

All are equal in God's eyes; a king must do well as all people must, by performing his duties in imitation of Christ. He owes this debt to his commons as they owe him food and labor, and as the knights owe both of them protection. But if the king does not do well, neither can his subjects, for they in turn will act out of self-interest rather than love. And this, Langland argues, is just what has happened. Into the scene of hierarchical order the poet introduces "an Aungel of heuene" (Pr. 128) to speak for the commons in warning the king:

> . . . for lewed men ne koude
> Iangle ne Iugge þat Iustifie hem sholde,
> But suffren and seruen; forþi seide þe Aungel,

"Sum Rex, sum princeps, neutrum fortasse deinceps.
O qui iura regis christi specialia regis,
Hoc quod agas melius es, esto pius!"

(Pr. 129–34)

The angel threatens the king with merciless judgment if he is a merciless judge, reminding him that only Christ is the true king and
judge. Earthly courts should imitate the divine court and are ordained in similitude for this purpose; the king's duty is to administer
Christ's laws of love, thereby doing well (*agas melius*). The angel
speaks to protect the commoners, who are too ignorant to speak in
their own defense; but in the next lines, through their misinterpretation of the Latin, the commons actually encourage the king to abuse
the Word of Christ's law of love, compounding the nonsimilitude
between letter and spirit:

Thanne greued hym a Goliardeis, a gloton of wordes,
And to þe Aungel an heiȝ answerde after:
"Dum rex a regere dicatur nomen habere
Nomen habet sine re nisi studet iura tenere."
Thanne [comsed] al þe commune crye in vers of latyn
To þe kynges counseil, construe whoso wolde,
"Precepta Regis sunt nobis vincula legis."

(Pr. 139–45)

Langland labels his bad minstrel "a gloton of wordes" as though the
metaphor linking gluttony and minstrelsy, which has not yet actually appeared in the poem, were already perfectly understood. The
man is a bad minstrel because his analysis of *"rex"* equivocates: it
could mean that a king is only a king as long as he administers the
laws properly, but it could also mean that since *rex* is from *regere*,
meaning "to rule," the king's primary duty is to enforce (mere) laws.
The latter is clearly the interpretation the commons choose, for they
equate the king's will with law. From the angel's injunction upon the
king to imitate Christ, the Latin has degenerated into a statement
that the king may do as he pleases. The minstrel's equivocation has
tainted the entire social hierarchy, and his abuse of the Word has as
tangible and pervasive a social impact as the hoarding of food. More
will be said of this analogy later.

The ensuing parable of the court of rats and mice—a belittling microcosm of the king's court that also literally lives in the king's court—depicts the mutual abuse to which king and commons have fallen. Social hierarchies, like the cosmic hierarchies, should be held together by love; instead, the nobility prey on the commons as a cat preys on mice. But as the wise mouse explains, without the cat the rats and mice would overrun and destroy the court: "For hadde ye rattes youre [raik] ye kouþe noȝt rule yowselue" (Pr. 201). Neither king nor commons are innocent; instead, as shown throughout the Prologue, each person in the society participates in all the others' sins.

The Prologue builds its cosmic system of similitude, nonsimilitude, and causation according to the blueprint of God's own creation; but this blueprint is assumed to be preunderstood. If we as modern readers do not understand that this is a Christian society founded on and by the grace of Christ, we are not likely to understand, for example, the genuine causal correspondence between the courts Langland describes. Not until Passus I, in Holy Church's tree image, does the poet provide any direct information about the way in which Christ's love binds the court of heaven and the courts of human society, and then we are likely to make no connection between this information and the Prologue's structure, and even to pass over Holy Church's tree imagery as mere poetry, mere allegory, unless we have already entered imaginatively into Langland's belief that allegory truly reflects reality. As with the imagery of trees first employed by Holy Church, the images of money, food, and court introduced in the Prologue do not develop in the course of the poem, but are reused in numerous combinations that imitate to varying degrees the same cosmic archetype of allegorical causation.

Our preunderstanding that money is a poor imitation of the divine bond of love is assumed throughout the Prologue in figures such as the bishops who opt to "tellen" silver rather than the Word and to "seruen þe kyng" of England rather than the King of heaven. The idea is more clearly articulated in Passus I, where Holy Church repeats Jesus' words to the Pharisees concerning taxes (I.46–53). Jesus' answer of "*Reddite Cesari*" already plays on both the similitude and the nonsimilitude between earthly and spiritual treasures, and the Lady Meed episode shows that the unlikeness between Truth and treasure predominates in contemporary society to the point of near-complete nonsimilitude: money and love, though they function similarly as personal treasures that bind people to one another, are actually near opposites. It is because the divine bond of love has been corrupted that money has come to dominate in human relationships, and it is because one person works only for money that another learns to do so, creating the network of mercenary lovelessness we see in the Prologue. Although money can still signify love, the money system is generally a very poor imitation of the system of grace; people must endeavor to distinguish signifier from signified and to make the signifier of money reflect what it signifies as much as possible by rewarding the just and not the wicked—hence the king's final realization that there are two Meeds, and that he must exercise Conscience and Reason to use his wealth properly in making his court a better imitation of the Court of Christ and its system of reward and punishment.

Money's continuing currency as a similitude for love is apparent in the poet's retelling of the parable of the minas in Passus VI, and in Piers's honest statement that he has his "hire" of Truth (V.550). But the similitude between grace and money receives a new twist in Anima's "ensample" of the "lussheburwes," which appears in the middle of his discourse on charity. Here money signifies not grace but the clergy whose duty it is to spread it:

"Forþi I counseille alle cristene to conformen hem to charite,
For charite wiþouten chalangynge vnchargeþ þe soule,
And many a prison fram purgatorie þoruȝ hise preieres
    deliuereþ.
Ac þer is a defaute in þe folk þat þe feiþ kepeþ,
Wherfore folk is þe febler and noȝt ferm of bileue.
As in lussheburwes is a luþer alay, and yet lokeþ he lik a
    sterlyng;
The merk of þat monee is good ac þe metal is feble;
And so it fareþ by som folk now; þei han a fair speche,
Crowne and cristendom, þe kynges mark of heuene,
Ac þe metal, þat is mannes soule, [myd] synne is foule alayed.

Both lettred and lewed beþ alayed now wiþ synne
That no lif loueþ ooþer, ne oure lord as it semeþ."

(xv.344–55)

Members of the clergy are good or bad coinage—bearers of a greater
or lesser likeness to God—specifically insofar as they give chari-
tably to the poor. But in addition to the money image, this allegory
shares with the others a literal message that is causally connected
to its spiritual significance: priests bear the form of grace without
the "metal," the content, when they preach lessons on charity but
fail to embody the "treasure" of Truth by giving materially to the
poor. Because clerics fail to embody true love for humanity in earthly
treasure, the laity perceives that they are false coinage, that they do
not really bind society together in love; and in this realization the
laity's treasure of faith is destroyed: "folk is þe febler and noȝt ferm
of bileue." In this way people are robbed of both physical and spiritual treasure by the failure of priests, and the failure of the clergy
causes the failure of the laity: "both lettred and lewed beþ alayed now
wiþ synne." The two social orders naturally resemble one another,
bound as they are in sin and mutual unlikeness to their divine pattern; thus the whole Christian society becomes false coinage. Just
as, in the parable sequence of Matthew 13, seed signifies first the
Word, then people, and finally the kingdom of heaven, so here Langland shifts the meaning of a fertile image so that his allegories exist
as a network of independent but related statements.

By far the most common image of social connectedness in the
poem is that of food, its production and its consumption.[15] In this
image Langland rings his own changes on Jesus' sowing parables,
both reiterating their original allegorical meanings and insisting also
upon their figural significance. The parable likening the man of God
to a sower and the Word to seed is the source of Langland's frequent
analogies between abuse of the Word and gluttony. The Word and
wheat are the life-giving staples of Christian society, uniting people
as they sustain the union of body and soul; hence Wit's description
of speech as the "spire of grace" (IX.103), a sprout of grain that feeds
human souls. This connection is assumed from the beginning of the
poem, not only in the unexplained description of the goliard as "a
gloton of wordes" (Pr. 139), but in less direct references to friars who

preach "for profit of [þe wombe]" (Pr. 59), to laymen who confess "[o]f falshed of fastynge [and] of Auowes ybroken" (Pr. 71), and to pardoners who falsely assume the powers of priests and are subsequently dubbed "glotons" (Pr. 76). In the confession of the Seven Deadly Sins, Glutton is also a waster of words, especially of the Word:

> "I, Gloton", quod þe [gome], "gilty me yelde
> That I haue trespased with my tonge, I kan noȝt telle how ofte;
> Sworen goddes soule [and his syde] and 'so me god helpe'
> There no nede was nyne hundred tymes;
> And ouerseyen me at my soper and som tyme at Nones
> That I, Gloton, girte it vp er I hadde gon a myle,
> And yspilt þat myȝt be spared and spended on som hungry. . . ."
>   (v.367–73)

Gluttony and word abuse are physically similar since they both involve a misuse of the mouth; but in Langland's view the two are also both analogically and causally related. Because they are similar, the poet often uses one as a metaphor for the other, but when Glutton goes to the tavern instead of to church, he seems naturally to indulge in both sins, and each seems to lead him back to the other: he enters the tavern with "grete oþes" (V.306), and he and his friends "seten so til euensong and songen vmwhile / Til Gloton hadde yglubbed a galon and a gille" (V.338–39). As Glutton later confesses:

> "For loue of tales in Tavernes [to] drynke þe moore I [hyed;
> Fedde me bifore] noon whan fastyng dayes were."
>   (v.376–77)

When the wasters refuse to help Piers in the half-acre scene, they "songen atte Nale / And holpen ere [þ]e half acre wiþ 'how trolly lolly'" (VI.115–16). Langland associates tavern life quite literally with both kinds of oral sin; but the two are also connected allegorically: where there is physical abuse, there must also be spiritual abuse, since one represents the other—gluttony represents a failure to receive the Word.

References to goliards, jongleurs, singers, and bawdy song add another element to the analogy between abuse of the Word and gluttony. Bad minstrelsy becomes an additional or alternative vehicle

expressing the abuse of the Word; like gluttony it is a material signifier of society's failure to receive and spread the Word of God. While
it is literally true that bawdy minstrels abuse their power of speech
and lead people away from holiness, the minstrel has an allegorical significance as well: minstrelsy becomes a vehicle to express the
duty all Christians have to spread the Word. The parish priests who
"syngen for symonie" in the Prologue (86) do so quite literally, and
Dame Study, in her lengthy description of the courts of faithless lords
(X.27–118), describes real clerks as performing the function of bawdy
minstrels at rich men's feasts (X.52–53). But Dame Study also opposes
"Iangleris of gestes" to those who "prechen" (X.31, 34); argues that
those who "[s]pitten and spuen" or "[d]rynken and dreuelen" actually
"konne na moore mynstralcie ne Musik men to glade / Than Munde
þe Millere of *Multa fecit deus*" (X.41, 42, 44–45); and insists that

> ". . . [mynstralcie and murþe] amonges men is nouþe
> Lecherie, losengerye and losels tales;
> Glotonye and grete oþes, þis[e arn games nowadaies]."
>
> (x.49–51)

And Patience refers to priests and the poor specifically as "goddes
minstrales" (XIII.439). Moreover, Haukyn/*Activa Vita*, described as
a waferer whose duty is to provide physical nourishment, introduces
himself as "a Mynstrall" (XIII.224)—as indeed he is, since all honest
labor spreads the Word by example. Clearly minstrelsy and music
making have a figurative as well as a literal significance in the poem:
to Langland everyone is a minstrel, whether lord, priest, laborer, or
beggar, and all speech is "goddes gleman" (IX.104), whether good or
bad. Although some people are "vntempred," all are God's "fiþeles,"
a word whose proximity to "feiþful fader" in IX.105 suggests a pun
on Latin *fidele:* the well-tuned "fiddle" is faithful, and gives a faithful rendering of God's Word in daily speech and labor. Conversely,
Patience describes real "kynges minstrales" as well as "flaters and
fooles" at court as "luciferis fiþele," destined to partake, not of the
feast of Christ, but of "Luciferis feste" (XIII.436, 456, 455). Langland's reference to both literal and figurative minstrelsy adds an
extra dimension to the play between similitude and nonsimilitude
in his allegory. On the literal level, he complains that the wealthy
feed bawdy minstrels rather than honest laborers, whose figurative

designation as "minstrels" emphasizes the distinction between the hardworking poor and the idle court followers and calls attention to the injustice of their relative treatment by the nobility. Allegorically, however, the lowly in society truly are "goddes minstrales," faithfully imitating Christ the Word in their lives of humble poverty.

Langland's numerous images of court feasts, like his representations of earthly courts in the Prologue, should be understood as weak signifiers of the Court of Christ, where all people are called to feast, sing God's praise, and receive their eternal reward. In her criticism of lords who feed minstrels and starve the poor, Dame Study emphasizes that these lords derive all their wealth from a higher Lord and yet fail to distribute it as their Lord would wish (X.27–29, 63–64). Through subsequent allusions to biblical feasts signifying the banquet hall in the Court of Christ, such as Scripture's "*Multi* to a mangerie and to þe mete were sompned" (XI.112) and Troianus's description of how "Crist to a commune womman seide, in [comen] at a feste, / That *Fides sua* sholde sauen hire" (XI.217–18), the reader is prepared for Will's own summoning to a feast:

> And as crist wolde þer com Conscience to conforte me þat
> tyme
> And bad me come to his court, wiþ clergie sholde I dyne.
> (XIII.22–23)

The scene that follows provides the most interesting blend of court and food images in the poem, while it demonstrates the richness of significance achieved through the interplay of similitude and nonsimilitude in Langland's allegorical imagery. The "meats" served at the feast of Conscience are passages from Scripture and the church fathers; but a certain "maister" of divinity, the honored guest at the feast, insists on different fare for himself and his servants:

> Conscience called after mete and þanne cam Scripture
> And seruen hem þus soone of sondry metes manye,
> Of Austyn, of Ambrose, of [alle] þe foure Euangelistes:
> *Edentes & bibentes que apud eos sunt.*
> Ac þis maister [of þise men] no maner flessh [eat],
> Ac [he eet] mete of moore cost, mortrews and potages.
> Of þat men myswonne þei made hem wel at ese,

Ac hir sauce was ouer sour and vnsauourly grounde
In a morte, *Post mortem*, of many bitter peyne.
(XIII.37–44)

Patience, who is seated beside Will, is delighted to receive "a sour
loof" of "*Agite penitenciam*" and a plain drink of "*Di[u] perseuerans*"
(XIII.49, 50), but Will notices with impatience the unlikeness between his spiritual repast and the doctor's more substantial fare:

. . . ac I mornede euere
For þis doctour on þe heiȝe dees drank wyn so faste:
Ve vobis qui potentes estis ad bibendum vinum.
He eet manye sondry metes, mortrews and puddynges,
Wombe cloutes and wilde brawen and egges yfryed wiþ grece.
(XIII.60–63)

Langland begins by contrasting the simple "meats" of Scripture with
the fancier but deadly "sauces" of certain divines who derive physical
sustenance from the spiritual privation of others ("*Vos qui peccata
hominum comeditis . . .*" [XIII.45a]). But soon the allegory shifts to
a direct contrast between physical and spiritual nourishment: Will
and the others get words, whereas the doctor gets food. Yet Langland
is not saying, as Priscilla Martin suggests, that spiritual nourishment
is useless when people are starving; after all, the doctor's food begins
as an allegorical "sauce," as well, and the poet states unambiguously
that these sauces are poison. The cause of Will's impatience with
the doctor is not some sudden, modern perception of opposition between spiritual ideals and material "realities" as reflected in the nonsimilitude between food and the Word; what Will perceives is the
doctor's hypocrisy, which creates the nonsimilitude, distorting the
feast's proper significance as an expression of charity, of the Word of
God. Anyone who truly knows the Word will sustain others physically as well as spiritually; but the doctor is guilty of both kinds of
gluttony, starving his fellow Christians of both food and the Word by
misrepresenting Scripture in his deeds:

Thanne seide I to myself so pacience it herde,
"It is noȝt foure dayes þat þis freke, bifore þe deen of Poules,
Preched of penaunces þat Poul þe Apostle suffrede
In fame & frigore and flappes of scourges. . . ."

"Ac þis goddes gloton", quod I, "wiþ hise grete chekes
Haþ no pite on vs pouere; he parfourneþ yuele
That he precheþ [and] preueþ noȝt [com]pacience", I tolde.

(XIII.64–67, 78–80)

The doctor's hypocritical attitude is in no way "realistic" (Martin's word);[16] rather, he shows a complete failure to comprehend the real allegorical significance of his disruption of the feast: his presence, and Will's impatience, distort the scene's proper likeness to the Court of Christ just as his gluttony distorts the real connection between the Word and the charitable sharing of food among people. Nor, later, when Patience offers Haukyn spiritual food, is Haukyn's initial response of disbelief to be taken as a "realistic" attitude:

"And I shal purueie þee paast", quod Pacience, "þouȝ no plouȝ
    erye,
And flour to fede folk wiþ as best be for þe soule;
Thouȝ neuere greyn growed, ne grape vpon vyne,
All þat lyueþ and lokeþ liflode wolde I fynde
And þat ynogh; shal noon faille of þyng þat hem nedeþ:
Ne soliciti sitis &c; celi deus pascit &c; pacientes
    vincunt &c."
Thanne laughed haukyn a litel and lightly gan swerye;
"Whoso leueþ yow, by oure lord! I leue noȝt he be blessed."
"No?" quod Pacience paciently, and out of his poke hente
Vitailles of grete vertues for alle manere beestes
And seide, "lo! here liflode ynough, if oure bileue be trewe."

(XIV.29–38)

Haukyn, whose faith is weak, can perceive only the unlikeness between food and the Word; but Patience teaches him Christ's promise to tend to all the needs of his faithful, and Haukyn's recognition of his sin brings him to full confession. The doctor, who persists in seeing only nonsimilitude between physical and spiritual realities, persists in faithlessness, unable to receive the Word Patience has to offer. Significantly, when Patience claims to have Dowel in a box containing the Eucharist, the doctor calls this riddle "a dido" and "a disours tale" (XIII.172), suggesting that there is no real connection between physical and spiritual food and that Patience is a bad minstrel as well as a bad pilgrim—"for pilgrymes konne wel lye" (XIII.178). But of course the Eucharist is the greatest material symbol of the Christian union of flesh and spirit, and Patience is both a true minstrel of the Word and a true pilgrim for Christ.

As *Activa Vita*, Haukyn represents the working classes upon whom the gluttonous doctor has been feeding, and whose hard labor sustains the whole of Christian society:

"For alle trewe trauaillours and tiliers of þe erþe
Fro Mighelmesse to Mighelmesse I fynde hem wiþ wafres.
Beggeris and bidderis of my breed crauen,
Faitours and freres and folk wiþ brode crounes.
I fynde payn for þe pope and prouendre for his palfrey . . ."

(XIII.239–43)

Unfortunately, Haukyn's is not the kind of minstrelsy that is likely to be rewarded, and Haukyn complains of his treatment by the courts of church and state:

"Couþe I lye [and] do men lauȝe, þanne lacchen I sholde
Ouþer mantel or moneie amonges lordes Mynstrals.
Ac for I kan neiþer taboure ne trompe ne telle no gestes,
Farten ne fiþelen at festes ne harpen,
Iape ne Iogele ne gentilliche pipe,
Ne neiþer saille ne [sautrie] ne synge wiþ þe gyterne,
I haue no goode giftes of þise grete lordes
For no breed þat I brynge forþ, saue a benyson on þe sonday
Whan þe preest preieþ þe peple hir Paternoster to bidde
For Piers þe Plowman and þat hym profit waiten.
And þat am I, Actif, þat ydelnesse hatie."

(XIII.228–38)

The failure of both the nobility and the church to sustain the common people in any real physical or spiritual sense is accentuated by Haukyn's insistence upon his allegorical identification with Piers Plowman: the honest laborer, God's minstrel, is as much the image of Christ as is the pope. All the disparate and warring factions of human society unite in the figure of Piers, which expresses their kinship to one another through their equal kinship to Christ. Hence the bitter irony of the clergy's directions to pray for the very people they daily starve of food and the Word, the very people who both feed them and exemplify the Word in their dutiful service. Of course the common people are guilty, too; they, too, have failed to do their duty for love of their neighbors, as Haukyn explains after complaining that the pope gives only paper pardons and not true grace to the lowly:

"Ac if myȝt of myracle hym faille it is for men ben noȝt worþi
To haue þe grace of god, and no gilt of [þe] pope.
For may no blessynge doon vs boote but if we wile amende,
Ne mannes masse make pees among cristene peple
Til pride be pureliche fordo, and [þat] þoruȝ payn defaute.
For er I have breed of mele ofte moot I swete,
And er þe commune haue corn ynouȝ many a cold morwenyng;
So er my wafres be ywroȝt muche wo I þolye."

(XIII.255–62)

As Piers is both the common man and the pope in their equal kin-ship to Christ, so Haukyn, like Piers, must be his own pope, gain grace through his own loving performance of good labor; the homely analogy to food production here emphasizes the need to work hard for spiritual nourishment. As in the courts of the king and rats in the Prologue—and indeed, as in the imagery of the poem throughout —sin has spread everywhere and is equally evident in all orders of society, which continually re-create and sustain one another in sin, instead of in love.

In Passus XIX the death and resurrection of Christ is followed by his establishment of the Christian social hierarchy and the church, the highest and lowest members of which are united in the figure of Piers Plowman. A highly allegorized plowing scene develops out of this description of contemporary society's spiritual foundation, as Piers sows the seeds of the four cardinal virtues and builds the barn of Unity Holy Church in which to gather the harvest of Christian souls. The Sins attack, threatening, in a brief allusion to the earlier image of the church as a tree, to "[b]low hem doun and breke hem and bite atwo þe mores" (XIX.338). As in the tree of Wrath image, sin here is depicted both as an external agent and as a characteristic of individual personalities. When Piers begins to plow, "pride it aspide / And gadered hym a greet Oost" (XIX.335–36); Conscience gathers all his Christians into Holy Church and they are beseiged by the Sins.

Once inside, Conscience, who had earlier invited Will to his court to dine, invites all Christians to partake of the Eucharistic feast:

> "Comeþ", quod Conscience, "ye cristene, and dyneþ,
> That han laboured lelly al þis lenten tyme.
> Here is breed yblessed, and goddes body þervnder.
> Grace, þoruȝ goddes word, [g]af Piers power,
> [Myȝt] to maken it and men to ete it after
> In help of hir heele ones in a Monþe."
>
> (xix.383–88)

Conscience invites all to join in the spiritual feast of the Word of God in Holy Church, an earthly representation of Christ's Court. But when Conscience stipulates that this feast is available only to "þo þat hadde ypaide / To Piers pardon þe Plowman *redde quod debes*," the people's response indicates that sin has already permeated the walls of Unity. Those who eat the body of Christ without love in their hearts are gluttonously corrupting the Eucharist's true significance, distorting the bond of likeness between the wafer and divine love; and it is just such love for one another through God that the representatives of internal discord refuse to promise Conscience. Each of the four sinful individuals Langland depicts represents one of the major social strata of the Christian hierarchy: a "Brewere" tells Conscience he would rather cheat his customers to make more money than be ruled by justice; a "lewed vicory" complains that the lower clergy and commons are so abused by the pope and cardinals (again the pun on cardinals is evoked) that they cannot be expected to love and be honest themselves; a "lord" insists that when he sends his reeve to steal from the poor he is only taking his due; and the "kyng," describing himself as the "Iugge" of all men, the ruler of the commons and defender of Holy Church, insists that he has an automatic right to receive Holy Communion. All wish to eat at Christ's feast, but none are willing to pay the debt of love that Conscience tells them they owe to one another.

This scene is interesting because, in addition to combining Langland's favorite images for depicting the social order, it offers final evidence that his imagery has not actually developed in the course of the poem but has only been reused in subtly shifting ways to make the same points: that for good or ill, Christian society is bound in true kinship through God; that because of this connection people are responsible for both their own and one another's salvation; and that each person's sin hurts the Christian society as a whole. The later plowing scene has often been viewed as a higher development of the earlier, expressing more fully the meaning that was only literal, or merely implicit or "pregnant," in the half-acre scene. But the two simply focus on different aspects of the same cosmic vision. The half-acre scene identifies the Christian's duty to spread the Word of love as the basis for the social contract, and its connection with the pilgrimage and pardon scenes shows that in performing their social duties of charity people also gain salvation. The later scene reemploys the plowing image (as Jesus reemploys it when he moves from the parable of the sower to the parable of the wheat and chaff) to depict the foundation of the church and its promise of salvation; but again, this scene is connected with a scene describing the founding of social hierarchies and Grace's command that all Christians work in love and harmony. The two plowing scenes provide the same vision of Christian society, of the essential unity of social and spiritual duties, and of each individual's equal value, responsibility, and hope of salvation. The emphasis alone has changed.

Nor does the closing description of contemporary social corruption present a fuller expression of that corruption than the Prologue. Although this later scene places contemporary society more expressly within a Christian historical context by showing that Christ himself founded it, the same context was preunderstood in the Prologue, where the courts of church and state are patterned on the "Consistorie" of Christ, and where Christ is the source of "þe power þat Peter hadde to kepe" (Pr. 99, 100). The whole vision of the Christian order is as fully preunderstood in the Prologue as it is in Passus XIX, and the Prologue's description of the goliard as "a gloton of wordes" (Pr. 139) presupposes later imagery as much as the passing reference to the church as a tree with "mores" presupposes earlier imagery.

As for the allegorical explanation of sin in Passus XIX, as compared to that in the confession of the Seven Deadly Sins, the scope has both widened and, in another sense, narrowed in the later scene. It has widened to show the attack of sin on the whole society rather than on individuals in it, and it has narrowed, like the plowing and feasting images, to discuss sin with specific reference to the church. But essentially the two visions say the same things about sin: as in Wrath's grafting image, sin is presented both allegorically and naturalistically in Passus XIX; the same closed system of allegorical causation is shown binding the temporal and spiritual worlds. The Sins lay siege to Unity Holy Church in a display of vertical causation that will be matched in Passus XX by Kind's own arrival from "out of þe planetes" (80); but even as the siege of Sin continues, we see that just as Christ's love pierces all walls and armor in Dame Holy Church's tree image, so sin, too, permeates society and spreads among brewers, vicars, cardinals, lords, and kings. Each of the scenes in which Langland employs his social imagery creates the same completely functional closed system of likeness and unlikeness, and vertical and horizontal causation, in order that readers may perceive the true spiritual significance of all human interactions. If we do not preunderstand the medieval Christian view of the material world as the vehicle of a divinely written allegory, we are as unlikely to understand Passus XIX as the Prologue.

This brings us to the other point of interest in Passus XIX: the four representatives of Christian society who refuse to pay the debt of love they owe their fellows do so on the basis of their own willful misinterpretations of *Spiritus Iusticie, Spiritus Prudencie,* and *Spiritus Fortitudinis,* three of the four cardinal virtues that Piers has sown and that ought to raise a crop of believers. As the personified Sins threaten that the "carte" of Christian faith will be "coloured . . . queyntely and couered vnder [oure] Sophistrie" (XIX.347), so the representative sinners deliberately misread the cardinal virtues to suit their own purposes. The brewer's is actually more a misinterpretation of himself: instead of misreading *Spiritus Iusticie,* he reinterprets his own "kynde" (XIX.400) as deceitful and mercenary. But the king uses his faulty logic to redefine both *Spiritus Iusticie* and himself by identifying one with the other:

> ". . . if me lakkeþ to lyue by þe lawe wole I take it
> Ther I may hastilokest it haue, for I am heed of lawe;
> Ye ben but membres and I aboue alle.
> And siþ I am youre aller heed I am youre aller heele
> And holy chirches chief help and Chieftayn of þe comune,

And what I take of yow two, I take it at þe techynge
Of *Spiritus Iusticie* for I Iugge yow alle.
So I may boldely be housled for I borwe neuere,
Ne craue of my comune but as my kynde askeþ."
(xix.468–76)

This is the same wrongheaded identification of justice with the king's will as that which we saw in the goliard's redefinition of *"rex"* in the Prologue. The vicar explains that because cardinals fail to signify the cardinal virtues in their behavior to commoners, the latter have also reinterpreted these virtues:

"For *Spiritus prudencie* among þe peple is gyle,
And alle þo faire vertues as vices þei semeþ.
Ech man subtileþ a sleiȝte synne to hide
And coloureþ it for a konnynge and a clene lyuynge."
(xix.455–58)

The names of the cardinal virtues themselves have become mere "colors," rhetoric in which to cloak sin: prudence means not wisdom but cunning self-interest. In the same way, when the lord sends out his reeve to collect his payment from an underling, the physical force the reeve employs to take it "wole he, nel he" is labeled *"Spiritus fortitudinis"* (XIX.464). The corruption of the last remaining virtue is discussed in the beginning of Passus XX, where Need attacks Will, tempting him to steal—but only moderately—in the name of *"Spiritus temperancie"* (XX.8), and arguing that this interpretation of temperance is allowable because the other three virtues have been redefined as well. For Langland, sin is a matter of misinterpretation, of misreading the Word of God expressed both in Scripture and in the material signifiers of this world. Misinterpretation is specifically the failure to "read" reality allegorically; the failure to recognize oneself and one's neighbor as kindred images of God is the initial sin, causing all other sinful acts. The sinner may misread the likeness between tenor and vehicle as sameness, as does the king who reads himself as a synonym for justice rather than merely a similitude. Or the sinner may fail to see the likeness altogether, as does the brewer who thinks there is no true connection between *Spiritus Iusticie* and his own "kynde." But in the cosmos of *Piers*, the proper way to read both allegory and reality is as a complex system of similitude, nonsimilitude, and causation, in which nonsimilitude is always a measure of human sin and failure of perception, not of some "reality" exclusive of Christian doctrine. Modern critics who read the nonsimilitude in Langland's allegory as a sign of disbelief are correct in a sense: but it is their own disbelief they are reading, not Langland's. They are reading nonsimilitude the way the faithless characters in the poem read it, characters who in Langland's vision figure as poor similitudes for Christ because they misinterpret the allegorical reality of their situation.

Langland presents his many variations on the same sets of allegorical images to explain the nature of human society, as Jesus presents his series of parables describing the kingdom of heaven, not in order to exclude nonbelievers from his audience, but because he knows nonbelievers cannot understand until they believe. Anyone can learn to read; but to read the allegorical Truth, faith is required. As we shall see in the next chapter, Langland is concerned throughout *Piers* with the question of reading and misreading; after all, salvation depends on finding the right interpretation of Scripture, the self, and the world. But since understanding is not to be achieved through the temporal learning process alone, Langland "teaches" his reader about human society, as the allegorical teachers in the poem "teach" Will, and as Jesus "teaches" the disciples, through numerous embodiments of the same Truth in a few select images.

4
Creating the Text
Ambivalence, Holy Play, and Salvation

✦

We saw in chapter 2 that Langland conceives Dowel as an innate capacity for both faith in Christ and good works in imitation of him; this is what Wit means when he explains to Will that people may do well because God used both his Word and work to create them in his image. But the "ensample" Wit uses to teach Will this lesson has an additional significance for poets:

> "For he was synguler hymself and seide *faciamus*
> As who seiþ, 'moore moot herto þan my word oone;
> My myȝt moot helpe forþ wiþ my speche'.
> Right as a lord sholde make lettres; [if] hym lakked parchemyn,
> Thouȝ he [wiste to] write neuer so wel, [and] he hadde [a]
>   penne,
> The lettre, for al þe lordshipe, I leue, were neuere ymaked.
> And so it semeþ by him [þere he seide in þe bible
> *Faciamus hominem ad imaginem nostram*]
> He moste werche wiþ his word and his wit shewe."
>
> (IX.36–44)

Just as in *Paradiso* Dante describes the cosmos as a book bound together by the glue of love, so here Langland explains God's act of creation by analogy to human writing. But Wit is also explaining how people may do well: if Dowel is faith and works in imitation of Christ, then the learned Christian who fails to express this faith in the work of pen and parchment has not done well, has not imitated divine creation. Dowel for the poet is the imitation of God's creation in his own work with words, and this is as much a moral imperative for the poet as works of love are necessary for everyone's salvation: "He moste werche wiþ his word and his wit shewe." Of course, Langland is showing his own wit in this passage, by letting his Wit tell us about Dowel. But the entire poem is also a product of the poet's playful wit, a verbal imitation of divine creation in which time and space are imperfect imitations of eternal presence, humanity is created in the image of God, and the spiritual and material worlds are linked by similitude, nonsimilitude, and causation. *Piers* is Langland's effort to imitate God; the poem is the Life of Dowel that guarantees the poet's salvation.

The verbal playfulness with which Langland pursues salvation cannot be too much stressed and should be properly understood; to discover why the poet plays with words is to understand both his motivation and his poem. Bernard Huppé has suggested that wordplay in *Piers Plowman* "is the basic method of achieving structural coherence for the entire poem," since for Langland, "[t]o play with the etymology or the sound of a word until it revealed an image, a symbol, or a moral was to move on the high road to Truth." A. V. C. Schmidt, too, finds in this wordplay "a profound awareness on Langland's part of his gift of language as a spiritual responsibility."[1] But Schmidt also asserts that "[t]o proclaim the message properly, not only the messenger but the medium also must be purified," and he suggests that this need to purify language in *Piers* derives from the poet's anxiety concerning the inherent weakness and duplicity of words: "In his effort to prevent words from breaking under the burden and tension of trying to communicate difficult truths, in his struggle to make words stay in place and stay still, Langland discovers, draws the veil from, their deceits as well as their depths."[2] As we have seen, the human inability to know the Truth, and the inability of human words to express it, were commonplaces in medieval Christian thought, as was the assurance that faith in Christ the Word removes this barrier of inadequacy, making the impossible possible. All that is required for transmission of the Truth is a faithful speaker and a faithful listener; and indeed, as Chaucer's Pardoner attests, even a faithless speaker may adequately transmit God's Word of Truth to listeners of good faith. But if the Word falls upon deaf ears, no amount of verbal purity will help; the seed of the sower may be uniformly good, but it often falls among stones and thistles. The suggestion that Langland is concerned with purifying language—as though the difference between "lele wordes" and "bele paroles" were intrinsic and not contingent on their representation of the speaker's heart—reflects the trend in *Piers* criticism that seeks to place words, and not faith, at the center of the poem. The tendency is to depict Langland's wordplay as a crusade against verbal ambivalence when in fact it is just the opposite: it is the poet's deliberate, faithful attempt to reproduce divine Truth through the proliferation of its image in verbal paradox. Each word Langland takes up in poetic play becomes an imitation of the divinely ambivalent Word made Flesh, a microcosm of visible and invisible creation, and a means of measuring the true relationship between God and humankind.

To Mary Carruthers Langland's wordplay seems to stem from his anxiety concerning the inadequacy of all verbal signs to signify Truth and hence the human inability to know Truth. Langland's poetic world, she argues, is one in which "words no longer have a stable referent," so that "Will's problem of understanding is located in language itself, its inexactness, ambiguity, and obscurity."[3] There are a number of problems with this theory, not the least of which is the assumption that if Will fails to understand the words of Holy Church, the words, and not Will, are to blame. Carruthers lists Avarice's and Envy's misinterpretations of Repentance's words, "restitution" and "sorry," as comic examples of the problem of verbal ambivalence: "Repentance uses a Latinate pedantry on the one hand and an ambiguous, unintended pun on the other, neither of which successfully communicates the intended meaning to its audience." But who is at fault here, the teacher or the pupils? Augustine himself heads off such criticism by writing, "[T]o those who do not understand what we write, I say this: I am not to blame because they do not understand. . . . Although I can lift my finger to point something out, I cannot supply the vision by means of which either this gesture or what it indicates can be seen."[4] The Sins' blind and willful misinterpretations of Repentance's honest words signify their own distance from Truth—for true restitution is certainly not avaricious "riflynge" (V.235), nor is sorrowful envy a true sign of repentance.

Verbal ambivalence suggests to Carruthers a "corruption of language" that makes it inadequate as a medium for the discovery of Truth:

> The corruption of language demonstrated in these passus is indeed of greater significance than is the corruption of society which the language generates. . . . Langland seems to demonstrate that words in his language have lost their inherent and generally stable relationship to those things which should signify them—the spiritually upright heart and the divine Word, which is the faith upon which Christian rhetoric is based. Lady Holy Church, Reason, and Repentance can no longer speak meaningfully to the folk on the field. And as the relationship between sign and significator becomes unstable and ambiguous, the whole foundation of knowledge—God's revelation of himself in signs—is also jeopardized.

The slip by which the upright heart and divine Word become signifiers for human words in this passage suggests the backward thinking that characterizes the whole thesis positing language as Langland's chief concern. Carruthers defends this idea by pointing out that "[a]t the heart of all medieval theories concerning knowledge is the problem of signs"; she especially cites Augustine's theory of language and his interest in developing a redeemed rhetoric, arguing that "Langland is in his own way searching for a truly Christian rhetoric as urgently as Augustine did, and for much the same reason—out of a sense that rhetoric has failed and has led men away from Truth rather than toward him." But Augustine's demonstration in *De Magistro* that words are merely signs is itself a part of his theory that understanding is achieved not through the teaching of words but through the interior illumination of Truth that is Christ:

> If we consider this a little more closely, perhaps you will find that nothing is learned even by its appropriate sign. If I am given a sign and I do not know the thing of which it is the sign, it can teach me nothing. If I know the thing, what do I learn from the sign? . . .
> But when we have to do with things which we behold with the mind, that is, with the intelligence and with reason, we speak

of things which we look upon directly in the inner light of truth which illuminates the inner man and is inwardly enjoyed. There again if my hearer sees these things himself with his inward eye, he comes to know what I say, not as a result of my words but as a result of his own contemplation. Even when I speak what is true and he sees what is true, it is not I who teach him. He is taught not by my words but by the things themselves which inwardly God has made manifest to him.[5]

Only if pupils already understand Truth can they assess the truth of their teacher's words, and their faith must precede their understanding. "[T]he relationship between sign and significator" is indeed "unstable and ambiguous" by nature; but faith in the Word made Flesh redeems ambiguity itself and provides a stable referent by which the degree of Truth in human language may be measured. Carruthers's idea that the ambivalence of language may actually jeopardize the divine Word is an impossibility for Langland; as his Clergy explains, even priests who distort the Word by failing to practice what they preach cannot destroy the Word, and may themselves ultimately be moved by it:

> "This text was told yow to ben ywar er ye tauȝte
> That ye were swiche as ye sey[d]e to salue wiþ oþere.
> For goddes word wolde noȝt be lost, for þat wercheþ euere;
> [Thouȝ] it auailled noȝte þe commune it myȝte auaille
>   yowselue."

(X.275–78)

Certainly Langland is interested in the ambivalence of language, and Carruthers is right to stress the danger of misinterpretation as a central focus of the poem. But corrupt language does not generate a corrupt society, although as Langland's many references to word abuse demonstrate, it does reinforce social corruption. Rather, it is because people are corrupt that their language is corrupt; ultimately, it is not language that must be redeemed but people, and only their faith in Christ can redeem them.

For Langland, as for Augustine, the "problem of signs" is solved through faith in the Word, the only perfect sign of God revealed to humankind. And it is already solved when the poet begins to write:

that is, he does not write to discover whether or not language may be redeemed in his poem but to demonstrate the way in which the Word has redeemed language, and to do so by imitating that Word. To Carruthers, the whole problem with Lady Meed is that she is a pun, and thus that her trial "is more of a trial of language and of true verbal comprehension than it is of the value of bribery, or of reward, in society."[6] But Langland's punning allegory of Lady Meed, we have seen, is derived from the Word of God as quoted by Holy Church in Passus I (the "Reddite Cesari" passage [I.46–53]); Langland is imitating Jesus' own punning distinction between spiritual and material treasure, and the ambivalent nature of Meed is already made clear when Will asks Holy Church to "[t]eche me to no tresor" but to tell how he may save his soul, and Holy Church answers that "[w]han alle tresors arn tried treuþe is þe beste" (I.83, 85). The truth is that earthly treasure both is and is not a good likeness of spiritual treasure, depending upon whether it is given and received in Christian love and charity. Lady Meed is indeed a pun, but like all Langland's puns she expresses in small the real relationship between spirit and flesh, between God and humanity—a relationship that incorporates both similitude and nonsimilitude. The extreme nonsimilitude we perceive between spiritual and material treasure reflects people's willful corruption of the image of God within them.

In *The Language of Allegory*, Maureen Quilligan expands Huppé's idea that wordplay is the source of the poem's structure to create her own theory that all allegory is built on the pun, that allegory is "the generation of narrative structure out of wordplay." Langland's generation of the Lady Meed episode out of scriptural wordplay demonstrates this theory nicely. Quilligan's argument is in many ways undeniable, and her revision of Carruthers's theory that Langland's central concern is language, goes far to make that theory more palatable: by its nature, Quilligan suggests, the pun calls attention to itself as language; and allegory, generated out of the pun's verbal ambivalence, is a genre whose subject is itself. An allegory is a text that calls attention to itself by functioning as both text and commentary. Nothing could be truer of Langland's use of puns, or of his allegory as a whole, the subject of which is largely how it should be interpreted. Quilligan writes: "Language is polysemous; if man recognizes the fact he can discover the truth. . . . If he does not perceive this basic fact of his language, his words will confuse and ultimately control him through their dangerous polysemousness." The reinterpretations of the four cardinal virtues at the end of Passus XIX and beginning of XX would seem to support this theory: if, for example, *Spiritus Fortitudinis* may mean either spiritual or physical strength, it appears that people cannot gauge the virtue of their actions even by the cardinal virtues. There are some problems with this idea, however. First, like Carruthers, Quilligan places the blame on language, arguing that "language must be redeemed" in the poem, which she sees as being primarily concerned with "the purging of puns"; but when the lord confuses *Spiritus Fortitudinis* with force, it is not the language that leads the lord astray, but the lord who willfully twists the language to serve his own sinful ends.[7] Second, the lord does not say that *Spiritus Fortitudinis* is both spiritual and physical strength, and hence ambiguous; instead he defines it merely as physical strength:

> "I holde it riʒt and reson of my Reue to take
> Al þat myn Auditor or ellis my Styward
> Counseilleþ me bi hir acounte and my clerkes writynge.
> Wiþ *Spiritus Intellectus* þei [toke] þe reues rolles
> And wiþ *Spiritus fortitudinis* fecche it, [wole he, nel he]."
>
> (XIX.460–64)

The double entendre, then, is Langland's, not the lord's, and the pun is the correct interpretation of the virtue: true fortitude for lords consists in using their physical strength in the service of spiritual virtue. The lord has distorted the meaning of the cardinal virtue by robbing it of its ambivalence, and the nonsimilitude between his actions and the spiritual virtue they should signify is itself signified by the nonsimilitude in Langland's pun. Langland's polysemous language reflects the Christian polysemous reality; it is not polysemousness that is dangerous but sinful, unambivalent misinterpretation. Langland describes the cardinal virtues as puns fraught with nonsimilitude, not to comment on human language but to signify through language the human failure to signify God. The subject of the poem, then, is the purging of sin rather than of puns, and people must learn to think in puns—must become puns themselves, signifying the union of flesh and spirit—in order to be saved. It is true, as Quilligan shows, that there is good wordplay and bad wordplay in *Piers*, but bad wordplay invariably robs the word of its whole ambivalent meaning: the Prologue's goliard sins by using the etymology of *rex* to suggest that the king's duty is simply to create and enforce rules, ignoring the spiritual similitude to the King of kings by which the angel attempts to explain the true meaning of kingship (pr. 139–45). Verbal ambivalence, for Langland, can never fail to signify Truth: the pun itself always indicates the similitude, nonsimilitude, and causation that order the cosmos. To abuse or misinterpret words is to choose to sin, and therefore any wordplay, good or bad, truly signifies the quality of the speaker's relationship to God.

In her assessment of the value of paradox in *Piers*, Quilligan assumes it to be problematic: "[A]ll allegorists . . . aim at redemption; and because they must work with language, they ultimately turn to the paradox at the heart of their own assumptions about words and make the final focus of their narratives not merely the social function of language, but, in particular, the slippery tensions between literalness and metaphor. They scrutinize language's own problematic polysemy."[8] The suggestion is that paradox is dangerous, and that it is up to the poet to untangle it for the reader: that Truth is to be found in the disarming of ambivalence. But Quilligan's view that paradox is a problem leads to difficulties in her interpretation of crucial passages in *Piers*. She rightly argues that Piers understands the "do well" of the pardon correctly as a command "which enjoins no specific action," but then she states that Piers decides not to plow any longer because plowing "is not a sufficient outward sign of the spiritual state commanded by the pardon."[9] The plowmen and common laborers for whom Piers has obtained the pardon would be dismayed to hear this judgment; indeed, it is exactly the opposite of what the pardon itself says: that any action is an adequate outward sign of Dowel if it is performed with love and faith. Quilligan sees Piers's pardon as problematic because it seems to collapse the "Law of Justice"—which she equates with Dowel—with the "Law of Love" in the form of the merciful pardon; in the image of the pardon, she believes, "Langland has condensed the central paradox of Christianity . . . the enduring conflict between works (doing well) and faith." What Piers's tearing of the pardon would mean in this context Quilligan does not say, concluding only that "the breakdown of the literal action is designed to make the reader become involved in the paradox."[10] But the pardon does not express conflict; rather, it expresses the resolution of conflict through paradox, since there is no Dowel without faith, and no pardon without Dowel. Piers tears the pardon when the priest fails to read Dowel as the faithful works of love that alone save the soul.

Finally, Quilligan argues that language is redeemed in the poem through the pervasive punning on "just" as both justice and jousting in the later passus. She suggests that Langland initiates the metaphor of Jesus as a jouster in order to purge this merely literal interpretation by shifting to the image of the court of justice in which Jesus is condemned by the Jews: the reader is cautioned by the pun against interpreting justice as the letter of the law, or as mere jousting. "When [justice] is merely jousting it is insufficient."[11] In the idea that "[t]he pun on 'just' . . . helps to correct the reader's tendency to misread," Quilligan is correct; but in assuming that the wordplay enacts a process through which the old ideas of justice and jousting are gradually redeemed by the new law of love that redefines them, she considers both the poem and redemption to be processes that are worked out through linear logic. She asserts that the allegory of Jesus as a jouster is first introduced in Passus XVI; but in fact it is already completely worked through in Passus VIII, where the friar defines Dowel as "charite the champion" (VIII.45), and in Passus XV, where Will first says he understands that "Charite is noȝt chaumpions fight," and Anima agrees that "Charite . . . ne chalangeþ" but then paradoxically explains, "For charite is goddes champion" (XV.164, 165, 216). Here the image of Jesus as a jouster for the human soul is already combined with the idea of Christian justice that is paradoxically also merciful, charitable. More important, Langland already demonstrates the paradoxical nature of puns, metaphors, and reality itself, by saying that charity both is and is not a champion, as Christ both is and is not man. Langland introduces the competing metaphors of jousting and the court of justice, as he introduces those of pilgrimage, plowing, and pardon in the *Visio*, not to show the inadequacy of one in favor of the other, but to guarantee the whole meaning of both. Jesus was literally tried and condemned by the Jews, but in a spiritually real sense he was jousting for the human soul at the same time; conversely, jousting is a perfectly sufficient metaphor as long as it is understood to signify the true justice of *caritas*. Quilligan argues that through "the purging of puns"—the exposing and cleaning up of verbal ambivalence and paradox—language is eventually redeemed in the course of the poem, when Christ is resurrected in Passus XVIII: "Language has definitely redeemed itself, or, as Langland himself might have said, Christ, who was the Word of God, has redeemed man's language and therefore the language of the poem."[12] But the wordplay throughout *Piers* is already redeemed in this same sense; Christ redeems human beings, and hence human language, because he reunites the spiritual and material planes, binds the Word and flesh; in short, because he is a pun, a paradox, an ambivalent signifier.[13] Langland uses wordplay as a means of salvation, but his method is not to purge ambivalence but to multiply it, not to eschew paradox but to embrace it in the faith that alone brings redemption.

The source of Langland's playfulness is faith rather than doubt, a fact that may be demonstrated by the very passage critics generally use to support the theory that the poet felt uneasy about his writing. When Imaginative first appears, he briefly chastises Will for poetizing, and Will, admitting his weakness, nevertheless defends his action:

> "And þow medlest þee wiþ makynges and myȝtest go seye þi
>   sauter,
> And bidde for hem þat ȝyueþ þee breed, for þer are bokes
>   y[n]owe
> To telle men what dowel is, dobet and dobest boþe,
> And prechours to preuen what it is of many a peire freres."
> I seiȝ wel he seide me sooþ, and somwhat me to excuse
> Seide, "Caton conforted his sone þat, clerk þouȝ he were,
> To solacen hym som tyme; [so] I do whan I make:
> *Interpone tuis interdum gaudia curis.*
> And of holy men I her[e]", quod I, "how þei ouþerwhile
> [In manye places pleyden þe parfiter to ben]."
>
> (XII.16–24)

As usual, Langland playfully demonstrates his subject as he discusses it, and this time the subject is play itself: Imaginative suggests that Will's poetry is frivolous, neither helping others nor saving Will as readily as serious prayer would do. Will admits this criticism to be just, but adds that such play is not only wholesome recreation but actually a holy, salvational activity in itself. At the same time, Langland is playing upon the formal pretense that he and Will are one —the same jest Chaucer employs with his narrator in *The Canterbury Tales*—and has placed an altercation between the poet and his own imagination at the center of the larger psychomachia of Will.[14] *Piers* at this moment is a playful poem condemning playful poetry, but it also seriously furnishes its own justification. Moreover, Will's classical and Christian justifications for playing with words place Langland in the context of a long tradition of Western rhetoric based on the idea of the *aner spoudogelaios,* the paradoxical "grave-merry man" who engages in holy play. In an excursus entitled "Jest and Earnest in Medieval Literature," E. R. Curtius discusses classical and Christian attitudes toward the mixture of serious and comic literary styles; he traces the medieval church's ambivalence toward humor, concluding that "the theoretical position of the church left all possibilities open—from rigoristic rejection to benevolent toleration of laughter," and demonstrating that "the mixture of jest and earnest was among the stylistic norms which were known and practised by the medieval poet." Citing the many classical justifications for play available to the medieval poet, Curtius suggests that "[l]ay morality would seem to have corresponded to the command of the *Dicta Catonis* (3, 6): *Interpone tuis interdum gaudia curis,* to the authority of which, in much later times, wags like the Archpriest of Hita and Rabelais appealed."[15] Langland's religious allegory cannot perhaps be accused of Rabelaisian waggishness, but his use of this traditional excuse for play is especially appropriate in its context as a moment of levity injected into a serious poem.

The relationship between Langland's comic and serious impulses goes much deeper, however, as evidenced by Will's second excuse: here play is not simply a momentary innocent diversion but a method of obtaining Christian perfection. Certainly this claim cannot be made of every kind of play—the virtuous plowmen of the Prologue "pleiden ful selde" (20)—but only of holy play: the kind Will witnesses when he peers into the bosom of Abraham and discovers "patriarkes and prophetes pleyinge togideres" (XVI.256). This is the play Johan Huizinga discusses in *Homo Ludens,* where he writes, "The playground of the saints and mystics is far beyond the sphere

of ordinary mortals, and still further from the rational thinking that
is bound to logic. Holiness and play always tend to overlap." Building upon Huizinga's study, Hugo Rahner attempts a "theological interpretation of the concept of play." Citing, among others, Plato's
description of humanity as God's plaything (*paignion theou*), the
image of Divine Wisdom playing like a child before the face of God
in Prov. 8:27–31, and a poem by Gregory Nazianzen in which God
creates the world through play, Rahner isolates the concept of *Deus
ludens*, which *homo ludens* attempts to imitate: "All play . . . is an
attempt to approximate to the Creator." Rahner explains that "play
is a human activity which engages of necessity both soul and body.
It is the expression of an inward spiritual skill, successfully realized
with the aid of physically visible gesture, audible sound and tangible
matter. As such it is precisely the process whereby the spirit 'plays
itself into' the body of which it is a part." We recall Wit's description of God creating with both Word and work, as a writer re-creates
with wit, pen, and parchment. Rahner also cites references to play
by saints and churchpeople: "The most serious part of the Christian
ideal of man is to be found in the fact that he who has faith and truly
loves God is also the man who can truly play, for only he who is
secure in God can be truly light of heart."[16] As Robert Levine points
out in his study of holy play in Wolfram von Eschenbach's *Parzival*,
"A firm sense of the sacred can generate a playfulness that readers
with few transcendant impulses may easily misinterpret; nonbelievers have particular difficulty with the techniques of *spoudogelaios*
in Christian medieval texts."[17] Such is the holy play of Langland's
poem: Rahner comments that "things that play, play only because of
their urge to attain to the vision of God,"[18] and Will further excuses
his impulse to write by implying that the purpose of his play is to
discover Dowel:

> "Ac if þer were any wight þat wolde me telle
> What were dowel and dobet and dobest at þe laste,
> Wolde I neuere do werk, but wende to holi chirche
> And þere bidde my bedes but whan ich ete or slepe."
> (XII.25–28)

What began in Imaginative's criticism as a contrast between the fri-
volity of poetry and the seriousness of prayer has suddenly been

reversed, so that now poetry is work, and prayer is the meditative reward for a life of labor. And in the final turn of Langland's poetic play, the momentary comic identification between the wise poet and the foolish Will is undermined. Will writes because he is ignorant of Dowel, but Langland writes because he understands and wishes to express it: as his Imaginative immediately explains, Dowel is faith:

"Poul in his pistle", quod he, "preueþ what is dowel:
Fides, spes, caritas, et maior horum &c.
Feiþ, hope and Charite, and alle ben goode,
And sauen men sondry tymes, ac noon so soone as Charite.
For he dooþ wel, wiþouten doute, þat dooþ as lewte techeþ."

(XII.29–32)

This same Lewte justified Will's wish to write in the previous passus; faith justifies poetry:[19]

"þyng þat al þe world woot, wherfore sholdestow spare
To reden it in Retorik to arate dedly synne?
Ac be [þow] neueremoore þe first [þe] defaute to blame;
Thouȝ þow se yuel seye it noȝt first; be sory it nere amended."

(XI.101–4)

The close reader may detect an inconsistency here: for if Lewte cautions Will to write only what is already generally known, Imaginative complains that his writing is useless because "þer are bokes y[n]owe / To telle men what dowel is." This is by no means the only instance of contradiction on the subject of writing in *Piers*; for after criticizing Will's writing Imaginative devotes the rest of his lecture to proving the value of learning, letters, and writing by drawing examples from classical texts, Scripture, and his own imagination. Clergy (scholastic learning) and kind wit (the perception of God through his traces in nature) cannot take the place of faith and divine grace—they are not in themselves redemptive—but Imaginative disproves Will's earlier statements that ignorance is better than learning by analogy to a swimmer and a nonswimmer thrown into the Thames: the educated man can better save himself "[i]f hym likeþ and lest" (XII.173). Moreover, writing imitates God, who wrote the Ten Commandments and whose writing in the sand saved the woman taken in adultery (XII.72–84). By playing on the definition of "clergie" as both clergymen, who keep the Eucharist, and literacy itself, Imaginative suggests that the divine writing of faithful people, like the Eucharist, is the investment of spirit into flesh, of the Word into human work, by which people are saved:

> "Holy kirke knoweþ þis þat cristes writyng saued;
> So clergie is confort to creatures þat repenten,
> And to mansede men meschief at hire ende.
> For goddes body myȝte noȝt ben of breed wiþouten clergie,
> The which body is boþe boote to þe riȝtfulle
> And deeþ and dampnacion to hem þat deyeþ yuele."
>
> (XII.82–87)

Through wordplay Imaginative also demonstrates that Christ reveals himself to poets and learned people. Having already equated clergy with writing, he now identifies the Gospel shepherds with clergy by a witty translation of *pastores:*

> "For þe heiȝe holy goost heuene shal tocleue,
> And loue shal lepen out after into þ[is] lowe erþe,
> And clennesse shal cacchen it and clerkes shullen it fynde:
> *Pastores loquebantur ad inuicem.*"
>
> (XII.139–41a)

Next he reminds Will that the wise men were not "lewed men, but of the hyeste lettred oute" (XII.414). His conclusion follows naturally, if only by the logic of puns:

> "To pastours and to poetes appered þe Aungel
> And bad hem go to Bethlem goddes burþe to honoure
> And songe a song of solas, *Gloria in excelsis deo.*
> [Riche men rutte þo and in hir reste were
> Tho it shon to shepherdes, a shewer of blisse].
> Clerkes knewen it wel and comen wiþ hir presentȝ
> And diden [hir] homage honourably to hym þat was almyȝty."
>
> (XII.148–54)

The angel inspires the singing of poets in praise of God, and the star that guides them to Christ is "a shewer of blisse," a mirror reflecting bliss onto poets, who in turn reflect it in song. By an imaginative analogy, Imaginative shows that the saving power of Christ's writing is reflected in human writing:

"Alþou3 men made bokes [þe maister was god]
And seint Spirit þe Samplarie, & seide what men sholde write.
[And ri3t as si3t serueþ a man to se þe hei3e strete]
Ri3t so [lereþ] lettrure lewed men to Reson."

(XII.101–4)

The image of God as the master clerk and the Holy Spirit as the master copy of all texts is blended with an image reminding us that reading and learning provide people with vision to perceive the "hei3e
strete" of reason. Similarly, as God's creation of nature provides the
"ensamples" of the peacock and the lark to explain the difference
between riches and poverty, so "þ[ise] poetes" (XII.237) may express
this divine similitude in their allegorical "ensamples," helping to
teach God's message.

The holy play of poets, then, is their faithful re-creation of God; it
is holy because it imitates Christ and thereby wins salvation, and it
is play because it recognizes the patent absurdity, the virtual impossibility, of its effort: "for not even the most inspired gesture of man
at play can be other than a clumsy, childish imitation of the Logos."[20]
The playful poet imitates the Logos by emulating divine allegorical
creation, but the resulting text is necessarily only a poor similitude
for Creation, embodying also nonsimilitude. Langland's awareness of
this ambivalence is not a source of angst but an occasion for play; indeed, play for Langland is the finding and embodying of ambivalences
that define Truth and the human condition within the Christian cosmos. Imaginative both condemns and condones poetry, and in the
Prologue Langland both condemns and condones minstrelsy:

And somme murþes to make as Mynstralles konne,
And geten gold with hire glee [gilt]lees, I leeue.
Ac Iaperes and Iangeleres, Iudas children,
[Fonden] hem fantasies and fooles hem makeþ,
And han wit at wille to werken if [hem liste].
That Poul precheþ of hem I [dar] not preue it here;
Qui loquitur turpiloquium is luciferes hyne.

(Pr. 33–39)

We have seen that there are good minstrels and bad minstrels in
the poem; but which is Langland? Langland does, after all, present a
fantasy, and his fantasy succeeds in making an increasingly greater

"fool" of Will, who has still not chosen a "craft," still not learned the work of Dowel, by the beginning of Passus XX. Moreover, as soon as the poet promises not to quote St. Paul on the subject of bad minstrels, because slander is the devil's tool, he immediately quotes him to show that slander is evil—thereby slanderously quoting St. Paul's accusations against bad minstrels (Eph. 5 : 3–5). The passage is a slanderous attack on slanderers, and the poet's playful use of Scripture proves him to be, like all people, both a good and a bad minstrel of the Word.[21] Like Will, the poet is both fool and Christ's fool, and in his poem he acknowledges the necessarily ambivalent nature of the poem as an imitation of divine creation. But Langland is quite comfortable with this ambivalence; he plays with it and uses it to show the paradox of the human predicament: the inevitability of sin and the assurance of salvation.

It is not the inevitably sinful and ambivalent nature of human texts that disturbs Langland but the inevitability of their misinterpretation by faithless readers. When Imaginative proves the value of "lettrure" by the example of God's writing in the Old and New Testaments, he presents these two writings, not so much to show the superiority of Christian grace to Hebrew law as to demonstrate that they are actually one Word interpreted differently by faithful and faithless people:

"For Moyses witnesseþ þat god wroot to wisse þe peple
In þe olde lawe as þe lettre telleþ, þat was þe lawe of Iewes,
That what womman were in auoutrye taken, whe[r] riche or
    poore,
Wiþ stones men sholde hir strike and stone hire to deþe.
A womman, as [we] fynde[n], was gilty of þat dede,
Ac crist of his curteisie þoruȝ clergie hir saued.
[For] þoruȝ caractes þat crist wroot þe Iewes knewe hemselue
Giltier as afore god, and gretter in synne,
Than þe womman þat þere was, and wenten awey for shame.
[Thus Clergie þere] conforted þe womman.
Holy kirke knoweþ þis þat cristes writyng saued;
So clergie is confort to creatures þat repenten,
And to mansede men meschief at hire ende.
For goddes body myȝte noȝt ben of breed wiþouten clergie,

The which body is boþe boote to þe riȝtfulle
And deeþ and dampnacion to hem þat deyeþ yuele,
As cristes caracte[s] confortede, and boþe coupable shewed
The womman þat þe Iuwes [iugged] þat Iesus þouȝte to saue."
(XII.72–89)

As part of his larger point that study and writing imitate divine creativity only when they are founded on faith, Imaginative shows that
God's writing speaks of salvation to the faithful but of damnation to
the faithless. Salvation, for Langland, lies in the faithful reading of
God's divinely ambivalent Logos: God's writing signifies both damnation and salvation, and readers incapable of understanding this ambivalence do not possess the full Truth. This is exactly what happens
to Will in Passus XI when he is terrified by the words of Scripture:

Ac þe matere þat she meued, if lewed men it knewe,
Þe lasse, as I leue, louyen þei wolde
[The bileue [of our] lord þat lettred men techeþ].
This was hir teme and hir text—I took ful good hede—
"Multi to a mangerie and to þe mete were sompned,
And whan þe peple was plener come þe porter vnpinned þe
    yate
And plukked in Pauci pryueliche and leet þe remenaunt go
    rome."
Al for tene of hir text trembled myn herte,
And in a weer gan I wexe, and wiþ myself to dispute
Wheiþer I were chosen or noȝt chosen.
(XI.108–17)

Will's response to Scripture's words underlines the difference between his fearful disbelief and the narrator's faithful certainty. Will,
being a "lewed" man, reads damnation in Scripture; he does not see,
as the present-tense narrator does, that his own ignorant faithlessness makes the passage a horrible judgment. Only after Will recalls
Holy Church's teaching does he begin to understand that all people
are called but few behave so as to be chosen (XI.117–24). The interpretations of Scripture Langland presents are often ambivalent:
Imaginative adds an optimistic twist to 1 Pet. 4:18, "Salvabitur vix
Iustus in die Iudicij," by concluding, "Ergo salvabitur" (XII.281–82);

and during the harrowing of hell in Passus XVIII, Jesus interprets the
very law that condemns mankind in such a way as simultaneously
to save man and to beguile Satan with his own wiles:

> ". . . þe olde lawe graunteþ
> That gilours be bigiled and þat is good reson:
> *Dentem pro dente & oculum pro oculo.*
> Ergo soule shal soule quyte and synne to synne wende,
> And al þat man haþ mysdo I man wole amende.
> Membre for membre [was amendes by þe old lawe],
> And lif for lif also, and by þat lawe I clayme
> Adam and al his issue at my wille herafter."
>
> (XVIII.338–44)

Human salvation, then, is accomplished through an act of divine ambivalence—through a divine multiplication of meaning—and subsequently through the human act of interpreting texts in their full,
redemptive polysemousness.

Many of the allegories in *Piers* that have traditionally been regarded as problematic are actually explained within the poem as
being matters of proper—that is, ambivalent—interpretation. In the
midst of the allegory of Lady Meed, when we are perhaps puzzled
about whether we should interpret her as Holy Church does or as
Theology does, Langland not only introduces Conscience to explain
that both of these interpretations are correct because "[t]her are two
manere of medes" (III.231), but also directly confronts the issue of
how we should read in the ensuing argument between Conscience
and Lady Meed. After Conscience quotes from Scripture to prophesy
a millennial era when "[s]hal na moore Mede be maister [on erþe]"
(III.290), Lady Meed angrily attempts to justify herself by quoting a
passage of her own:

> "I kan no latyn?" quod she, "clerkes wite þe soþe!
> Se what Salomon seiþ in Sapience bokes!
> That ȝyuen ȝiftes, [takeþ yeme], þe victorie wynneþ
> And [muche] worshipe ha[þ] þerwiþ as holy writ telleþ:
> *Honorem adquiret quo dat munera &c.*"
>
> (III.332–36)

But Conscience demonstrates that Lady Meed has willfully read only half of the passage, and that the other half condemns her:

"I leue wel, lady", quod Conscience, "þat þi latyn be trewe.
Ac þow art lik a lady þat radde a lesson ones
Was *omnia probate,* and þat plesed hire herte
For þat lyne was no lenger at þe leues ende.
Hadde she loked þat [left] half and þe leef torned
She sholde haue founden fel[l]e wordes folwynge þerafter:
Quod bonum est tenete; truþe þat text made.
And so [mys]ferde ye, madame; ye kouþe na moore fynde
Tho ye [souȝte] Sapience sittynge in your studie.
This text þat ye han told were [trewe] for lordes,
Ac yow failed a konnynge clerk þat kouþe þe leef han torned.
And if ye seche Sapience eft fynde shul ye þat folweþ,
A ful teneful text to hem þat takeþ Mede:
Animam autem aufert accipientium &c.
And þat is þe tail of þe text of þat [teme ye] shewed,
That þeiȝ we wynne worship and with Mede haue victorie,
The soule þat þe soude takeþ by so much is bounde."

(III.337–53)

Half of the text seems to praise Meed, but the other half exposes her; Conscience insists that the whole text be read: only the whole text is the text of Truth.[22] The priest in Passus VII, on the other hand, reads the whole two-line text of Truth's pardon—both the line that saves and the line that condemns—but fails to interpret these two lines properly as the twin components of the only true pardon. The literal paper pardon he expects would contain a simple, unconditional guarantee and would not be a text of Truth. Moreover, Langland proves this priest to be a bad reader in the next few lines, when the priest and Piers exchange scriptural insults. Piers states that it was Conscience who taught him how to read (VII.138–39), but the priest's response is snide:

"Were þow a preest, [Piers]", quod he, "þow myȝtest preche
    [whan þee liked]
As diuinour in diuinite, wiþ *Dixit insipiens* to þi teme."

(VII.140–41)

But Piers has said nothing foolish; he has been quoting Scripture to prove that people should not be materialistic, since God has promised that he will provide (VII.118–30). It is the Word of God at which the priest is scoffing, and the whole text from which he quotes proves him the fool ("The fool hath said in his heart: there is no God" [Ps. 13:1]). Piers retorts that the priest is a bad reader, and he quotes Scripture concerning the punishment of ignorant scoffers:

> "Lewed lorel!" quod Piers, "litel lokestow on þe bible;
> On Salomons sawes selden þow biholdest:
> E[ji]ce derisores & iurgia cum eis ne crescant &c."
> (VII.142–43a).

Throughout the poem, Langland returns repeatedly to the two kinds of misreading evinced by Lady Meed and the priest: failure to read the whole physical text and failure to interpret the text's whole meaning. Both crimes—"overskipping" and "glosing," as Langland calls them—dangerously distort the Word of God, and both occur most frequently and most dangerously among priests and friars, the men whose duty it is to teach the whole Word. Thus when the king's confessors are required to "construe" Reason's prophecies, one promises Meed, "I am youre man what so my mouþ Iangle. / I falle in floryns . . . and faile speche ofte" (IV.155–56); and when Conscience and Christ's fools lie sick in the besieged Holy Church at the end of the poem, the same kind of confessor comes and "gloseþ þere he shryueþ" (XX.368). But the "preest and person" who "kan noȝt rede a lyne" (V.415, 421), Langland suggests, is as culpable as the friars who "[g]losed þe gospel as hem good liked" (Pr. 60), and Troianus both discusses and demonstrates the problem of priests who are poor readers:

> "A chartre is chalangeable bifore a chief Iustice;
> If fals latyn be in þat lettre þe lawe it impugneþ,
> Or peynted parentrelynarie, parcelles ouerskipped.
> The gome þat gloseþ so chartres for a goky is holden.
> So is it a goky, by god! þat in his gospel failleþ,
> Or in masse or in matyns makeþ any defaute:
> Qui offendit in vno in omnibus est reus.
> And also in þe Sauter seiþ Dauid to ouerskipperis,

Psallite deo nostro; psallite quoniam rex terre deus Israel;
  psallite sapien[ter].
The bisshop shal be blamed bifore god, as I leue,
That crouneþ swiche goddes knyȝtes, þat konneþ noȝt
  sapienter
Synge ne psalmes rede ne seye a masse of þe day."

(XI.303–14)

Troianus wittily demonstrates the dangers of "overskipping" by showing that the meaning of the psalm is destroyed if the single word *sapienter* is left off: those who leave it off will literally not be singing wisely, and will be both distorting and disobeying the very command they quote. Like Lady Meed, Troianus's ignorant priests leave out the part of the text that proves their own guilt; and as in a court of law a text is worthless unless it is perfect, so to leave out one word of God's Word is to distort its whole meaning: "*Qui offendit in vno in omnibus est reus.*" Anima also complains about clerical illiteracy:

"Grammer, þe ground of al, bigileþ now children,
For is noon of þise newe clerkes, whoso nymeþ hede,
[That kan versifie faire ne formaliche enditen],
[Ne] nauȝt oon among an hundred þat an Auctour kan
  construwe,
Ne rede a lettre in any language but in latyn or englissh."

(XV.372–76)

But although it is clear to Langland that glosers and overskippers are dangerous, it is also clear that they cannot destroy true faith; Anima concludes his argument with this reaffirmation:

"Wherfor I am afered of folk of holy kirke,
Lest þei ouerhuppen as ooþere doon in office and in houres.
[Ac] if þei ouerhuppe, as I hope noȝt, oure beleue suffiseþ,
As clerkes in *Corpus Christi* feeste syngen and reden
That *sola fides sufficit* to saue wiþ lewed peple."

(XV.385–89)

Ultimately, each person is responsible for his or her own salvation, and only those whose faith is already weak may be led astray by poor teachers. If an overskipper leaves out a vital word, or if a gloser interprets Meed merely literally, the laity's simple faith protects them from fatal misunderstanding.

The danger of these glosers and overskippers, again, is not that they will render the Word ambivalent but that they will leave out part of its whole polysemous significance. Langland's misreaders tend to limit meaning, whereas he is intent on multiplying it; his equal concern with the reader's perfect reception of both the spirit and the letter of the text is a manifestation of his insistence on the whole message of the Word made Flesh. The distinction between the misreaders' limitation of meaning and Langland's multiplication is made apparent in the poet's punning attack on friars in Passus XIII. It begins with Will's angry denunciation of the gluttonous doctor's hypocrisy, but soon Langland himself is speaking playfully to his audience:

> Thanne seide I to myself so pacience it herde,
> "It is noȝt foure dayes þat þis freke, bifore þe deen of Poules,
> Preched of penaunces þat Poul þe Apostle suffrede
> In *fame & frigore* and flappes of scourges:
> *Ter cesus sum & a iudeis quinquies quadragenas &c*—
> Ac o word þei ouerhuppen at ech tyme þat þei preche
> That Poul in his Pistle to al þe peple tolde:
> *Periculum est in falsis fratribus.*"
> Holi writ bit men be war—I wol noȝt write it here
> In englissh on auenture it sholde be reherced to ofte,
> And greue þerwiþ [þat goode ben]—ac gramariens shul re[d]e:
> *Vnusquisque a fratre se custodiat quia vt dicitur periculum*
>   *est in falsis fratribus.*
> Ac I wiste neuere freke þat as a frere yed bifore men on
>   englissh
> Taken it for his teme and telle it wiþouten glosyng.
>
> (XIII.64–75)

As the doctor fails to interpret his text's whole significance for his own life and actions, so the friars hypocritically leave out the part of the text that, according to Langland, condemns them. But Langland's witty glosing of the passage provides an additional, contemporary meaning for *"fratres,"* and in his mock-respectful refusal to translate the passage he plays upon the fact that the pun works only in

Latin: when the friar gloses it in English, Langland's double entendre naturally vanishes.

We have already seen how lay society, too, from king to commons, misinterprets the Word: in the Prologue the angel's command that the king govern by the Law of Love degenerates into the commons' cry that the *"Precepta Regis sunt nobis vincula legis"* (Pr. 128–45), and in Passus XIX and XX a king, a lord, a brewer, and Need reinterpret the cardinal virtues in purely material terms (XIX.399–483, XX.1–50). Dame Study describes lords who misinterpret Scripture as part of an evening's amusement:

"I haue yherd heiȝe men etynge at þe table
Carpen as þei clerkes were of crist and of his myȝtes,
And leyden fautes vpon þe fader þat formede vs alle,
And carpen ayein cler[gie] crabbede wordes:
'Why wolde oure Saueour suffre swich a worm in his blisse
That bi[w]iled þe womman and þe [wye] after,
Thoruȝ whic[h werk and wil] þei wente to helle,
And al hir seed for hir synne þe same deeþ suffrede?
Here lyeþ youre lore', þise lordes gynneþ dispute,
'Of þat [ye] clerkes vs kenneþ of crist by þe gospel:
Filius non portabit iniquitatem patris &c.
Why sholde we þat now ben for þe werkes of Adam
Roten and torende? Reson wolde it neuere!
Vnusquisque portabit onus suum &c.'
Swiche motyues þei meue, þise maistres in hir glorie,
And make men in mys bileue þat muse on hire wordes."

(x.104–18)

There is heavy irony in these lords' choice of Scripture, for the passages they gleefully misinterpret to exonerate themselves and to blame God for sin actually condemn them when interpreted properly: it is they who, serpentlike, deceive innocents through their "wyles and wordes," they who perpetuate sin in this world from parent to child, teacher to pupil. In their sophistry they ignore the fact that if each man must carry his own burden (Gal. 6:5), then they, and not God, are responsible for their own sins. Nor do they turn the page to Gal. 6:6—"Let him who is taught the word share all good things with him who teaches"—or they would understand that they sin not only in refusing to feed honest clerics at their feast but also in failing to transmit their learning properly to the ignorant; in this way they are indeed responsible for the sins of others, as well as for their own sins.

But some of the best examples of nonclerical misinterpretation may be seen in Will's many confrontations with the divine texts in which he has no faith, and it is partly by his misinterpretations that we learn how to read the difficult allegory of Dowel.[23] At the end of the *Visio* Will understands that Dowel is the only guarantee of salvation, but he does not understand exactly what Dowel is; hence the pilgrimage he undertakes in the *Vita* "for to seke dowel" (VIII.2). It has been argued that Will's problem throughout the *Vita* is that he is searching for Dowel as a physical being when it is actually an abstraction, an "infinite."[24] It has also been argued that his problem lies in his looking for Dowel as an abstraction when in fact he should simply be doing well.[25] But the problem with both of these interpretations, as with Will himself, is that they do not read Dowel allegorically—that is, ambivalently. Will's first encounter in the *Vita* shows that he understands Dowel as both a spiritual essence and a human action, but cannot understand how these two things may be united, how spirit and flesh may be one. Will first meets two friars and asks them "[i]f þei knewe any contree or costes [aboute] / 'Where þat dowel dwelleþ'" (VIII.12–13). The friars, being part of the allegory, do not tell Will that Dowel is actually just an abstraction, or that Dowel is human deeds of love and hence lives nowhere; instead, they politely tell him that Dowel dwells among them. Will's attempt at a scholarly response is revealing:

> "*Contra!*" quod I as a clerc and comsed to disputen:
> "*Sepcies in die cadit Iustus.*
> Seuene siþes, seiþ þe book, synneþ þe rightfulle;
> A[c] whoso synneþ, I sei[e, certes], me þynkeþ
> [That] dowel and do yuele mowe noȝt dwelle togideres.
> Ergo he nys noȝt alwey [at hoom] amonges yow freres;
> He is ouþerwhile elliswhere to wisse þe peple."
> (VIII.20–25)

Will understands that Dowel is an absolute, since he cannot see Dowel in any way mixed with Do-Evil; he also understands that

Dowel is the good action people learn from this absolute Dowel who comes "to wisse þe peple." What Will does not understand, here and throughout the *Vita*, is how this incarnation can happen, how spirit and flesh may be made one; Will is searching for the way to express Dowel in human life, but he cannot understand this without first having faith in the paradox of the Incarnation. His faithlessness makes him a poor reader, unable to accept ambivalent allegory as Truth. Like Lady Meed, Will quotes only partially a passage that in its entirety controverts his own argument: "For a just man shall fall seven times and shall rise again" (Prov. 24:16). When one of the friars tries to explain that Dowel "strengþeþ [þee] to stonde" after every fall (VIII.46), Will rejects him and goes on his way, establishing himself in this scene as both a gloser and an overskipper.

Will appears to listen to his various allegorical teachers dutifully, if uncomprehendingly; but when Clergy concludes his denunciation of bad priests by prophesying that a "kynge" will come to purify the church and that Dowel will defeat Antichrist (X.334–35), Will demonstrates his growing confusion: " 'Thanne is dowel and dobet', quod I, '*dominus* and knyȝthode?' " (X.336). Will is correctly trying to find the way in which the spirit of Dowel may be made flesh in human action; but Clergy is not speaking merely of an earthly king, nor do human kings necessarily embody Dowel. Scripture tries to explain that rich men such as kings and knights are actually less likely to be saved than the poor; but Will testily interrupts:

"*Contra!*" quod I, "by crist! þat kan I [wiþseye],
And preuen it by [þe pistel þat Peter is nempned]:
That is baptiȝed beþ saaf, be he riche or pouere."
(x.349–51)

In the A-text Will quotes Mark 6:16 at this point—"He who believes and is baptised will be saved"—although he claims to quote Peter; Langland is perhaps thinking of 1 Pet. 3:21: "Baptism . . . saves you, not as a removal of dirt from the body but as an appeal to God for a clear conscience, through the resurrection of Jesus Christ."[26] Whichever passage he has in mind, Will is here translating only half of it; he is missing faith and conscience, the spiritual connection with God of which baptism should be a symbol. Will reads the physical sign of baptism as self-referential because he lacks the faith to read it allegorically. When Scripture again tries to correct him by demonstrating that "lele bileue" (X.355) and love for God and one's neighbor are also necessary for salvation, Will angrily launches into a veritable sermon of misinterpretation, proving his complaint that he is "litel . . . þe wiser" (X.377) for all his lessons. He cites John 3:13 as proof that human salvation is unfairly predetermined and seems not to depend on Dowel at all; but this passage is part of Jesus' lesson to Nicodemus chastising him for his lack of faith and promising that "whoever believes . . . should not perish but have eternal life" (John 3:16). Will complains that learned people often fail to do well and that therefore it is better to be ignorant, citing Jesus' words in Matt. 23:2: "*Super cathedra[m] Moysi &c*" (X.404a) ("The scribes and Pharisees sit on Moses' seat"). But the next verse, the other half of the sentence, counsels people simply to learn from what these scholars say rather than from what they do. He quotes Jesus' advice to his disciples in Mark 13:11 to prove that ignorance speaks better than education, but fails to notice that the disciples speak well because their faith allows the Holy Spirit to enter them. Lastly, Will quotes from Augustine's *Confessions* as final proof that ignorance is better than wisdom: "*Ecce ipsi ydiot[e] rapiunt celum ubi nos sapientes in inferno mergimur*" (X.461). There is double irony here. On the one hand Augustine is saying exactly what Will's teachers have said—that study is useless without faith; on the other hand Will is quoting from the *Confessions* at the point just before Augustine's own conversion to faith, where he speaks in an agony of willful disbelief: "I was disquieted in spirit, being most impatient with myself that I entered not into thy will and covenant, O my God, which all my bones cried out unto me to enter, extolling it to the skies."[27] Will's position here is the same as the faithless Augustine's: his lessons have made him no wiser because he has no faith and therefore lacks the understanding to read them correctly.

Then Will falls into the inner dream of worldliness and concupiscence, and his degeneration is accomplished through the misinterpretation of yet another text. Elde warns him that when he grows old "Thow shalt fynde Fortune þee faille at þi mooste nede" (XI.29), but Recklessness advises him not to worry:

"Folwe forþ þat Fortune wole; þow hast wel fer til Elde.
A man may stoupe tyme ynoȝ whan he shal tyne þe crowne.

'*Homo proponit*', quod a poete, and Plato he hiȝte,
'And *Deus disponit*', quod he; 'lat god doon his wille'.
If truþe wol witnesse it be wel do Fortune to folwe
Concupiscencia carnis ne Coueitise of eiȝes
Ne shal noȝt greue þee [graiþly], ne bigile [þee], but þow wolt."

(XI.35–41)[28]

Recklessness's gross misinterpretation of the proverb as signifying that to do well is to follow Fortune is the logical consequence of Will's fatalism and abnegation of personal responsibility for salvation. Under the cover of "Thy will be done," Will does his own will, and Langland shows that Will is abusing his wit as he degenerates quickly from mere recklessness to childishness:

"Ye! farewel, Phippe", quod Faunteltee, and forþ gan me drawe
Til *Concupiscencia carnis* acorded alle my werkes.
"Allas, eiȝe!" quod Elde and holynesse boþe,
"That wit shal torne to wrecchednesse for wil to haue his
     likyng!"

(XI.42–45)

Through the teachings of Lewte, Scripture, Troianus, and Imaginative, Will learns that study and books alone do not save, but that they may help to strengthen faith. Will is thus brought back to his search for Dowel. But he has by no means yet learned how to read allegorically, how to accept the divine ambivalence of all God's texts. At the beginning of Passus XV he still does not understand Dowel (XV.1–2), and Anima defines Dowel, again, as both the Word and human works:

" '*Beatus est*', seiþ Seint Bernard, '*qui scripturas legit
Et verba vertit in opera* fulliche to his power.' "

(XV.60–61)[29]

Will still does not understand how works may represent the Word; his failure to read allegorically is never more apparent than in his frustrated complaint to Anima about the nature of charity:

"Where sholde men fynde swich a frend wiþ so fre an herte?
I haue lyued in londe", quod [I], "my name is longe wille,
And fond I neuere ful charite, bifore ne bihynde.

Men beþ merciable to mendinauntȝ and to poore,
And wollen lene þer þei leue lelly to ben paied.
Ac charite þat Poul preiseþ best, and moost plesaunt to oure
    [Saueour]—
Non inflatur, non est ambiciosa, non querit que sua sunt—
I seiȝ neuere swich a man, so me god helpe,
That he ne wolde aske after his, and ouþerwhile coueite
Thyng þat neded hym noȝt and nyme it if he myȝte.
Clerkes kenne me þat crist is in alle places
Ac I seiȝ hym neuere sooþly but as myself in a Mirour:
[Hic] in enigmate, tunc facie ad faciem."

(XV.151–62a)

In his conversation with the friars Will knew but could not understand *how* Dowel could be both Christ and human actions; and here again Will knows that *caritas* is both Christ and charity, but still cannot understand how this may be so. He cynically rejects all human actions as cheap imitations of the real thing, rejects even the image of God he sees in himself, not believing in the genuine kinship these images have to their Creator. As always, Will withholds faith because he is presented with a paradox, when only his faith in the paradox will enable him to understand the allegorical truth: that people are created in God's image, both like and unlike their Creator, and that through faith in Christ they may reunite with God at last. During his analysis, in *De Trinitate*, of both the likeness and the unlikeness between God and his image in humankind, Augustine focuses at length on this same passage from 1 Corinthians, pointing out that an enigma is a Greek rhetorical trope signifying "an obscure allegory."[30] Augustine shows that the enigma or allegory through which we discern God as in a mirror is his image in our own minds; thus Will must learn to read himself allegorically, *in enigmate*, if he is ever to be granted the grace to see God face to face.

Of course, paradoxically, this is not something that can be learned through human words. Although Augustine acknowledges that "God's Word may be seen in this likeness of our human word," it is not primarily this kind of word through which God may be perceived *in enigmate*. Augustine speaks instead of an unspoken internal word:

The Word of God of which now we seek to gain some scanty vision by way of this likeness, is that of which it is written, that "the Word was God". . . . We must arrive at that human word which is the word of a reasonable creature, the word of an image of God not born of God but made by him, a word neither producing itself in sound nor object of thought in a likeness of sound, such as must needs belong to a particular language; but the word that precedes all the tokens by which it is signified, and is begotten of the knowledge which remains in the mind, in the moment when that knowledge is spoken inwardly and with truth to itself.[31]

Human words can only imitate this inner word of knowledge that is the image of the Word; in his allegorical wordplay Langland attempts to reproduce the allegoricity of humanity itself, in the hope that if his readers comprehend one they will comprehend the other. However, Langland would seem to argue, if readers, like Will, have not perceived in their own souls the word that is God's Word *in enigmate*, they will not be able to read the poem either. Instead, like Will they will go on to misinterpret the message of Abraham/Faith and Moses/Hope, thinking them opposed and contradictory lessons rather than a single lesson united in the Samaritan/Charity (Passus XVII). Like Will they will not understand Kind's injunction to "konne som craft" (XX.206) as a requirement to put God's Word of love into action, and will ask, "What craft is best to lerne?" (XX.207). It is possible that when Kind at last expresses the ultimate paradox of the poem—"Lerne to loue"—readers will suddenly understand with Will how to read the allegorical Truth, will understand that love may be "learned" only "in the moment when that knowledge is spoken inwardly." But this paradoxical Truth has been available to both Will and Langland's readers from the beginning; it has been embodied in every allegory in the poem, each requiring readers to read the whole ambivalent Truth of all God's texts: the text of the poem, of humankind, of society, and of the cosmos.

The paradoxical nature of *Piers* suggests Langland's understanding both that faithless readers will not read his allegory correctly and that he cannot teach them faith. But Langland also understands that in making his poem he is imitating God, recreating in his own life the salvational life of Dowel. And he retains the hope that by writing an allegory—by enclosing within his text a gloss on how to read—he may inspire an allegorical reading that, with God's grace, may help to kindle the faith of others. This is the purpose of his holy play and the meaning of his insistence on the ambivalence of everything in the poem, even to the names of the characters themselves: the two Meeds; Dowel, Dobet, and Dobest, who are all Dowel; Haukyn/*Activa Vita*; Anima, who has a dozen names; Abraham/Faith, Moses/Hope, and the Samaritan/Charity, who are all united in Christ, who is Dowel; and of course Will himself, who, as both the human will and the poet's faithless persona, is bound in dissimilar similitude to the faithful narrator who is also the voice of God. Like God, Langland strives to approach Unity through multiplicity and plenitude in his poetic cosmos. It is the unambivalent word that lies, for it cannot represent the medieval Christian perception of language, humanity, and creation as signifiers that are both like and unlike their divine Signified.

Notes

Introduction

1 J. P. Migne, *Patrologia Latina* (Paris, 1865) 38: 672; Etienne Gilson, *The Christian Philosophy of St. Augustine*, trans. L. E. M. Lynch (New York: Random House, 1960), p. 27.

2 Rosemary Woolf, "Some Non-medieval Qualities of *Piers Plowman*," *Essays in Criticism*, 12 (1962): 111; Charles Muscatine, "Locus of Action in Medieval Narrative," *Romance Philology*, 17 (1963): 116.

3 Priscilla Jenkins [Martin], "Conscience: The Frustration of Allegory," in *Piers Plowman: Critical Approaches*, ed. S. S. Hussey (London: Methuen, 1969), p. 142; Priscilla Martin, *Piers Plowman: The Field and the Tower* (London: Macmillan, 1979); Mary Carruthers, *The Search for St. Truth: A Study of Meaning in Piers Plowman* (Evanston, Ill.: Northwestern University Press, 1973), p. 10.

4 John Burrow, "The Action of Langland's Second Vision," *Essays in Criticism*, 15 (1965): 247–68, rpt. in *Style and Symbolism in Piers Plowman*, ed. Robert J. Blanch (Knoxville: University of Tennessee Press, 1969), pp. 209–27, and "Words, Works and Will: Theme and Structure in *Piers Plowman*," in Hussey, *Piers Plowman: Critical Approaches*, pp. 111–24. More recently A. J. Colaianne has in part echoed Burrow's argument in suggesting that *Piers* lacks "foreconceit"—a unifying organizational plan—because Langland "had a profound distrust of the moral worth and instructive validity of poetry"; the result is that "[t]he well-paced and controlled fiction of the initial vision of the fair field rapidly disintegrates giving way to a disquieting series of fragmentary and frustrated attempts to forge ideas into poetry" ("Structure and 'Foreconceit' in *Piers Plowman B*: Some Observations on Langland's Psychology of Composition," *Annuale Mediaevale*, 22 [1982]: 110, 107–8).

5 David Mills, "The Role of the Dreamer in *Piers Plowman*," in Hussey, *Piers Plowman: Critical Approaches*, pp. 205, 204; Anne Middleton, "Two Infinites: Grammatical Metaphor in *Piers Plowman*," *ELH*, 34 (1972): 183; Barbara Nolan, *The Gothic Visionary Perspective* (Princeton: Princeton University Press, 1977),

p. 205; John M. Bowers, *The Crisis of Will in Piers Plowman* (Washington, D.C.: Catholic University of America Press, 1986), p. xv; Daniel Murtaugh, *Piers Plowman and the Image of God* (Gainesville: University Presses of Florida, 1978), pp. 123–24; Charles Muscatine, *Poetry and Crisis in the Age of Chaucer* (London: University of Notre Dame Press, 1972), p. 72.

6   Compare Kane's analysis of *Piers* in *Middle English Literature: A Critical Study of the Romances, the Religious Lyrics, Piers Plowman* (Folcroft, Pa.: Folcroft Press, 1951), pp. 182–248, with his recent assessment of the poem in "The Perplexities of William Langland," in *The Wisdom of Poetry: Essays in Early English Literature in Honor of Morton W. Bloomfield*, eds. Larry D. Benson and Siegfried Wenzel (Kalamazoo, Mich.: Medieval Institute Publications, 1982), esp. pp. 83–84.

7   Anne Middleton, "Narration and the Invention of Experience: Episodic Form in *Piers Plowman*," in Benson and Wenzel, *The Wisdom of Poetry*, esp. pp. 96–98.

8   This idea is in fact implied on more than one occasion in the criticism: George Kane, for example, writes that Langland "senses unmistakably that he is living within and writing about a major crisis of ethics, the outcome of which will affect the future of his world" ("Perplexities," p. 89).

9   Unless otherwise noted, all quotations from the poem are taken from George Kane and E. Talbot Donaldson, eds., *Piers Plowman: The B Version* (London: Athlone, 1975).

10   E. R. Curtius, *European Literature and the Latin Middle Ages*, trans. Willard R. Trask (Princeton: Princeton University Press, 1953), pp. 83–85, 159–62; Marcia Colish, *The Mirror of Language: A Study in the Medieval Theory of Knowledge* (New Haven: Yale University Press, 1968), p. 3.

11   Carruthers, *Search for St. Truth*, p. 26; Eugene Vance, "Mervelous Signals: Poetics, Sign Theory, and Politics in Chaucer's *Troilus*," *New Literary History*, 10 (1979): 293.

12   Augustine, *On Christian Doctrine*, II.ii.3, trans. D. W. Robertson, Jr. (Indianapolis: Bobbs-Merrill, 1958). All quotations are taken from this edition.

13   Vance, "Mervelous Signals," p. 295.

14   Augustine, *On Christian Doctrine*, III.v.9, I.x.10; all quotations from Chaucer are taken from *The Riverside Chaucer*, 3d ed., ed. Larry D. Benson (Boston: Houghton, 1987); *The Cloud of Unknowing*, ed. William Johnston (Garden City, N.Y.: Image, 1973), pp. 52–53.

15   See, for example, William C. Strange, "The Willful Trope: Some Notes on Personification with Illustrations from *Piers (A)*," *Annuale Mediaevale*, 9 (1968): 26–39. Strange cites the classical and medieval rhetorical distinction between figures of thought, *figurae sentiarum*, and figures of words, *figurae verborum*, the former referring to "the stuff of what [the writer] has to say" and the latter "more [to] the saying than the thing said" (p. 28). He sees Piers's journey to St. Truth as a *figura verborum*, nothing more than "a kind of grammatical cuteness" (p. 28).

16   [Martin], "Conscience," p. 125.

17 Ibid., p. 126; *Dantis Aligherii Epistolae,* ed. and trans. Paget Toynbee (London: Oxford University Press, 1920), pp. 199–200.

18 Martin is not alone in this assumption; A. J. Colaianne, for example, assumes it in commenting that "[p]eriodically the veil of allegory is torn by a plaintive, impatient voice from the real world" and that "Langland then delivers a prediction concerning the arrival of Hunger in the real world as opposed to the allegorical field" ("Structure and 'Foreconceit,'" pp. 110, 108). If the impatient voice comes from the fair field of folk, and a figure named Hunger visits the "real world," where does the "real" end and the "allegorical" begin in *Piers?*

19 Edwin Honig, *Dark Conceit: The Making of Allegory* (1959; rpt. Hanover, N.H.: University of New England, 1982), pp. 7, 12; Angus Fletcher, *Allegory: The Theory of a Symbolic Mode* (Ithaca, N.Y.: Cornell University Press, 1964), p. 223; Hans Robert Jauss, "The Alterity and Modernity of Medieval Literature," *New Literary History,* 10 (1978–79): 202.

20 Fletcher, *Allegory,* pp. 75–81; Muscatine, "Locus of Action"; Fletcher, *Allegory,* pp. 100–108.

21 Johan Chydenius, *The Theory of Medieval Symbolism,* Commentationes humanarum litterarum, 27, no. 2 (Helsingfors: Societas Scientarum Fennica, 1960), p. 9.

22 Ibid., pp. 10–11; Curtius, *European Literature,* pp. 310–32; Alan de Lille, *Rhythmus alter, PL,* 210: 579A, quoted in Chydenius, "Theory of Medieval Symbolism," p. 11.

23 Upon the assumption that humans and language naturally reflect one another—that, as John of Salisbury states, "grammar . . . imitates nature"—Langland builds his many grammatical metaphors in the poem (*The Metalogicon,* trans. Daniel D. McGarry. Gloucester, Mass.: Peter Smith, 1971, I.14, p. 39). Margaret Amassian and James Sadowsky show, in "Mede and Mercede: A Study of the Grammatical Metaphor in *Piers Plowman* C:IV:335–409" (*Neuphilologische Mitteilungen,* 72 [1971]: 457–76), that men are the "relative" to God's "substantive" in *Piers.* And John Alford demonstrates that this way of thinking was not unique to Langland in "The Grammatical Metaphor: A Survey of Its Use in the Middle Ages," *Speculum,* 57 (1972): 731–34.

24 C. S. Lewis, *The Discarded Image: An Introduction to Medieval and Renaissance Literature* (Cambridge: Cambridge University Press, 1964), pp. 203–4.

25 G. R. Evans, *Old Arts and New Theology: The Beginnings of Theology as an Academic Discipline* (Oxford: Clarendon Press, 1980), pp. 101–2.

26 F. C. Copleston, *A History of Medieval Philosophy* (New York: Harper and Row, 1972), pp. 50–51.

27 Margaret W. Ferguson, "Saint Augustine's Region of Unlikeness: The Crossing of Exile and Language," *Georgia Review,* 29 (1975): 844.

28 Ibid., pp. 861, 860.

29 M. D. Chenu, "The Symbolist Mentality," in his *Nature, Man, and Society in the Twelfth Century: Essays on New Theological Perspectives in the Latin West,* ed. and trans. Jerome Taylor and Lester K. Little (Chicago: University of Chicago Press, 1968), p. 114.

30   Ibid., p. 103.

31   Ibid., p. 123.

32   Ibid., p. 124.

33   Ibid., p. 142; Edgar De Bruyne, *The Esthetics of the Middle Ages*, trans. Eileen B. Hennessy (New York: Ungar, 1969), pp. 75–78.

34   De Bruyne, *Esthetics*, p. 78.

35   Chenu, "The Symbolist Mentality," pp. 126, 125.

36   Ibid., p. 125.

37   D. W. Robertson, Jr., *A Preface to Chaucer: Studies in Medieval Perspectives* (Princeton: Princeton University Press, 1962); Robert M. Jordan, *Chaucer and the Shape of Creation: The Aesthetic Possibilities of Inorganic Structure* (Cambridge, Mass.: Harvard University Press, 1967).

38   Jordan, *Chaucer*, p. 2. I also agree with David Aers's recent criticism of Robertson's methodology for its "monumental disregard" of historical context ("Reflections on the 'Allegory of the Theologians,' Ideology and *Piers Plowman*," in *Medieval Literature: Criticism, Ideology, and History*, ed. David Aers [New York: St. Martin's, 1986], p. 58). Aers further comments on the irony that makes strange bedfellows of Robertson and the "openly anti-historical" American poststructuralists, although Aers seems to assume that the poststructuralist claim "that allegory affirms the arbitrariness of the sign" has not yet influenced American medievalists: "But if this movement ever attracts medievalists, it will not encourage a more serious interest in relationships between allegorical modes and historical practices" (p. 59).

1   Creating the Cosmos

1   This definition of evil is part of the larger idea Augustine adopted from the Neoplatonists, of a supremely good spiritual reality of which the created world is a lesser imitation: "And Thy righteousness displeaseth the wicked; much more the viper and little worm, which Thou hast created good, fitting in with inferior parts of Thy creation; with which the wicked themselves also fit in, the more in proportion as they are unlike Thee, but with the superior creatures, in proportion as they become like to Thee. And I inquired what iniquity was, and ascertained it not to be a substance, but a perversion of the will, bent aside from Thee, O God, the Supreme Substance, towards these lower things" (*The Confessions*, VII.xvi.22, trans. J. G. Pilkington [New York: Liveright, 1943], pp. 153–54; all quotations are taken from this edition). F. C. Copleston describes the importance of Neoplatonism in helping Augustine to convert to Christianity: "For Neoplatonism convinced him of two things. First, there could be, and indeed was a spiritual reality, the possibility of which Augustine had come to doubt. Secondly, the presence of evil in the world could be reconciled with the doctrine of divine creation. For evil, according to Plotinus, was not a positive thing but a privation. To say this was not to say that evil was unreal, an illusion. Blindness, a physical evil, is the privation of sight; but it is a real privation. Similarly, moral

evil is a privation of right order in the will; but it is real enough" (*History of Medieval Philosophy*, p. 27).

2 Of Langland's realism it should be noted that his approach appears to be from a theological rather than a philosophical perspective. In her work on Langland's personification, Lavinia Griffiths sees clearly that in *Piers* "the term *truth* becomes polyvalent, referring to God" and "to god-like behaviour in the man 'trewe of his tonge'" (*Personification in Piers Plowman* [Cambridge: Brewer, 1985], p. 20). But later she argues that Langland is a nominalist on the basis of his partially naturalistic presentation of the Seven Deadly Sins, assuming that a realist would depict the Sins as rarefied eternal beings and that any representational detail in a poem must point to a certain modern materialism on the poet's part (pp. 47–63). Since Langland appears to accept Augustine's theological definition of evil as the absence of good, however, there is no need to assume he is a nominalist simply because he does not adopt the ultrarealistic philosophical view that even sin must be a distinct substance. Copleston discusses this theological solution to the philosophical problem of sin's universal nature (*History of Medieval Philosophy*, pp. 69–70). In chapter 3 I discuss the Seven Deadly Sins according to Fletcher's theory of demonic agency in allegorical poetic thought.

3 Dante, *La divina commedia*, ed. and trans. Charles S. Singleton (Princeton: Princeton University Press, 1970–75), *Paradiso*, XXXIII.85–96; all quotations are taken from this translation.

4 For an interesting discussion of Dante's image of the universe as his own newly bound book, see J. Ahern, "Binding the Book," *PMLA*, 97 (1982): 800–809.

5 Dante, *Paradiso*, IV.37–45.

6 Mary Carruthers, "Time, Apocalypse, and the Plot of *Piers Plowman*," in *Acts of Interpretation: The Text in Its Contexts, 700–1600*, ed. Mary J. Carruthers and Elizabeth D. Kirk (Norman, Okla.: Pilgrim Books, 1982), p. 176; Oscar Cullman, *Christ and Time*, trans. F. V. Filson (1946; rpt. London: SCM, 1962), pp. 54, 61.

7 Herman Hausheer, "St. Augustine's Conception of Time," *Philosophical Review*, 46 (1937): 503–12, rpt. in *Aspects of Time*, ed. C. A. Patrides (Toronto: University of Toronto Press, 1976), pp. 36–37.

8 "Let them therefore see that there could be no time without a created being, and let them cease to speak that vanity. Let them also be extended unto those things which are before, and understand that Thou, the eternal Creator of all times, art before all times, and that no times are co-eternal with Thee" (Augustine, *The Confessions*, XI.xxx.40).

9 Ferguson, "Saint Augustine's Region of Unlikeness," pp. 861–62; Morton Bloomfield, "Chaucer's Sense of History," in his *Essays and Explorations: Studies in Ideas, Language, and Literature* (Cambridge, Mass.: Harvard University Press, 1970), p. 14; Erich Auerbach, *Mimesis: The Representation of Reality in Western Literature*, trans. Willard R. Trask (1953; rpt. Garden City, N.Y.: Doubleday, 1957), pp. 64, 64–65.

10 Georges Poulet, *Studies in Human Time*, trans. Elliott Coleman (1956; rpt. Westport, Conn.: Greenwood, 1979), p. 3. Poulet quotes from Suarez, *Metaphysical Disputations* (Geneva, 1636), 1:385.

11 Poulet, *Studies in Human Time*, pp. 4–5. Quotation is from Thomas's *Contra gentilium*, I.ii.19.

12 Georges Poulet, *The Metamorphoses of the Circle*, trans. Carley Dawson and Elliott Coleman (Baltimore: Johns Hopkins Press, 1966), p. xvii. Quotation is from Bonaventure, *Itinerarium Mentis ad Deum*, cap. v, 8.

13 Dante, *La vita nuova*, trans. Mark Musa (Bloomington: Indiana University Press, 1973), p. 18; and *Paradiso*, XXX.103–8.

14 Quoted in Poulet, *Metamorphoses*, p. xxi.

15 The use of this and related geometric paradoxes to describe the Incarnation was common practice in medieval Latin hymns to Mary and Christ and found its way into vernacular poetry as well. See Erich Auerbach, "Dante's Prayer to the Virgin (*Paradiso*, XXXIII) and Earlier Eulogies," *Romance Philology*, 3 (1949): 1–26; Peter Dronke, *Fabula: Explorations into the Uses of Myth in Medieval Platonism* (Leiden: Brill, 1974); and Robert Levine, "The Pearl-Child: Topos and Archetype in the Middle English *Pearl*," *Medievalia et Humanistica*, 8 (1977): 243–51, and "Squaring the Circle: Dante's Solution," *Neuphilologishe Mitteilungen*, 86 (1985): 280–84.

16 Ferguson, "Saint Augustine's Region of Unlikeness," p. 861.

17 "Comme, en réalité, la Parole éternellement prononcée est unique, ainsi maintenant son audition humaine, car le temps et l'éternité sont joints dans le Verbe fait chair" (Henri de Lubac, *Exégèse médiévale: Les quatres sens de l'écriture* [Paris: Aubier, 1959], pt. 2. 1:188).

18 Burrow, "Langland's Second Vision," p. 212.

19 The plowman, of course, is also commonly used as an image of the poet; Chaucer's Knight describes himself in these terms at the beginning of his tale: "I have, God woot, a large feeld to ere, / And wayke been the oxen in my plough." Langland, too, may have had this image in mind when he chose a plowman as his central figure.

20 A. V. C. Schmidt suggests something similar in his analysis of the second inner dream: "To the extent that it is a vision of history, it is *diachronic*; but to the extent that it presents the Fall existentially, it partakes of the *synchronic*" ("The Inner Dreams in *Piers Plowman, Medium Aevum*, 55 [1986]: p. 35]. Schmidt sees this paradoxical structuring of the second inner dream as resolving the dilemma he outlines in the first inner dream.

21 D. W. Robertson, Jr., and Bernard F. Huppé, *Piers Plowman and Scriptural Tradition* (Princeton: Princeton University Press, 1951), pp. 6–7, 18; Carruthers, *Search for St. Truth*, p. 10.

22 Imaginative later explains Troianus's salvation by quoting 1 Pet. 4:18: "*Salvabitur vix Iustus in die Iudicij*" (XII.281–82). The *Glossa ordinaria* interprets this passage to mean that justice alone does not save: "*Propter quod et peccata proclivia sunt et laboriosa justitia, nisi amantibus: sed charitas quae homines amantes facit, ex Deo est*" (*PL*, 114:688).

23 Augustine, *On Christian Doctrine*, I.xxxvii.41.

24 Middleton, "Two Infinites," p. 173.

25 The temporality of human words is for Augustine a central characteristic of their unlikeness to God's Word: "[The intelligent mind] compared these words sounding in time with Thy eternal word in silence, and said, 'It is different, very different. These words are far beneath me, nor are they, since they flee and pass away; but the Word of my Lord remaineth above me for ever'" (*The Confessions*, XI.vi.8).

26 R. E. Kaske, "*Ex vi transicionis* and Its Passage in *Piers Plowman*," *Journal of English and Germanic Philology*, 62 (1963): 236.

27 Poulet, *Metamorphoses*, p. xviii; Lawrence Clopper, "Langland's Trinitarian Analogies as Key to Meaning and Structure," *Medievalia et Humanistica*, 9 (1977): 102.

28 Claud A. Thompson also argues "that the Holy Trinity is *the* organizing principle for the entire poem," in "Structural, Figurative, and Thematic Trinities in *Piers Plowman*," *Mosaic*, 9 (1976): 106. Thompson sees C. S. Lewis's two dominant principles of medieval thought—the Principle of the Triad and the Principle of Plenitude—as being at work in the numerology, the triple alliteration, and the three main characters in the poem: Will, Piers, and Christ.

29 This is the case with readings of the *Visio* and *Vita* as chronicling the shift from law to love, reason to faith, or nature to grace, and of the whole poem as delineating a progressive plan for individual and social perfection. Two analyses along these respective lines are Carruthers, *Search for St. Truth*; and Morton W. Bloomfield, *Piers Plowman as a Fourteenth-Century Apocalypse* (New Brunswick, N.J.: Rutgers University Press, 1961). Carruthers argues that "[a]ll the efforts at order in the *Visio* seem to be based upon justice and law but lacking in grace," and that "Piers's understanding is . . . bounded in Passus VI by the terms of his allegorical map, the Ten Commandments of the Old Law" (pp. 73, 74). But it is not mere obedience to the Ten Commandments that brings the sinner to Grace and Truth in Piers's pilgrimage, but the love for God and one's neighbor that is Christ's version of the Ten Commandments. And this love is itself the motivating grace behind the redemptive good works of the folk who help Piers to plow and sow the half acre. Indeed, love is understood to be prior to law throughout the *Visio*, as in Holy Church's definition: "Right so loue is a ledere and þe lawe shapeþ" (I.161). Bloomfield's discussion of *Piers* focuses on the poem as a discourse on the earthly process of Christian perfection, both individual and social; he interprets the *Vitae* as delineating three grades of perfection: the ordering of the self to the natural world, the ordering of the self to Christ, and the ordering of the self to "the Kingdom of God and to the regenerated society" (p. 6). As I shall argue in the next chapter, however, the individual conversion to faith that Langland sees as the only means of correcting human and social ills is not attainable through any merely temporal process. Bloomfield's view also needs modification in light of the fact that the vision of Christian society's original foundation by Grace in Passus XIX rapidly decays in Passus XX into a vision of contemporary fallen Christian society, which is where the poem begins. The shape of Langland's cosmos is more suggestive of repeated falling and

degeneration than of regeneration, and this suggestion is in keeping with the traditional view that the world will continue to worsen until the Apocalypse; as Carruthers points out in "Time, Apocalypse," an eschatological view of history generally precludes any possibility of utopian social regeneration before the Second Coming that is to end all human time (pp. 186–87n).

30   Elizabeth D. Kirk, *The Dream Thought of Piers Plowman* (New Haven: Yale University Press, 1972), pp. 10, 12.

31   Ibid., pp. 33, 35. Kirk argues that although God is all-powerful in the universe, in creating the physical world he "has created a hierarchical and, in a sense, autonomous sphere of finite reality which functions according to natural and ethical laws that may be understood in their own right" (ibid., p. 33n). But nothing in Langland's cosmos may be understood in its own right; a person, word, or thing signifies only insofar as it imitates divine exemplars.

32   Muscatine, *Poetry and Crisis*, pp. 82, 78–79.

33   Middleton, "Narration," p. 92.

34   Middleton, "Narration," p. 98.

35   Ibid., p. 99.

36   John Ganim, *Style and Consciousness in Middle English Narrative* (Princeton: Princeton University Press, 1983), pp. 3, 11–12.

37   All biblical quotations are taken from *The New Oxford Bible, Revised Standard Version* (New York: Oxford University Press, 1973).

38   In the *Glossa ordinaria* Jesus' *qui enim habet* is specifically interpreted as a reference to "*apostolis habentibus fidem*" (*PL*, 114:130).

39   In fact, the divisions of *Visio* and *Vita* themselves cannot certainly be said to exist; as A. V. C. Schmidt notes in the introduction to his edition of the B-text, "There is no authority in the B-MSS for this division, though many A-MSS speak of a 'Visio de Petro Plowman' and a 'Vita de Dowel, Dobet & Dobest secundum Wyt & Reson'" (*The Vision of Piers Plowman: A Complete Edition of the B-Text* [New York: Dutton, 1978], p. xx).

40   Ganim, *Style and Consciousness*, p. 119.

41   Kirk, *Dream Thought*, p. 12.

2   *Creating Humankind*

1   Augustine, *The Teacher*, xii.40, xi.38, in *Augustine: Earlier Writings*, Library of Christian Classics, vol. 6, ed. and trans. John H. S. Burleigh (London: SCM, 1943), pp. 96, 95. All quotations are taken from this edition.

2   Augustine, *The Confessions*, VIII.xii.29, IX,i.1.

3   Margaret E. Goldsmith, "Will's Pilgrimage in *Piers Plowman* B," in *Medieval Literature and Antiquities*, ed. Myra Stokes and T. L. Burton (Cambridge: Brewer, 1987), pp. 120, 131.

4   Much has been written about Langland's poem, and especially his three Do's, as an allegory for the degrees of spiritual perfection. Henry Wells thought of *Piers* as an analysis of psychological states on the path to Christian perfection, whereas Nevill Coghill perceived it as a discussion of sociological degrees (Henry W.

Wells, "The Construction of *Piers Plowman*," *PMLA*, 44 [1929]: 123–40; Nevill Coghill, "The Character of Piers Plowman Considered from the B Text," *Medium Aevum*, 2 [1933]: 108–35). More recently, Morton Bloomfield has seen in *Piers* a blueprint for the process of both personal and social transformation (*Fourteenth-Century Apocalypse*), whereas Edward Vasta has argued that Langland presents the Christian mystic's progress toward perfection (*The Spiritual Basis of Piers Plowman* [The Hague: Mouton, 1965]).

5 *Pearl, Cleanness, Patience, Sir Gawain and the Green Knight*, eds. A. C. Cawley and J. J. Anderson (New York: Dent, 1976), lines 590, 601–4.

6 Colish, *Mirror of Language*, pp. ix, 3.

7 Carruthers, *Search for St. Truth*, p. 10.

8 Aquinas, *Contra gentilium*, I.ii.19, quoted in Poulet, *Studies in Human Time*, p. 4.

9 R. W. Frank, *Piers Plowman and the Scheme of Salvation: An Interpretation of Dowel, Dobet, and Dobest* (New Haven: Yale University Press, 1957), p. 47; Vasta, *Spiritual Basis*; Mary Clemente Davlin, "*Kynde Knowyng* as a Major Theme in *Piers Plowman* 'B,'" *Review of English Studies*, 22 [1971]: 19; Britton J. Harwood, "Langland's *Kynde Knowyng* and the Quest for Christ," *Modern Philology*, 80 [1983]: 245, 248.

10 Harwood, "Langland's *Kynde Knowyng*," p. 246.

11 Ibid., pp. 255, 247.

12 My argument at this point bears some resemblance to that of James Hala in "The *Meening* of the Word in *Piers Plowman* B," paper presented at the Twenty-First International Congress on Medieval Studies at the Medieval Institute of Western Michigan University, Kalamazoo, 9 May 1986. Hala argues for the connection between Will's dilemma and Augustine's theory of learning, but to him the solution is to be found in teaching by the nonverbal demonstration of Christ's death and resurrection in Passus XVIII. But of course the poem itself cannot escape verbal demonstration, nor does Will seem any less confused when he first speaks to Kind in Passus XX.

13 Richard E. Palmer, *Hermeneutics* (Evanston, Ill.: Northwestern University Press, 1969), pp. 87, 25.

14 Ibid., pp. 87, 24.

15 William C. Spengemann, *The Forms of Autobiography: Episodes in the History of a Literary Genre* (New Haven: Yale University Press, 1980), p. 32.

16 Ibid., pp. 9, 11, 12–13.

17 Carruthers, *Search for St. Truth*, p. 5; Nolan, *Gothic Visionary Perspective*, pp. 217, 206; Martin, *Piers Plowman: The Field and the Tower*, pp. 5–6.

18 David Mills, "The Role of the Dreamer in *Piers Plowman*," in *Piers Plowman: Critical Approaches*, ed. S. S. Hussey (London: Methuen, 1969), p. 187. See also J. V. Holleran, "The Role of the Dreamer in *Piers Plowman*," *Annuale Mediaevale*, 7 [1966]: 33–50.

19 In *Time in Literature* (Berkeley: University of California Press, 1955), Hans Meyerhoff has much of interest to say concerning the relationship between time and the self in literature, although his interest is primarily in the modern novel.

He argues, for example, that the religious denial of the self is manifested specifically in literary efforts to escape time: "As time is evil and illusory, so is the self born and bred in time. All mystic literature describes time as an illusion and/ or evil. Perfect reality is invariably envisaged as being beyond and outside time; hence, the ideal life can be achieved only through a liberation from time, craving, and personality" (p. 31). Meyerhoff also discusses the literary "reconstruction of the self through memory" as itself containing "an aspect of timelessness"; "since the self is envisaged as a functional unit in which different elements are always potentially co-present or simultaneous with each other, it also has the status of a permanent 'now,' that is, it manifests a sense of being released from the chronological order of time" (p. 56). Meyerhoff adds that "[t]his sense of eternity does not entail or prove the fact of a physical or spiritual immortality of the self— even though Proust sometimes talks as if it does" (p. 56). But for Augustine and Langland, the godlike narrating self is in fact the representative of that which is immortal in humanity.

20   In his description of the trinity of Dowel by analogy to social hierarchies that work together as one, Thought suggests not only that Dowel is the image of the triune God impressed upon the social structure but also, by the familiar analogy between the state and the body, that Dowel is the image of the triune God in humankind. These are, after all, "þre faire vertues" (VIII.79), and when Thought explains that Dobest naturally rules over Dowel and Dobet, he is discussing the united hierarchy of virtues in each person as much as in the social contract (VIII.100–110). One is reminded of Augustine's trinity of memory, understanding, and will as the image of God in the mind (De Trinitate X). But it is most interesting that Thought should suggest the possibility of internal discord here:

> "[Thei han] crowne[d a] kyng to [kepen] hem [alle],
> That if dowel [and] dobet dide ayein dobest
> [And were vnbuxom at his biddyng, and bold to don ille],
> Thanne [sholde] þe kyng come and casten hem in [prison]. . . ."
>
> (VIII.101–4)

Traditionally the similitude between the state and the body is invoked to depict the absurdity of social rebellion: the hand does not revolt against the head, nor should the peasant rise up against his lord. But in the allegory of this scene, Will rebels against Thought, commits an act of spiritual insurrection.

21   The idea of the marriage of Wit and Study seems to derive from Martianus Capella's De nuptiis Philologiae et Mercurii, in which the union between human study and divine eloquence renders the former immortal. By introducing the shrewish Study just after her husband's rapturous description of marriage as "heaven on earth," Langland momentarily suggests an irony similar to that of Chaucer's Merchant, who applauds January's marriage on the grounds that it is "paradys terrestre." But Langland also aims at deeper irony by using Study to insist that study alone does not earn immortality.

22   Murtaugh, Image of God, pp. 94, 95.

3   *Creating Society*

1   Robertson, *Preface to Chaucer*, p. 7.

2   Robertson and Huppé, *Scriptural Tradition*.

3   Frank, *Scheme of Salvation*, p. 2; Rosemond Tuve, *Allegorical Imagery: Some Medieval Books and Their Posterity* (Princeton: Princeton University Press, 1966), pp. 222, 391, 391–92.

4   Auerbach, *Mimesis*, p. 171; Elizabeth Salter, "Medieval Poetry and the Figural View of Reality," *Proceedings of the British Academy*, 54 (1968): 80; David Aers, *Piers Plowman and Christian Allegory* (New York: St. Martin's, 1975), p. 19.

5   Kane and Donaldson emend this line to "crist wolde [it als]," but list numerous variant endings involving "wroughte." I have chosen W. W. Skeat's version here (*The Vision of William Concerning Piers Plowman, in Three Parallel Texts, Together with Richard the Redeless, by William Langland* [London: Clarendon, 1886]).

6   Dorothy L. Owen, *Piers Plowman* (London: University of London Press, 1912); [Martin], "Conscience"; Martin, *Piers Plowman: The Field and the Tower*.

7   A recent example is Lavinia Griffiths's argument, in *Personification in Piers Plowman*, that the naturalism in Langland's presentation of the Sins proves he was a nominalist. See my comments on Griffiths's theory in n. 2 to chapter 1 above.

8   Roman Jakobson, "The Cardinal Dichotomy in Language," in *Language: An Enquiry into Its Meaning and Function*, ed. Ruth N. Anshen (New York: Harper and Row, 1957), p. 171; Fletcher, *Allegory*, pp. 189, 196.

9   Fletcher, *Allegory*, pp. 193, 199.

10   Ibid., pp. 199, 198–99.

11   Ibid., pp. 201, 202, 188.

12   William J. Brandt, *The Shape of Medieval History: Studies in Modes of Perception* (1966; rpt. New York: Schocken, 1973), esp. pp. 65–76; Morton W. Bloomfield, "Episodic Motivation and Marvels in Epic and Romance," in his *Essays and Explorations*, pp. 115, 112.

13   John Lawlor, *Piers Plowman: An Essay in Criticism* (New York: Barnes and Noble, 1962), pp. 255–56; Greta Hort, *Piers Plowman and Contemporary Religious Thought* (1936; rpt. Folcroft, Pa.: Folcroft Press, 1969), p. 25; Stephen A. Barney, "The Plowshare of the Tongue: The Progress of a Symbol from the Bible to *Piers Plowman*," *Mediaeval Studies*, 35 (1973): 261–93; A. C. Spearing, "Development of a Theme in *Piers Plowman*," *Review of English Studies*, 11 (1960): 252.

14   In *Traditional Imagery of Charity in Piers Plowman* (The Hague: Mouton, 1966), pp. 56–73, Ben Smith builds on earlier studies of traditional Christian tree imagery to show that Langland's blending of and shifting between similar images from Christian tradition, far from denoting uniqueness or the decay of allegory, is a common tendency in medieval writing; especially useful in supporting this point are D. W. Robertson, Jr., "The Doctrine of Charity in Medieval Literary Gardens: A Topical Approach Through Symbolism and Allegory," *Speculum*, 26

(1951): 24–49; and Eleanor Greenhill, "The Child in the Tree: A Study of the Cosmological Tree in Christian Tradition," *Traditio*, 10 (1954): 323–71.

15   Two good studies of Langland's food imagery are Jill Mann, "Eating and Drinking in *Piers Plowman*," *Essays and Studies*, 32 (1979): 26–43; and A. V. C. Schmidt, "Langland's Structural Imagery," *Essays in Criticism*, 30 (1980): 311–25. Mann is especially interested in "the relationship between physical and moral laws" in Langland's imagery (p. 31), whereas Schmidt demonstrates that "the issue of temporal feeding is inseparable from the spiritual one of man's true needs as a creature made in the image of God" (p. 313). Schmidt also notes that the poet's metaphors work "by opposition as much as by reciprocity" (p. 315).

16   In *Piers Plowman: The Field and the Tower*, Martin uses the feast scene to argue that Langland had serious doubts about allegory as an idealizing mode; she sees the doctor's attitude as "realistic" and suggests that "[t]he use of allegory can seem almost comically idealistic to the literal characters" (p. 118).

4   *Creating the Text*

1   Bernard F. Huppé, "*Petrus id est Christus:* Word Play in *Piers Plowman*, the B-Text," *ELH*, 17 (1950): 179, 163; A. V. C. Schmidt, "*Lele Wordes* and *Bele Paroles:* Some Aspects of Langland's Word-Play," *Review of English Studies*, 34 (1983): 138.

2   Schmidt, "*Lele Wordes* and *Bele Paroles*," p. 141.

3   Carruthers, *Search for St. Truth*, p. 36.

4   Ibid., p. 4; Augustine, *On Christian Doctrine*, Pr. 3, para. 3.

5   Carruthers, *Search for St. Truth*, pp. 52, 11, 19; Augustine, *The Teacher*, x.33, xii.40.

6   Ibid., p. 52.

7   Maureen Quilligan, *The Language of Allegory: Defining the Genre* (Ithaca, N.Y.: Cornell University Press, 1979), pp. 22, 63.

8   Ibid., p. 64.

9   Ibid., p. 69.

10 Ibid., p. 70.

11 Ibid., p. 79.

12 Ibid.

13 James Hala, too, in "The *Meening* of the Word," describes Christ as "God's pun."

14 In his edition of the B-text, A. V. C. Schmidt notes that Imaginative's name suggests *vertu imaginatif* in *MED* sense 1(c): "The ability to form images of things not experienced, eg. of past or future events" (Schmidt, p. 336). Britton J. Harwood takes the idea of Imaginative's psychomachic significance further, identifying it with "the mind's power for making similitudes," in "Imaginative in *Piers Plowman*," *Medium Aevum*, 44 (1975): 249. But I find untenable Harwood's assertion that in the whole course of the poem, "Imaginative alone . . . attempts to prove a point with a serious and exact analogy" (p. 256); the friars' allegory of the man in the boat is no different, in kind or degree, from Imaginative's allegory

of two men swimming in the Thames, and a moment's reflection should provide sufficient evidence that Imaginative's part of the poem is neither more nor less allegorical than any other part. Just as Dame Holy Church appears only in Passus I though her doctrine pervades the entire poem, so Imaginative appears only here though his similitudes are everywhere.

15   Curtius, excursus IV in *European Literature*, pp. 422, 424, 422–23.

16   Johan Huizinga, *Homo Ludens: A Study of the Play-Element in Culture* (1950; rpt. Boston: Beacon, 1955), pp. 139–40; Hugo Rahner, *Man at Play*, trans. Brian Battershaw and Edward Quinn (London: Burns and Oates, 1965), pp. 7, 28, 6, 57–58.

17   Robert Levine, "Wolfram von Eschenbach: Dialectical 'Homo Ludens,' " *Viator*, 13 (1982): 177. See also Samuel Overstreet's assessment of the grammatical metaphor in the C-text of *Piers* as spiritually motivated wordplay: " 'Grammaticus Ludens': Theological Aspects of Langland's Grammatical Allegory," *Traditio*, 40 (1984): 251–96.

18   Rahner, *Man at Play*, p. 29.

19   The *MED* defines "leaute" both as truth and justice and as loyalty and faithfulness. Langland's usage of the word throughout *Piers* suggests all of these definitions.

20   Rahner, *Man at Play*, p. 9.

21   Interestingly, E. Talbot Donaldson, in attempting to reconcile opposed attitudes toward minstrelsy in the three texts of *Piers*, concludes that "all the texts agree and disagree with themselves and each other" on the subject (*Piers Plowman: The C-Text and Its Poet* [New Haven: Yale University Press, 1949], p. 137). But Donaldson does not take into account Langland's extensive use of minstrelsy as a metaphor for all people's expression of the Word; he attributes the ambivalence to the poet's weak vocabulary: "For want of a couple of terms that would distinguish good from bad minstrels and minstrelsy, the A- and B-poets perplex their readers" (p. 141).

22   In a study that provides an interesting corollary to Quilligan's thesis, John Alford suggests that Langland's entire allegory is generated out of his analysis of and commentary on passages from Scripture, only parts of which he actually cites in the poem. Alford contends that the reader, like Lady Meed, must not forget to "turn the leaf," to read the whole scriptural passage from which Langland quotes in part, since the true meaning of his poem is to be found in Langland's play upon verbal concordances he finds in Scripture ("The Role of the Quotations in *Piers Plowman*," *Speculum*, 52 [1977]: 80–99). The present analysis occasionally follows Alford's advice.

23   Margaret Goldsmith has also recently noticed Will's misuse of Scripture; see "Will's Pilgrimage," p. 125.

24   Anne Middleton, in "Two Infinites," asserts that the three lives are not specific, timebound examples of doing well but "the essence of Christian action" (p. 175), and that "Dowel and Dobet in themselves have no substance" (p. 180).

25   In "Role of the Dreamer," David Mills writes, "What the Dreamer seeks in the

Vitae section is to know Dowel, Dobet and Dobest, but paradoxically this knowledge involves 'doing' " (p. 189).

26 See Kane and Donaldson, *Piers Plowman: The A Version* (London: Athlone, 1960).

> "*Contra*," quaþ I, "be crist! þat can I þe wi[þsigg]e,
> And prouen it be þe pistil þat petir is nempnid:
> *Qui crediderit et baptizatus fuerit saluus erit.*"
>   (XI.232–34)

27 Augustine, *The Confessions*, VIII.viii.19.

28 In this quotation I must take a small liberty with Kane and Donaldson's text, which presents the quotation from Plato as if Plato himself were speaking, not Recklessness. This not only disrupts the frame allegory (since it makes little sense for Will to degenerate from recklessness to Plato to childishness) but also puts words in Plato's mouth, with the result that he seems to be misinterpreting himself. I follow Skeat's punctuation instead.

29 Anima also warns Will that the "man þat muche hony eteþ his mawe it engleymeþ" (XV.57), paraphrasing Prov. 25:27. Henri de Lubac shows that this passage was often cited specifically to warn against hyperintellectual misinterpretations of Scripture (*Exégèse médiévale*, pt. 2, 1:304–5).

30 Augustine, *The Trinity*, XV.ix.15, in *Augustine: Later Works*, Library of Christian Classics, vol. 8, ed. and trans. John Burnaby (London: SCM, 1945), pp. 17–181.

31 Ibid., XV.xi.20.

Bibliography

Texts of Piers Plowman

Kane, George, and E. Talbot Donaldson, eds. *Piers Plowman: The A Version.* London: Athlone, 1960.
———. *Piers Plowman: The B Version.* London: Athlone, 1975.
Schmidt, A. V. C., ed. *The Vision of Piers Plowman: A Complete Edition of the B-Text.* New York: Dutton, 1978.
Skeat, W. W., ed. *The Vision of William Concerning Piers Plowman, in Three Parallel Texts, Together with Richard the Redeless, by William Langland.* London: Clarendon, 1886.

Secondary Sources

Aers, David. *Piers Plowman and Christian Allegory.* New York: St. Martin's, 1975.
———. "Reflections on the 'Allegory of the Theologians,' Ideology and *Piers Plowman.*" In *Medieval Literature: Criticism, Ideology, and History.* Ed. David Aers. New York: St. Martin's, 1986, pp. 58–73.
Ahern, J. "Binding the Book." *PMLA,* 97 (1982): 800–809.
Alford, John. "The Grammatical Metaphor: A Survey of Its Use in the Middle Ages." *Speculum,* 57 (1972): 731–34.
———. "The Role of the Quotations in *Piers Plowman.*" *Speculum,* 52 (1977): 80–99.
Amassian, Margaret, and James Sadowsky. "Mede and Mercede: A Study of the Grammatical Metaphor in *Piers Plowman* C: IV:335–409." *Neuphilologishe Mitteilungen,* 72 (1971): 457–76.
Auerbach, Erich. "Dante's Prayer to the Virgin (*Paradiso* XXXIII) and Earlier Eulogies." *Romance Philology,* 3 (1949): 1–26.
———. *Mimesis: The Representation of Reality in Western Literature.* Trans. Willard R. Trask. 1953; rpt. Garden City, N.Y.: Doubleday, 1957.
Augustine of Hippo, St. *The Confessions.* Trans. J. G. Pilkington. New York: Liveright, 1943.

——. *On Christian Doctrine.* (*De doctrina Christiana.*) Trans. D. W. Robertson, Jr. Indianapolis: Bobbs-Merrill, 1958.

——. *The Teacher.* (*De magistro.*) In *Augustine: Earlier Writings.* Library of Christian Classics, vol. 6. Ed. and trans. John H. S. Burleigh. London: SCM, 1943, pp. 64–101.

——. *The Trinity.* (*De Trinitate.*) In *Augustine: Later Works.* Library of Christian Classics, vol. 8. Ed. and trans. John Burnaby. London: SCM, 1945, pp. 17–181.

Barney, Stephen A. "The Plowshare of the Tongue: The Progress of a Symbol from the Bible to *Piers Plowman.*" *Mediaeval Studies* 35 (1973): 261–93.

Bloomfield, Morton W. "Chaucer's Sense of History." In his *Essays and Explorations: Studies in Ideas, Language, and Literature.* Cambridge, Mass.: Harvard University Press, 1970, pp. 13–26.

——. "Episodic Motivation and Marvels in Epic and Romance." In his *Essays and Explorations: Studies in Ideas, Language, and Literature.* Cambridge, Mass.: Harvard University Press, 1970, pp. 97–130.

——. *Piers Plowman as a Fourteenth-Century Apocalypse.* New Brunswick, N.J.: Rutgers University Press, 1961.

Bowers, John M. *The Crisis of Will in Piers Plowman.* Washington, D.C.: Catholic University of America Press, 1986.

Brandt, William J. *The Shape of Medieval History: Studies in Modes of Perception.* 1966; rpt. New York: Schocken, 1973.

Burrow, John. "The Action of Langland's Second Vision." *Essays in Criticism,* 15 (1965): 247–68. Rpt. in *Style and Symbolism in Piers Plowman.* Ed. Robert J. Blanch. Knoxville: University of Tennessee Press, 1969, pp. 209–27.

——. "Words, Works and Will: Theme and Structure in *Piers Plowman.*" In *Piers Plowman: Critical Approaches.* Ed. S. S. Hussey. London: Methuen, 1969, pp. 111–24.

Carruthers, Mary J. *The Search for St. Truth: A Study of Meaning in Piers Plowman.* Evanston, Ill.: Northwestern University Press, 1973.

——. "Time, Apocalypse, and the Plot of *Piers Plowman.*" In *Acts of Interpretation: The Text in Its Contexts, 700–1600.* Ed. Mary J. Carruthers and Elizabeth D. Kirk. Norman, Okla.: Pilgrim Books, 1982, pp. 175–88.

Chenu, M. D. "The Symbolist Mentality." In his *Nature, Man, and Society in the Twelfth Century: Essays on New Theological Perspectives in the Latin West.* Ed. and trans. Jerome Taylor and Lester K. Little. Chicago: University of Chicago Press, 1968, pp. 99–145.

Chydenius, Johan. *The Theory of Medieval Symbolism. Commentationes humanarum litterarum.* 27, no. 2. Helsingfors: Societas Scientiarum Fennica, 1960.

Clopper, Lawrence. "Langland's Trinitarian Analogies as Key to Meaning and Structure." *Medievalia et Humanistica,* 9 (1977): 87–110.

The Cloud of Unknowing. Ed. William Johnston. Garden City, N.Y.: Image, 1973.

Coghill, Nevill. "The Character of Piers Plowman Considered from the B Text." *Medium Aevum,* 2 (1933): 108–35.

Colaianne, A. J. "Structure and 'Foreconceit' in *Piers Plowman B:* Some Observations on Langland's Psychology of Composition." *Annuale Mediaevale*, 22 (1982): 102–11.

Colish, Marcia. *The Mirror of Language: A Study in the Medieval Theory of Knowledge.* New Haven: Yale University Press, 1968.

Copleston, F. C. *A History of Medieval Philosophy.* New York: Harper and Row, 1972.

Cullmann, Oscar. *Christ and Time.* Trans. F. V. Filson. 1946; rpt. London: SCM, 1962.

Curtius, E. R. *European Literature and the Latin Middle Ages.* Trans. Willard R. Trask. Princeton: Princeton University Press, 1953.

Dante Alighieri. *The Divine Comedy.* (*Divina commedia.*) Ed. and trans. Charles S. Singleton. Princeton: Princeton University Press, 1970–75.

——. *La vita nuova.* Trans. Mark Musa. Bloomington: Indiana University Press, 1973.

Dantis Aligherii Epistolae. Ed. and trans. Paget Toynbee. London: Oxford University Press, 1920.

Davlin, Mary Clemente. "*Kynde Knowyng* as a Major Theme in *Piers Plowman* 'B.' " *Review of English Studies*, 22 (1971): 1–19.

De Bruyne, Edgar. *The Esthetics of the Middle Ages.* Trans. Eileen B. Hennessy. New York: Ungar, 1969.

Donaldson, E. Talbot. *Piers Plowman: The C-Text and Its Poet.* New Haven: Yale University Press, 1949.

Dronke, Peter. *Fabula: Explorations into the Uses of Myth in Medieval Platonism.* Leiden: Brill, 1974.

Evans, G. R. *Old Arts and New Theology: The Beginnings of Theology as an Academic Discipline.* Oxford: Clarendon, 1980.

Ferguson, Margaret W. "Saint Augustine's Region of Unlikeness: The Crossing of Exile and Language." *Georgia Review*, 29 (1975): 842–64.

Fletcher, Angus. *Allegory: The Theory of a Symbolic Mode.* Ithaca, N.Y.: Cornell University Press, 1964.

Frank, R. W. *Piers Plowman and the Scheme of Salvation: An Interpretation of Dowel, Dobet, and Dobest.* New Haven: Yale University Press, 1957.

Ganim, John. *Style and Consciousness in Middle English Narrative.* Princeton: Princeton University Press, 1983.

Gilson, Etienne. *The Christian Philosophy of St. Augustine.* Trans. L. E. M. Lynch. New York: Random House, 1960.

Goldsmith, Margaret E. "Will's Pilgrimage in *Piers Plowman* B." In *Medieval Literature and Antiquities.* Ed. Myra Stokes and T. L. Burton. Cambridge: Brewer, 1987, pp. 119–32.

Greenhill, Eleanor. "The Child in the Tree: A Study of the Cosmological Tree in Christian Tradition." *Traditio*, 10 (1954): 323–71.

Griffiths, Lavinia. *Personification in Piers Plowman.* Cambridge: Brewer, 1985.

Hala, James. "The *Meening* of the Word in *Piers Plowman* B." Paper presented at the Twenty-First International Congress on Medieval Studies, at the Medieval Institute of Western Michigan University, Kalamazoo. 9 May 1986.

Harwood, Britton J. "Imaginative in *Piers Plowman.*" *Medium Aevum*, 44 (1975): 249–63.

————. "Langland's *Kynde Knowyng* and the Quest for Christ." *Modern Philology*, 80 (1983): 242–55.

Hausheer, Herman. "St. Augustine's Conception of Time." *Philosophical Review*, 46 (1937): 503–12. Rpt. in *Aspects of Time*. Ed. C. A. Patrides. Toronto: University of Toronto Press, 1976, pp. 30–37.

Holleran, J. V. "The Role of the Dreamer in *Piers Plowman*." *Annuale Mediaevale*, 7 (1966): 33–50.

Honig, Edwin. *Dark Conceit: The Making of Allegory*. 1959; rpt. Hanover, N.H.: University Press of New England, 1982.

Hort, Greta. *Piers Plowman and Contemporary Religious Thought*. 1936; rpt. Folcroft, Pa.: Folcroft Press, 1969.

Huizinga, Johan. *Homo Ludens: A Study of the Play-Element in Culture*. 1950; rpt. Boston: Beacon, 1955.

Huppé, Bernard F. "*Petrus id est Christus:* Word Play in *Piers Plowman*, the B-Text." *ELH*, 17 (1950): 163–90.

Jakobson, Roman. "The Cardinal Dichotomy in Language." In *Language: An Enquiry into Its Meaning and Function*. Ed. Ruth N. Anshen. New York: Harper and Row, 1957, pp. 155–73.

Jauss, Hans Robert. "The Alterity and Modernity of Medieval Literature." *New Literary History*, 10 (1978–79): 181–227.

John of Salisbury. *The Metalogicon*. Trans. Daniel D. McGarry. Gloucester, Mass.: Peter Smith, 1971.

Jordan, Robert M. *Chaucer and the Shape of Creation: The Aesthetic Possibilities of Inorganic Structure*. Cambridge, Mass.: Harvard University Press, 1967.

Kane, George. *Middle English Literature: A Critical Study of the Romances, the Religious Lyrics, Piers Plowman*. Folcroft, Pa.: Folcroft Press, 1951.

————. "The Perplexities of William Langland." In *The Wisdom of Poetry: Essays in Early English Literature in Honor of Morton W. Bloomfield*. Ed. Larry D. Benson and Siegfried Wenzel. Kalamazoo, Mich.: Medieval Institute Publications, 1982, pp. 73–89.

Kaske, R. E. "*Ex vi transicionis* and Its Passage in *Piers Plowman*." *Journal of English and Germanic Philology*, 62 (1963): 228–63.

Kirk, Elizabeth D. *The Dream Thought of Piers Plowman*. New Haven: Yale University Press, 1972.

Lawlor, John. *Piers Plowman: An Essay in Criticism*. New York: Barnes and Noble, 1962.

Levine, Robert. "The Pearl-Child: Topos and Archetype in the Middle English *Pearl*." *Medievalia et Humanistica*, 8 (1977): 243–51.

————. "Squaring the Circle: Dante's Solution." *Neuphilologische Mitteilungen*, 86 (1985): 280–84.

————. "Wolfram von Eschenbach: Dialectical 'Homo Ludens.'" *Viator*, 13 (1982): 177–201.

Lewis, C. S. *The Discarded Image: An Introduction to Medieval and Renaissance Literature*. Cambridge: Cambridge University Press, 1964.

Lubac, Henri de. *Exégèse médiévale: Les quatres sens de l'écriture.* Paris: Aubier, 1959–62.

Mann, Jill. "Eating and Drinking in *Piers Plowman.*" *Essays and Studies,* 32 (1979): 26–43.

[Martin], Priscilla Jenkins. "Conscience: The Frustration of Allegory." In *Piers Plowman: Critical Approaches.* Ed. S. S. Hussey. London: Methuen, 1969, pp. 125–42.

Martin, Priscilla. *Piers Plowman: The Field and the Tower.* London: Macmillan, 1979.

Meyerhoff, Hans. *Time in Literature.* Berkeley: University of California Press, 1955.

Middle English Dictionary. Ed. Hans Kurath, Sherman M. Kuhn, John Reidy, and Robert E. Lewis. Ann Arbor: University of Michigan Press, 1954–.

Middleton, Anne. "Narration and the Invention of Experience: Episodic Form in *Piers Plowman.*" In *The Wisdom of Poetry: Essays in Early English Literature in Honor of Morton W. Bloomfield.* Ed. Larry D. Benson and Siegfried Wenzel. Kalamazoo, Mich.: Medieval Institute Publications, 1982, pp. 91–122.

———. "Two Infinites: Grammatical Metaphor in *Piers Plowman.*" *ELH,* 34 (1972): 169–88.

Migne, J. P. *Patrologia Latina.* Paris, 1844–1891.

Mills, David. "The Role of the Dreamer in *Piers Plowman.*" In *Piers Plowman: Critical Approaches.* Ed. S. S. Hussey. London: Methuen, 1969, pp. 180–212.

Murtaugh, Daniel. *Piers Plowman and the Image of God.* Gainesville: University Presses of Florida, 1978.

Muscatine, Charles. "Locus of Action in Medieval Narrative." *Romance Philology,* 17 (1963): 115–22.

———. *Poetry and Crisis in the Age of Chaucer.* London: University of Notre Dame Press, 1972.

Nolan, Barbara. *The Gothic Visionary Perspective.* Princeton: Princeton University Press, 1977.

Overstreet, Samuel. "'Grammaticus Ludens': Theological Aspects of Langland's Grammatical Allegory." *Traditio,* 40 (1984): 251–96.

Owen, Dorothy L. *Piers Plowman.* London: University of London Press, 1912.

Palmer, Richard E. *Hermeneutics.* Evanston, Ill.: Northwestern University Press, 1969.

Poulet, Georges. *The Metamorphoses of the Circle.* Trans. Carley Dawson and Elliott Coleman. Baltimore: Johns Hopkins Press, 1966.

———. *Studies in Human Time.* Trans. Elliott Coleman. 1956; rpt. Westport, Conn.: Greenwood, 1979.

Quilligan, Maureen. *The Language of Allegory: Defining the Genre.* Ithaca, N.Y.: Cornell University Press, 1979.

Rahner, Hugo. *Man at Play.* Trans. Brian Battershaw and Edward Quinn. London: Burns and Oates, 1965.

Robertson, D. W., Jr. "The Doctrine of Charity in Medieval Literary Gardens: A Topical Approach Through Symbolism and Allegory." *Speculum,* 26 (1951): 24–49.

———. *A Preface to Chaucer: Studies in Medieval Perspectives.* Princeton: Princeton University Press, 1962.

Robertson, D. W., Jr., and Bernard Huppé. *Piers Plowman and Scriptural Tradition.* Princeton: Princeton University Press, 1951.

Salter, Elizabeth. "Medieval Poetry and the Figural View of Reality." *Proceedings of the British Academy*, 54 (1968): 73–92.

Schmidt, A. V. C. "The Inner Dreams in *Piers Plowman*." *Medium Aevum*, 55 (1986): 24–40.

———. "Langland's Structural Imagery." *Essays in Criticism*, 30 (1980): 311–25.

———. "*Lele Wordes* and *Bele Paroles*: Some Aspects of Langland's Word-Play." *Review of English Studies*, 34 (1983): 137–50.

Smith, Ben. *Traditional Imagery of Charity in Piers Plowman*. The Hague: Mouton, 1966.

Spearing, A. C. "Development of a Theme in *Piers Plowman*." *Review of English Studies*, 11 (1960): 241–53.

Spengemann, William C. *The Forms of Autobiography: Episodes in the History of a Literary Genre*. New Haven: Yale University Press, 1980.

Strange, William C. "The Willful Trope: Some Notes on Personification with Illustrations from *Piers (A)*." *Annuale Medievale*, 9 (1968): 26–39.

Thompson, Claud A. "Structural, Figurative, and Thematic Trinities in *Piers Plowman*." *Mosaic*, 9 (1976): 105–14.

Tuve, Rosemond. *Allegorical Imagery: Some Medieval Books and Their Posterity*. Princeton: Princeton University Press, 1966.

Vance, Eugene. "Mervelous Signals: Poetics, Sign Theory, and Politics in Chaucer's *Troilus*." *New Literary History*, 10 (1979): 293–337.

Vasta, Edward. *The Spiritual Basis of Piers Plowman*. The Hague: Mouton, 1965.

Wells, Henry W. "The Construction of *Piers Plowman*." *PMLA*, 44 (1929): 123–40.

Woolf, Rosemary. "Some Non-medieval Qualities of *Piers Plowman*." *Essays in Criticism*, 12 (1962): 111–25.

Index

Abraham: defines marriage, 52; holy play in bosom of, 149. *See also* Abraham/Faith
Abraham/Faith, Moses/Hope, Samaritan/Charity, 4, 58, 167, 168; as paradoxical trinity, 45–48
Aers, David, 103–4, 172 (n. 38)
Ahern, J., 173 (n. 4)
Alford, John, 171 (n. 23), 181 (n. 22)
Allan de Lille, 18
Allegory: "inadequacy" of, 1–4, 14–15, 41, 58–59, 104–5, 171 (n. 18), 172 (n. 38), 179 (n. 14), 180 (n. 16); anxiety theory founded on, 5; incorporates everything, 7, 11, 13; imitates polysemous cosmos, 14; both literal and allegorical, 15, 102, 104–6; "language of religion," 15; "poetry of the invisible," 15–16; generic impurity of, 16, 25, 103–4; expresses medieval reality, 21–22; vs. symbolism, 23–24; imitates medieval time, 34–35, 40, 59; trinitarian vision underlies, 57; imitates parables, 59–61, 104; imitates paradox of faith, 69, 98, 100; more than extended metaphor, 108; causation in, 108, 110, 111; "generated out of wordplay," 144; humanity as, 166–67; generated out of Scripture, 181 (n. 22). *See also* Symbolism; Similitude/Nonsimilitude

Alterity: of medieval texts, 15; of God, 20
Amassian, Margaret, 171 (n. 23)
Angel, 122–23, 146, 161
Anima, 84, 165; criticizes ignorant priests, 51, 159; multiplicity of names, 91, 168; warns against knowledge without faith, 92–93, 182 (n. 29); describes church as tree, 114–15; describes clergy as coinage, 125–26; defines charity, 147
Antichrist, 96, 163
Aquinas, St. Thomas, 18, 37–38, 72
Aristotle, 20, 71
Auerbach, Erich, 37, 103
St. Augustine of Hippo, 6, 13, 83, 178 (n. 20); on faith, 1, 54, 90, 164; on language and signification, 8, 10–11, 12–18, 20–21, 24, 55, 142, 166–67, 175 (n. 25); Dame Study quotes, 9; on good and evil, 30, 172 (n. 1), 173 (n. 2); on time, 36–37, 173 (n. 8), 175 (n. 25); on learning and teaching, 68, 71, 80–82, 141–43, 177 (n. 12); Will quotes, 90, 164; served at feast of Conscience, 129. *See also* Autobiography; Narrator
Autobiography, 79, 80; of Will, 26, 67, 71–72, 79, 82, 97; of St. Augustine, 80–82

Barney, Stephen, 112
Bible: Apocalypse, 3, 35, 97, 175–76